Theology of My Life

Theology of My Life

A Theological and Apologetic Memoir

John Frame

Foreword by Andrée Seu Peterson

CASCADE *Books* • Eugene, Oregon

THEOLOGY OF MY LIFE
A Theological and Apologetic Memoir

Copyright © 2017 John Frame. All rights reserved. Except for brief quotations in critical publications or reviews, no part of this book may be reproduced in any manner without prior written permission from the publisher. Write: Permissions, Wipf and Stock Publishers, 199 W. 8th Ave., Suite 3, Eugene, OR 97401.

Cascade Books
An Imprint of Wipf and Stock Publishers
199 W. 8th Ave., Suite 3
Eugene, OR 97401

www.wipfandstock.com

PAPERBACK ISBN: 978-1-5326-1376-0
HARDCOVER ISBN: 978-1-5326-1378-4
EBOOK ISBN: 978-1-5326-1377-7

Cataloguing-in-Publication data:

Names: Frame, John M., 1939–

Title: Theology of my life : a theological and apologetic memoir / John M. Frame.

Description: Eugene, OR: Cascade Books, 2017.

Identifiers: ISBN 978-1-5326-1376-0 (paperback) | ISBN 978-1-5326-1378-4 (hardcover) | ISBN 978-1-5326-1377-7 (ebook)

Subjects: LCSH: Frame, John M., 1939– | Theologians—United States—Biography | Apologetics

Classification: BX4700 F75 2017 (print) | BX4700 (ebook)

Manufactured in the U.S.A.

To Steve Childers

Table of Contents

Foreword by Andrée Seu Peterson ix

Preface xvii

Abbreviations xix

1. God Found Me in Pittsburgh 1
2. I Was a Teenage Theologian 14
3. Evangelical at Princeton 25
4. Reformed at Westminster 50
5. The Most Tendentious Guy at Yale 73
6. Westminster Again: The Boy Wonder 88
7. Collegiality in California 123
8. Confessionalism in California 141
9. Winsomely Reformed at RTS 164

Name, Subject Index 217

Scripture Index 229

Foreword

I COULDN'T FIGURE OUT why John Frame would ask me to write a foreword to his theology book when he knows what I'm likely to say. Then it dawned on me: he knows what I'm likely to say.

But let us not begin there. The work you have in your hand is in the ancient tradition of Ecclesiastes and old people appraising their lives for the edification of younger people. This is the peculiar duty and privilege of our elders: "O God, do not forsake me, until I declare your strength to this generation, your power to everyone who is to come" (Ps 71:18).

In hindsight, I should not be surprised by the book's appearance. Why wouldn't Frame, champion of biblical perspectivalism, round out his life oeuvre with an existential perspective on his theology's formation? Not that a man's theology can be reduced to his lifetime influences: John would never have that. Indeed, the testimony you are about to read in *Theology of My Life* defies reductionism of all kinds and exults in the free and mysterious coursing of the Spirit's wind.

Your unworthy foreword writer has only this to recommend her in the present task: no prospective reader will be able to pigeonhole the author's theology in advance by skipping to the name affixed below this text. For I am the most unknown of quantities, neither Conservative nor Liberal nor Klinean nor Van Tillian nor any other debatable thing I might be that fits nicely into a camp. No spoiler here.

My connection with John Frame dates from 1977 as a new student at Westminster Theological Seminary. I came knowing no theology. In fact, I came not of my own design at all, but as a favor of sorts to the guy who led me to the Lord, who was rejected for admission to the post-graduate institution, for lack of college and even high school diploma, and who offered to pay my way in exchange for a promise that I pass him my notes.

A large portion of those notes were from John Frame's Apologetics classes, and sorry to say that they ended up lost at sea en route to Beirut circa 1980 when the aforementioned friend found himself in the middle of a civil war in Lebanon. All that beautiful Framian pacing back and forth dodging microphone cords while lost in Platonic thought before a packed amphitheater seemed forever forfeit. Praise God for publishing companies! In the old days a theologian wanting to get the goods on a fellow theologian he or she considered a heretic was known to say, "Would that the man would write a book!" My publication wish fulfillment is of a happier kind.

Besides the pacing low-wire act at the front of Van Til Auditorium, I spied Frame from the back at a large pipe organ in a church I was invited to around Easter of '78 or '79, where he played with great emotion a piece of music that, to the surprise of my companion, I had never heard before—Handel's *Messiah*. I do not hail from the Reformation tradition, and classical music was unheard of in my childhood home, except what could be gleaned of Liszt's Hungarian Rhapsodies and Rossini operas on Saturday morning *Popeye* and *Bugs Bunny* cartoons (Remember the "Rabbit of Seville"?).

Frame writes glowingly of his WTS colleagues: "Nobody on the faculty reproduced all of [WTS founder] Machen's qualities. . . . I've sometimes thought that E. J. Young best represented Machen's pleasant, conversational writing style; Ned Stonehouse replicated his careful academic research; Woolley reproduced his social and cultural stances; Van Til best resembled Machen's courageous, antithetical approach to theological error—and his sense of humor; and John Murray best expressed the theological position Machen wanted to inculcate in his students" (page 58).

I saw things on a more Kim Kardashian level. For me, twenty-six in 1977, these towering figures about campus were "as trees walking." Woolley, whom I occasionally sighted, but never once heard open his mouth, I saw as . . . woolly. Like a sheep. John Skilton, retired when I arrived on the scene, seemed an avuncular old bachelor with a big heart for the city. I went to his modest Philadelphia row home a few times in tow with an older woman student and nurse named Audrey. There was always a revolving door of down-and-out characters loitering there freely, like in a *Seinfeld* episode, and once I walked into Skilton's kitchen and spotted well-developed mold on a cold pot of rice on the stove.

John Murray, then recently deceased, I knew through the anecdotes of his erstwhile car mechanic at the corner of Glenside Avenue and Limekiln Pike in Glenside.

The venerated octogenarian Van Til made one special appearance in a class I attended and scribbled on the blackboard what may as well have been medieval Dutch. The only other encounter was at his little house in the suburbs with another female student (there were only half dozen of us) who was a bit of a groupie and liked to call the professors by first names, even making a habit of borrowing one of their cars. I asked Van Til who the gray-haired woman in the framed picture on the end table was. He said, "That was my wife, and if I'm not careful it's my idol." In his kitchen over tea I asked him what his major life-sin struggle had been, and he answered, "Humility."

Dr. Vern Poythress, overcome by the Holy Spirit, stopped in the middle of a lecture on Revelation one day and sang a full-throated chorus of "Holy, holy, holy!" I have forgotten most of the content of most of my classes at Westminster, but I hid this one away in my heart.

A professor named Norman Shepherd walked back and forth to the library like a hunted man, always alone. I wish I had tried to strike up a conversation with him, but I heard he was a heretic.

I don't say I understand everything in Frame's *Theology of My Life*. To wit: "The philosophical language I learned at Princeton was that of Anglo-American language analysis, which was not easily translatable into Van Til's language derived from philosophical idealism" (page 60). *Say what?* If you are in the same boat as I, read on anyway. There is an education in this chronicle of the state of the church two thousand years after Christ walked in sandals and told stories about farmers—and much of it is not pretty. If you are tender of heart you will hardly get through the chapter "Confessionalism in California" or the section on Norman Shepherd without weeping. Afterward, do this exercise: return in your mind to the Christianity of the Gospels, Acts, and Epistles, and try to imagine Peter, Paul, John, and Stephen suddenly catapulted by time machine into the twenty-first century and forced to observe the events narrated in chapter 8. Would they not tear their robes and don sackcloth and ashes?

In 2 Kings 6 there was a king who did that. During a severe famine he overheard two women dispassionately discussing a personal fairness issue regarding the cooking and eating of their respective infant sons. The sight shocked the monarch sober. He suddenly realized what Israel had come to. A similar calculated effect is produced on us by the final chapters of Judges, told, again, with blasé matter-of-factness. Everyone had drifted from the Word and ways of God and was doing what was right in his own eyes.

Chapter 8 of TML forces the question on us: how did we come to this pass? How did the mandate to spread the good news and "the fragrance of the knowledge of God" become so Byzantine, esoteric, and cutthroat? How can it be that men who are considered to be among the deepest biblical thinkers of their generation could fail to practice toward their colleagues the most elementary biblical principles, principles that a Sunday School child knows, like Matthew 18:15 and Ephesians 4:32 (See pages 143, 152–54, for example)? Certainly, "all who desire to live godly in Christ Jesus will suffer persecution." But it's too bad when that persecution comes from other Christians.

Come to think of it, why does the training of ministers look so different from when Paul took Titus and Timothy out on missions trips, and talked and prayed with them along the way? Did we take a wrong turn somewhere in history? Thinking to have rejected the Enlightenment, did we succumb to its vapors wafting in under the door? (I once challenged Dr. D. Clair Davis to summarize 2,000 years of Christianity in one sentence. He thought a moment and replied, "There is a tendency to lose Jesus.")

Are we paying now for mistakes that were not properly appraised at the start of the journey? Why this pox on all our houses—40,000 denominational houses that are so queerly at odds with Paul's vision that "there be no divisions among you, but that you be perfectly joined together in the same mind and in the same judgment" (1 Cor 1:10)?

In his masterful 1975 work *The Socialist Phenomenon*, Igor Shafarevich says that in the face of the repeated failures of Socialism wherever the political theory has been tried, its proponents continue to doggedly argue "that an idea cannot be judged by the unsuccessful attempts at its implementation," and that Socialism's stumbles are merely "due to the shortcomings of certain individuals." Presumably, when we finally have better people implementing it, Socialism will work just fine.

Ditto for the Seminary model of the Great Commission. We keep stubbornly clinging to it in spite of all the evidence that it is not a setting likely to produce the attributes the Holy Spirit is looking for in a minister of the gospel. (Cf. Paul's training manual to Timothy: "be strengthened by the grace that is in Christ Jesus"—2 Tim 2:1.) Evidently we reckon the scandalous in-fighting and bad results are "due to the shortcomings of certain individuals." But what if it's not just a few bad apples but a systemic problem? Here is Frame's experience:

> My purpose in going to seminary was to immerse myself in the word of God, our only weapon against Satan (Eph 6:10–18).... I had hoped that seminary would provide me with the ability to share the gospel with unbelievers. I had hoped to become like Dr. Fullerton, able to direct a conversation to the subject of Christ and salvation.... I had come to seminary for many reasons.... But to a large extent I hoped most of all to be equipped to be a pastor. And my failure to achieve that goal was my greatest disappointment at WTS. Particularly, I had hoped to become an evangelist—to be able to talk to seekers like Don Fullerton did.... But WTS was not the place. Their interest was

in correct, intellectually sophisticated doctrine, and not much else." (pp. 55, 72, 72)

Interest in "correct, intellectually sophisticated doctrine, and not much else" is the worldly wineskin of Ivy League university respectability, not conducive to the new wine of gospel ministry preparation. It is the very thing that Paul the apostle rejected when he got converted. Or to put it another way: What's a nice Christian boy like you doing in a "publish or perish," secular accreditation-driven place like this?

Note the name Fullerton that keeps popping up throughout the book. This is interesting because Donald B. Fullerton was a non-Reformed evangelical chaplain Frame had at Princeton. The campus group he founded, Princeton Evangelical Fellowship (snootily called "fundamentalist" by some), was a setting in which Frame, though ever torn between the academicians and the "fundamentalists," actually grew in Christian character.

(This scenario reminds me of a chick flick movie I once saw in which a teenaged guy is pursuing a beautiful girl he thinks he is in love with. But as a matter of fact, if he is honest with himself, he always has a better time with the girl next door whom he considers just a friend. By the end of the movie he realizes that it is this other girl who really does him good.)

Over the course of his life, Frame's thirst for a joyful, living relationship with God—more tangible in the theologically unsophisticated Fullertons than in the theologically sophisticated academicists—brings him to a stance increasingly at odds with some of his colleagues, especially the Confessionalists. At this point one has to ask oneself, it seems to me, especially as a self-proclaimed triperspectivalist: If my existential self keeps nudging me in a different direction from my normative or situational self, may it be that the heart knows something the head knows not?

(Here is my simple diagnostic test for knowing if you're in the right Bible school: If you can exclaim "Oh, how I love Jesus!" at your lunch table in a crowded seminary cafeteria and not cause major awkwardness, you're good. Such an exclamation by a young girl named Florrie Evans in 1904 is what ignited the Welsh Revival, by the way.)

As Frame's self-described "tension" seeks a satisfactory balance in his teaching days, he writes of his course outline preparation: "I did not want to eliminate the theoretical questions that had traditionally been the subject matter of theology, but I wanted to deemphasize them so that the practical questions of ministry were given equal importance" (page 94).

By page 209 he is speaking of the training of Christian ministers solely from Scripture and not from the Confessions of men (Hey! Maybe that's what *sola scriptura* should mean!): "In 1 Tim 3:1–7, Paul tells us that most of the qualifications for overseers are traits of character: 'above reproach, the husband of one wife, sober-minded, self-controlled....'" "Theology" Frame defines not in some ponderous jargon to impress the inner ring, but as "the application of Scripture by persons to every area of human life" (p. 94).

Implicit reservations about the academic model become explicit: "Yet in the history of the church, academic learning has played a larger and larger role in the training of our church leaders. The church fathers often took pride in their knowledge of Greek philosophy and incorporated that into their theological teaching. Greek thought came to dominate medieval theology. In the modern period, university education was considered an advantage to pastors, even though that education was dominated by secularist unbelief" (p. 209).

In *The Academic Captivity of Theology* Frame writes: "It was nice to know that I could analyze and evaluate Anselm's ontological argument..., but the question kept recurring, 'who cares?' [Echoes of Ecclesiastes' 'All is vanity.'] Of course some people do care. We call them scholars. They care because they have those specialized interests, and their passion (I assume that they are honest scholars) is to learn the truth about them. But my passion (and I do not boast of this) was different: to help people to know Jesus."[1]

There is a darker possibility:

Brutus rightly observed to Lucillius regarding Cassius in Shakespeare's *Julius Caesar*: "Thou hast described a hot friend cooling. Ever note, Lucillius, when love begins to sicken and decay, it useth an enforced ceremony. There are no tricks in plain and simple faith. But hollow men, like horses hot at hand, make gallant show and promise of their mettle."

When "first love" dies, Christianity doesn't go away; it becomes Western theology. To be specific, it morphs into a delight in systems and controversies and subtle semantic distinctions. Not able to bear the truth of an emptiness at the core, we surround that empty core with little projects and academic hobbies. No one will be saved by it, of course. Jesus, at his coming, will blast it with the breath of his mouth, like a gnat in a furnace.

In feudal Scotland a church would hold Communion service once a year. The good thing about that is that the preaching the week before was sharp and clear because there was no time to dither. It was now or never to search oneself and confess any sins, and to start obeying God: "If you're not ready to take Communion, you're not ready to die," was the urgent message.

If we had a lot of time on our hands, leisurely discussions of pluriformity and intralapsarianism would be fine. My personal takeaway from two

---

[1] John Frame, *The Academic Captivity of Theology* (Lakeland, FL: Whitefield Media Publishing, 2012), 2.

years in seminary (on my friend Bob's nickel) was that seminary is okay as long as you don't mistake it for preparation for ministry. There is a need for research, to be sure, and I own a few commentaries.

"It will be night presently," as the Intelligent Man says in *The Great Divorce*. People around us are slipping into hell. (Or is it tactless to speak of hell nowadays?) If the trumpet is uncertain who will rouse to battle? We need a certain trumpet, and training in godliness and spiritual warfare, not a Mensa club or glorified debate society. This is what Frame urges in this book, at the cost of critiquing the very institution that is his bread and butter.

I sense there is nobody Frame knew at some stage in his life who does not appear in *Theology of My Life*. This gives the book the feel of a last will and testament. Frame asks forgiveness of some, thanks others, and others he confronts in love—all the things God bids us do.

If anyone reading this book is convicted of any of the sins narrated in this story (I am), let us ask God's forgiveness, "Today, while it is today." If we have been prideful, if we have been uncharitable, if we have been divisive, if we lusted after respectability rather than pining after God, if we have drifted from "the faith once delivered" and "the simplicity of Christ," Father, forgive us, in the name of Jesus. Thus, I draw this foreword to a close, risking to add a hortative dimension to Frame's tri-perspective modes. I think that Donald Fullerton would approve.

"Oh, how I love your law; it is my meditation all the day. You, through your commandments, make me wiser than my enemies; for they are ever with me. I have more understanding than all my teachers, for your testimonies are my meditation. I understand more than the ancients, because I keep your precepts" (Ps 119:97–100).

Andrée Seu Peterson

Preface

LIKE MANY IN THEIR later years, I have spent some time, perhaps too much, mulling over the course of my past life. I have wanted to assure myself of what really happened and why, and whether I would make again the same decisions that I made then. I am especially interested in the transactions between me and God, the "spiritual realm," as some would put it. As it turns out, I have invested my whole life in the theology of Scripture and of evangelical Christianity. That has not brought me great financial rewards, and other vocational choices may have opened up better ways for me to help others.

Still, on reflection, I stand by that major decision and many of the minor decisions that have led me to this point. This is not to deny that I regret huge numbers of my choices. There is no getting around the fact that I have been foolish in many situations, especially that I have been unkind to countless people, including people I have loved very much. If I could go back and rectify all of those relationships, I certainly would.[1] But there is not sufficient time for that. Still, I want to affirm the general course of my life, which is at the same time to praise God for his grace and his leading. He has always forgiven me, for Jesus' sake. And in many cases he has turned my foolishness into good, for him, for others, and for myself.

I am publishing these reflections, because I think they can be of use to some readers. I have written much about apologetics, that is, about the grounds for believing in the God of the Bible. I think my books and articles

---

1. I have long hesitated to write anything autobiographical (though see John Hughes, ed., *Speaking the Truth in Love* [Phillipsburg, NJ: P & R, 2009], 3–30), fearing that a really honest autobiography would be full of criticisms of people who have opposed me in one way or another, as well as confessions of my own sinful role in these controversies. I have no heart for reviewing all of that. In this book, there will necessarily be some allusions to the conflicts in my life, because they have been formative in my thinking. But this book is, chiefly, an apologetic, a theology, in which the central thing is to show how God, and his word, have proved true in my life. That is, of course, the most important thing. So in other respects, this memoir will be far from complete.

in this field are still useful. But it has often occurred to me that the arguments I have used in these writings differ considerably from the ways God has actually led me into assured conviction. And as I hear testimonies from other believers, I get the impression that few of them (perhaps C. S. Lewis was an exception) came to faith through intellectual arguments. I think, therefore, that it might be helpful for me to share with readers the actual events and thinking by which God led me to faith in Christ and to deepened assurance. That's what an "autobiographical apologetic" can do.[2]

I would also describe this book as an "autobiographical theology." Theology and apologetics are inseparable in my thinking. Both seek to set forth the teachings of Scripture (theology) in the most winsome manner possible (apologetics), but they use different pedagogical devices for different audiences. So inevitably, especially since I have spent much of my life teaching systematic theology, this book will indicate how my theology got to be the way it is. I'm hoping that the theology of the book, as well as the apologetic, will carry some exemplary value for younger theologians, and also for all Christians, since on my understanding every believer is a theologian.

For those readers who are interested in my perspectival triads: my *Systematic Theology* is normative, my *History of Western Philosophy and Theology* is situational, and the present volume is existential.

---

2. There are other examples of this genre. Much of Augustine's *Confessions* is in this category. Recent examples are C. S. Lewis, *Surprised by Joy* (New York: Harcourt, Brace, Jovanovich, 1955, 1966), and G. C. Berkouwer, *A Half Century of Theology* (Grand Rapids: Eerdmans, 1979).

Abbreviations

ACT	*The Academic Captivity of Theology* (Lakeland, FL: Whitefield Media, 2013)
AGG	*Apologetics to the Glory of God* (Phillipsburg, NJ: P&R, 1994)
CPC	Covenant Presbyterian Church
CRC	Christian Reformed Church
CVT	*Cornelius Van Til: An Analysis of His Thought* (Phillipsburg, NJ: P&R, 1995)
CWM	*Contemporary Worship Music* (Phillipsburg, NJ: P&R, 1997)
DCL	*Doctrine of the Christian Life* (Phillipsburg, NJ: P&R, 2008)
DG	*Doctrine of God* (Phillipsburg, NJ: P&R, 2002)
DKG	*Doctrine of the Knowledge of God* (Phillipsburg, NJ: P&R, 1987)
DWG	*Doctrine of the Word of God* (Phillipsburg, NJ: P&R, 2010)
ER	*Evangelical Reunion* (Grand Rapids: Baker, 1991)
ESV	English Standard Version
HWPT	*A History of Western Philosophy and Theology* (Phillipsburg, NJ: P&R, 2014)
JETS	*Journal of the Evangelical Theological Society*
KJV	King James Version
ME	*Medical Ethics: Principles, Persons, and Problems* (Phillipsburg, NJ: P&R, 1988)

NASB	New American Standard Bible
NIV	New International Version
NOG	*No Other God* (Phillipsburg, NJ: P&R, 2001)
NT	New Testament
OPC	Orthodox Presbyterian Church
OT	Old Testament
PCA	Presbyterian Church in America
RTS	Reformed Theological Seminary
RTSO	Reformed Theological Seminary in Orlando
SBL	*Salvation Belongs to the Lord* (Phillipsburg, NJ: P&R, 2006)
SSW 1	*Selected Shorter Writings 1* (Phillipsburg, NJ: P&R, 2014)
SSW 2	*Selected Shorter Writings 2* (Phillipsburg: P&R, 2015)
ST	*Systematic Theology* (Phillipsburg, NJ: P&R, 2013)
TET	*The Escondido Theology* (Lakeland, FL: Whitefield, 2011)
UP	United Presbyterian
WCF	Westminster Confession of Faith
WLC	Westminster Larger Catechism
WSC	Westminster Shorter Catechism
WST	*Worship in Spirit and Truth* (Phillipsburg, NJ: P&R, 1996)
WTJ	*Westminster Theological Journal*
WTS	Westminster Theological Seminary
WTSP	Westminster Theological Seminary in Philadelphia
WTSC	Westminster Seminary in California

1

God Found Me in Pittsburgh

WESTERN PENNSYLVANIA IS NOT usually considered part of the Bible belt, but it is, even today, one of the more religious parts of the United States.[1] A recent statistic says that in the Pittsburgh area 71.85% of the people are affiliated with a church, compared with 50.2% of the nation as a whole.[2] 68.7% of these adherents are Roman Catholic. By far the largest Protestant membership, 6.5%, belongs to the Presbyterian Church, USA. That last percentage reflects the large number of Scotch-Irish immigrants, mostly Presbyterians of various kinds, who settled there in the eighteenth century. Nineteenth- and twentieth-century immigration, especially from Eastern Europe, was mostly Roman Catholic. But one writer described Western Pennsylvania in the eighteenth century as the "Presbyterian Valley."

In our family lore, the first of our Frame line to migrate there was "Irish Jimmy" Frame, who lived from 1727–94. My father, Clark Crawford Frame, was born in 1908 in Erie, PA, but was raised largely in Franklin, a small town eighty miles north of Pittsburgh. He studied industrial engineering at Penn State and the University of Pittsburgh. After graduation he worked for Westinghouse Electric. He played a major role in solving a labor dispute at the Westinghouse plant in East Pittsburgh and was then promoted to be

---

1. We recall how in 2008, Senator Obama, campaigning for the Presidency, said this about out-of-work Pennsylvanians: "And it's not surprising then they get bitter, they cling to guns or religion or antipathy toward people who aren't like them or anti-immigrant sentiment or anti-trade sentiment as a way to explain their frustrations." Ben Smith replied, "That's a pretty broad list of things to explain with job loss." See http://www.politico.com/blogs/bensmith/0408/Obama_on_smalltown_PA_Clinging_religion_guns_xenophobia.html, accessed Feb. 15, 2014.

2. "Religion Statistics Profile," http://www.city-data.com/county/religion/Allegheny-County-PA.html, accessed Feb. 14, 2014.

the Director of Labor Relations for the whole company, with an office in one of the new high-rise buildings on the "point" in Pittsburgh—where the Monongahela and Allegheny rivers combine to form the Ohio. He kept that job until his retirement in 1973. On retirement, he was honored both by the company and by the labor unions. He and Mom moved to Boca Raton, FL shortly after that, and in 1980 Dad died of leukemia.

My mother, Violet McElphatrick Frame, born in 1911, was also raised in Franklin. Her father, G. Domer McElphatrick, in his youth had been on course to become a Christian minister. He was named after a pastor respected by the family. But he reported losing his faith after discovering various problems in the Bible. Instead, he became an oil prospector. The American oil business had begun in western Pennsylvania, but Domer traveled wherever there were rumors of oil discoveries. So he went throughout the country and later told his grandchildren exciting stories of the Wild West. After he married, he remained for the most part in the Franklin area where he managed an oil lease into his old age. But on one occasion, he took his family west. He had heard stories of oil discoveries in Texas, so he moved his family to Fort Worth for a time. But his wife and three daughters (including my mother) complained so persistently about leaving their Franklin friends, and about the conditions in Texas, that Domer moved them back to Franklin.

Mother experienced a major trauma through an auto accident that killed her mother. She was a teenage passenger at the time. I don't think she ever felt safe in a car again. But she persevered at learning to drive and at teaching her four children to drive as well. Occasionally she would place unreasonable restrictions on us (e.g., "drive five miles under the speed limit"). But we made allowances and tried to ease her discomfort when we were behind the wheel.

A talented actress and musician, Mom studied at the University of Wisconsin. But money for tuition ran out in the Great Depression, and she did not graduate. The family sold their musical instruments, among many other things, and mother resumed her life in Franklin. After marrying Clark Frame, she was a homemaker and occasional volunteer worker. Early on, she acted in community theater. She was my first piano teacher and also taught me to read and write before I went to school. That was the main source of my academic success. She died in 1996, from a combination of illnesses. The top priority of both my parents was their children, and they provided everything we needed for our physical and educational well-being.

Sunday School

I was born in 1939, the oldest of four.[3] Religion was not a major component of our family life, but Dad came from a long line of Presbyterians, some of them devout, and he and Mom thought that the kids should have a religious education. So they took me to Sunday School at the Edgewood Presbyterian Church, near the apartment where we first lived. When I was six, they moved us to Mt. Lebanon, a more upscale suburb of Pittsburgh, with a reputation for excellent schools. The nearest Presbyterian church was the Beverly Heights United Presbyterian Church,[4] and we kids joined the Sunday School there.

For me, Sunday School was first of all a place to meet friends and for us to play practical jokes on one another. I remember once entering a contest with another boy to see who could accumulate the biggest pile of hymnbooks. We would steal them from other kids and put them in a pile near where we were sitting. In time the teacher would

Me, with siblings at our grandmother's house in Franklin, PA, probably around 1955. John, Martha, David, and Clark in order of age

---

3. My sister Martha is a mostly retired public school math teacher in Northbrook, IL. My brother David is a retired orthopedic surgeon and lives near Allentown, PA. My youngest brother Clark started two banks and lives in a historic farmhouse in Perkasie, Bucks County, near Philadelphia.

4. The "United Presbyterian Church of North America" (UPNA) was not the large Presbyterian body that was at the time called "Presbyterian Church in the United States of America" (PCUSA). The UPNA was a smaller body that had resulted from a nineteenth-century merger of two "Covenanter" denominations, which historically sang only Psalm versions in worship. By the 1940s, most congregations of the UPNA had relinquished their exclusive Psalmody, but the denomination had remained more theologically conservative than the PCUSA. Beverly Heights was strongly evangelical, though not sensitive to all the theological issues that were debated in the larger church culture. Pittsburgh was the center of the UPNA, and there the denomination was large and well-established. The denomination's two largest presbyteries were in the Pittsburgh area, and the PCUSA presbytery was also one of its largest, which added to the impression that the Pittsburgh area was the Presbyterian Valley. (The Reformed Presbyterian Church of North America, the "Covenanter" church, was also headquartered in Pittsburgh. Its seminary and college were in the Pittsburgh area.) In 1958, the UPNA and the PCUSA merged (exactly 100 years after the UPNA was formed by another merger) and became the "United Presbyterian Church of the USA." When the church later merged with the Southern Presbyterian Church (PCUS), the denomination went back to its earlier name, PCUSA. All of that is somewhat confusing, of course. I think my parents believed that Beverly Heights was part of the PCUSA; but at that time it was UPNA.

intervene, and we would try something else. The Bible lesson was not much more than ambient noise to accompany our games. Some have told me that I had the reputation of being the worst-behaved kid in the class. To that charge I plead no contest.

I say this not to be cute or to solicit admiration for my roguishness. I was a sinner, and what I describe above is the least of my sins. What I did was hurtful to others, rebellion against the teachers, and opposition to the word of God they were trying to teach us. Several people in the congregation took on teaching our class as a divine calling, praying earnestly that God would enable them to present the Scriptures so that we would believe. But they regularly failed, so far as anyone could tell. I heard of women teachers who were in tears because of us. One year we had our class around a table, and one kid brought a penknife. Every time a teacher quit, that kid would put a notch in the table, as one cowboy villain put a notch in his gun for everybody he put away. The knife was not mine, and the notches were not my doing. But the loss of each teacher was in part my responsibility.

But something got through to us. Beverly Heights had a Bible memory program. They gave every child a booklet called "Bible Verses to Remember." In that book were fairly long passages of Scripture: the Ten Commandments, Psalms 1, 23, 121, 1 Cor 13, and others. My parents had little thought for our spiritual nurture, but they cared a lot about our academic reputations, and they didn't want the humiliation that would result if one of their children failed to complete the Bible memory program. So every Sunday morning they drilled my siblings and me on the Bible verses we were supposed to remember for that day. In time I completed the memory program and received a Bible (King James Version, of course), the first I ever owned.

Another positive influence on me was the general impression I had of the church as an institution. For a period, our Sunday School met at Markham School, the same school I attended from Monday through Friday. At Markham, in the grade school, there was Scripture reading and prayer before each class. Some students (not I) were excused once a week to go to religious education classes at various churches, of which one was Beverly Heights. This was before two Supreme Court decisions declared these practices unconstitutional. But while they persisted, they gave me the impression that the church and the school were partners in our education. The church taught the Bible; the schools taught about the world in general. It never occurred to me that there was any conflict between these. None of my public school teachers ever criticized what the church was teaching me, nor vice versa. What I learned at church and what I learned in school were just two aspects of the great fund of human knowledge. As much as I respected the one, I respected the other. I misbehaved in both contexts and therefore was not very receptive to either type of instruction. But I saw both institutions equally as embodiments of the authority of society, authority that, for all my childish disdain, I had to respect.

In the Presbyterian Valley, not only Catholics, but also Presbyterians, had cathedral-like church buildings.[5] Some were financed by multi-millionaires (billionaires easily in today's dollars). So even by sheer weight of physical architecture and wealth, the church was an impressive institution. The church administered colleges and seminaries, and the opinions of pastors appeared in the newspapers. As a young child I could not have described all this, let alone appreciate its meaning. But I certainly had no reason to question that the church was the equal of any other social institution, and so what the church said was worthy of acceptance.

My point here is not to say that the social status of the church is a reason for trusting its message. Later I would come to believe, as I do today, that big buildings and concentrations of wealth are most often distractions from the gospel. The wealthiest churches are often the least trustworthy. But as a child, the position of the church in society seemed to me to be worth something: what the church said came with at least the same force as the message of my family, of the schools, of government officials, of the newspapers and radio. I had no reason for distrusting the church, any more than I had reason for distrusting any social institution. And later in life, when others in society objected to the teachings of the church, I placed the burden of proof on them, and concluded that they could not bear that burden.

My problem with the church was not intellectual, then, but moral. I simply did not *like* the thought of obeying God, or obeying anybody other than myself. I cultivated the image of the rebel, the dissenter, the kid who knew more than anyone around him.

Markham Elementary

At Markham, I did not find that image difficult to cultivate. My mother had taught me to read phonetically before I entered first grade, and that gave me a huge advantage over my peers. The school itself had abandoned phonics and had begun to teach what we would later call a "whole language"[6] approach to reading. So in my reading group, the teacher would encounter a word, say *fish*, and would not even suggest that the kids could sound it out.

---

5. Not cathedrals, for a cathedral is a church presided over by a bishop, and Presbyterians, we say, are ruled by elders, not bishops. (But in Presbyterian theology "elder" is synonymous with "bishop," so that difference may not be very great.)

6. Less reverently, "look and guess."

She asked questions like "have we learned that word yet?" I was frustrated waiting for everybody, and regularly I blurted out the word. Eventually I got a reputation. When I was in first grade, sixth graders would bring their geography texts to me and I would read them fluently (without, of course, understanding them very well). Eventually the teachers put me at my own table in the classroom and gave me more advanced books to read, "enrichment" projects, to keep me interested. That privilege failed to ease my boredom, but I did everything they asked of me, hoping in vain that I could be promoted to a higher grade.

Markham School

Of course, sitting at a table by myself did not do much good for my social standing at the school. I was, and still am, socially maladept, and I was even less adept in athletics. Regularly I was chosen last for sports teams, with good reason. One gym teacher, when I was in, I think, fourth grade, set a bar for a high jump and told my group that we didn't have to jump over the bar, but we could try. Given that option, I elected not to try, having an accurate assessment of my jumping skills. But I was the only one who refused the challenge, and the gym teacher called me "yellow belly" in front of all the other kids. That was the end of my athletic career, and that in turn ended any hope I ever had for general social acceptance. Readers can draw the lesson that a single traumatic event can cast a shadow over a person's whole life.[7]

Of course, the opposite was the case in the academic area. In classroom academic games, I was usually the first kid chosen, and I looked down on the others with an ungodly contempt that today I cannot bear to recall. Other kids resented this, of course, and I got beaten up more than once on the walk to and from school. So the story of my elementary school

---

7. Psychologists tend to draw attention to childhood traumas. But the worst traumas in my life occurred in adulthood, and I will describe them later in this book. They occurred in 1979 and 1999.

experience was a story of rejection, rejection that was my own fault. I was the prototypical smarty-pants.

God Calls Me at Beverly Heights

But it was different at Beverly Heights, even though my behavior there was at least equally as obnoxious as my behavior at Markham. The story of my Markham years was one of predictable rejection, but the story of my life at Beverly Heights was one of astonishing acceptance.

I had been taking classical piano lessons since fourth grade from the wonderful Joseph Esposito, who showed incredible patience with my failure to follow his directions. In spite of that failure, I loved the music and I became a good enough pianist that people from Beverly Heights began to call and ask if I could play hymns for this meeting or that. So I became a regular Sunday School pianist and eventually came to play for Vacation Bible School, Youth Fellowship meetings, conferences, and even some adult gatherings. Had they known the spiritual condition of my heart, they might have thought twice about asking me to do such things. But they had no thought of that, or perhaps they thought that getting me to play would be a way for God to get through to me.

Meanwhile, Alberta Meadowcroft, the church organist, was developing a multiple choir program that not only taught young people to sing church anthems, but changed their lives as well. She started a junior high school choir in 1951, the year I graduated from Markham to Mellon Junior High. Someone at the church encouraged me to get involved. Choirs were certainly not my preferred activity. I could not stand the thought of wearing a robe. My athletic failure had compromised perceptions of my masculinity, and wearing a choir robe was not going to help, to say nothing of singing hymns in front of a lot of pious people.

But I went to the first rehearsal. When I walked in, I wanted to exit immediately, for I was the only boy in a group of maybe ten or twelve girls. But Mrs. M., as we called her, was aware of the problem immediately. She had heard of my musical prowess, such as it was, and commended it, suggesting that we could possibly play some duets during the church worship service. And in time she assigned me to be the narrator who introduced an anthem. Staying in that choir went against all my natural instincts. It was completely out of character. But something new was happening in my life.[8]

---

8. One other time I recall acting entirely out of character: when I first wrote to my future wife in 1983. To act out of character may sometimes be the same thing as acting in the Spirit of God.

That year, Mrs. M. also began taking on organ students. Various people in the church suggested that I become one of them. I was fascinated with the pipe organ at Beverly Heights, excited about all the different tone qualities it could produce. At first I didn't dare ask my parents if I could take still another weekly music lesson. But in time Dad and Mom asked me if I would like to do it: people had been making the suggestion to them, as well. So I began to study organ, and in time people at the church asked me to play the organ for various functions, as they had asked me to play the piano. I became a regular substitute organist.

One result of this was that I came to love hymns and choir anthems. I also loved the pop music of the day, Crosby, Sinatra, Como, and the rest. (Elvis Presley came along a bit later, and my nerdy group of friends determined that I should not like him.) I enjoyed everything that came from the Broadway stage. But the music of God overshadowed everything else. The songs went through my head, through the day, every day. At home (often at the expense of Joseph Esposito's piano assignments) I would go through the church hymnals (adult, youth, and Sunday school) and play the songs over and over again. I would experiment with harmonies and textures and drill myself on anything that contained technical difficulty.

I practiced on the little Baldwin electronic organ in the Beverly Heights chapel room, and occasionally on the pipe organ in the sanctuary. My parents had always found it difficult to get me to practice for an hour a day on the piano. But I loved to play the organ and spent hour after hour in the chapel. There the genius of Bach overwhelmed me, and the ingenuity of more recent composers like Alexandre Guilmant, Thomas Crawford, and Leo Sowerby.

Eventually I had to face the question: how could I lead the church in singing these wonderful songs without believing their message?

But there was more. As a junior high student, I also became a member of "Pioneers," the youth group that met on Sunday nights at Beverly Heights. I was not eager to spend still another two hours at church each week, but of course someone told me they needed me as a pianist. The someone in this case was Bob Kelley,[9] first a seminary intern at the church, later associate pastor. Bob made it his business to know all of the church kids on a one-on-one basis. With the athletes, he played ball; with academics like me, he taught, discussed, and debated. Despite my awful reputation, he was determined to be my friend. And he kept track of me and everyone else in the youth group until he died in his eighties. Bob, and subsequent Beverly

---

9. We kids always called him by his first name, despite the fact that Mrs. M. thought that was quite improper.

Heights youth pastors, formed my early images of Jesus. Energetic, wise, loving, pursuing each of us, leaving none behind.

Bob was also a biblical scholar. He later earned a doctorate at Princeton University (about the same time I earned my B.A. there) and became a professor of New Testament at Pittsburgh Theological Seminary. So Bob was not only my friend, but my first contact with the world of academic theology. He challenged us to study the Bible for ourselves, but in ways that would be fun. Case in point: during the 1952 election season, he set up a political contest between two tickets of candidates: Moses and Joseph (Biblicrats) against David and Abraham (Religicons). We kids were to search the Bible for points for or against the candidates. Some painted posters, some wrote up talking points, some made speeches. Though I don't remember who won, I can't say that I have ever had more fun with a theological project.

Bob worked with the Pioneers only one or two years, then left to supervise the senior high group, the "Builders." A new seminary intern named Bill Boder replaced him as the leader of us junior high kids. Bill emphasized that our relation to Christ was not primarily a matter of learning the content of the Bible and the church's teaching. It was coming to know Jesus as a real, living person.

At the time, the early 1950s, Billy Graham was becoming famous and controversial. Some churches felt challenged by him and took a critical attitude toward his mass evangelism. But Beverly Heights welcomed him as an ally, and they arranged for a number of our young people to attend one of his meetings at Forbes Field. I attended, but I did not respond to Graham's invitation to "come forward." Some of my friends did respond, however, and in the following months I noticed real changes in their lives. Among them were some who had beaten me up on the way home from Markham School. I couldn't deny that after the Graham meeting they were different people.

Then in Pioneers one Sunday night, Bill Boder invited one of his fellow seminary students to give an evangelistic message, essentially channeling Billy Graham. The student stressed that it wasn't enough to believe in sin; it was necessary for each of us to regard *himself* as a sinner, to hate that sin, and to turn from it. Then it was necessary for each of us to understand, not just that Christ died for the sins of the world, but that he died for *me*. Further, God raised him from the dead, so that he still lives today and calls on us to make him our personal friend.

Afterward, the young preacher gave an invitation, again like Graham. He asked us to put up our hands if we trusted Jesus as our *personal* lord and savior. Somehow I felt that I ought to raise my hand, and I did. After that, the preacher asked those of us who had raised our hands to stand and tell everybody why. He had not warned us in advance that he would ask this, and I felt (and still do feel) that request was an imposition, at least that it was probably not age-appropriate. But I couldn't refuse to testify of what my heart had expressed. My testimony was mealy-mouthed, something like this: "I raised my hand, not to profess Christ for the first time, but to reaffirm a faith that I have had for a long time."

But was that testimony untrue? To this day, I cannot say. Jesus teaches us that the Spirit works invisibly (John 3:8), and I do not know the date and time of my new birth. If you had asked me two years before that Pioneers meeting whether I believed that Jesus was the Son of God, and whether I believed that he died, was raised, and was ascended to save his people from their sins, I would have replied that I did. In fact, a year or two before, in sixth grade, I had attended the Beverly Heights communicants class and received the privilege of taking the Lord's Supper and of voting in congregational meetings.

Did I have a *personal* relation to Jesus? As I attended the youth group and sang the songs of God in the choir, Jesus became to me more and more a friend. I prayed to him, thought affectionately of him. When others rejected me, I turned to him and found acceptance. Was there a moment when all of this suddenly clicked into shape? I cannot say that there was. Certainly it was not what happened in Pioneers that Sunday night. God had transformed my heart long before that, so my testimony was essentially true. But the evangelistic preacher forced me to "Stand Up for Jesus" for the first time in a public way.

At any rate, whether my new birth took place that night or some time before, I was by age fourteen a follower of Jesus Christ. Church was not a game anymore, not a mere social club. Christ was truly the center of my life. God had sought me out (John 4:23) and had found me. The church youth ministry had taught me the gospel, Mrs. M's music had driven it deep into my heart, and God's Spirit had worked through it all, making me a new creation.

Reflections

As I look back on those days from my present perspective, I naturally have questions to ask. Was I justified, as a young teenager, in choosing to believe Christ and, along with him, all the teachings of the Bible? Christianity is a highly complex system of ideas, and in 1953 I hadn't had the education, the understanding, or the discernment to wrestle through all the problems raised by learned people against that system. What right did I have to say, "it is all true"?

Today I have a higher degree of learning and analytic competence, and I have employed my mature thought to many of these problems. I believe that I have found satisfactory answers to some of them. But not all of them. Mysteries remain, and to a large extent I am still a young adolescent, following Jesus "through a mirror dimly" (1 Cor 13:13). Even today, I depend on the same faith commitment that I expressed in the early 1950s. Some might think that this sort of commitment is utterly unreasonable. For in my youth I committed myself to believing a vast number of things without anything approaching what some intellectuals would consider to be sufficient reasons.

But there are ways of responding to this kind of criticism.

1. The most important is to reiterate what the Bible itself says about conversion. It is, in the end, a supernatural event. In conversion, the gospel comes to us "not only in word, but also in power and in the Holy Spirit and with full conviction" (1 Thess 1:5). Like millions of others, I came to believe *because God made me believe.*

That is an entirely sufficient account of why I came to believe in Jesus in my early teens. But it will usually not be enough to show a skeptic that this decision was a rational one. For skeptics, it is not enough to say "God made me believe." For people say things like this about any number of crazy beliefs.

For every belief, however, there is a divine side and a human side. The divine side is the supernatural work of the Holy Spirit. But belief is also a matter of human responsibility, a human choice. Human reason is a means of justifying such choices to ourselves and to others. So the question becomes: is there a rational justification for a teenage conversion? I would say yes.

2. In a teenage conversion, the young person rarely has arguments or evidences for his or her new beliefs sufficient to persuade skeptics. But many philosophers today[10] argue that we are often justified in holding beliefs without adequate argument or evidence (or even without any argument or evidence at all). Examples of such beliefs include "The earth has existed for more than five minutes"; "other people have minds like mine"; and "the sun will rise tomorrow." Among these beliefs are those accepted as "basic" (Plantinga's term) in the communities where we grow up. If a child's parents teach him that robins fly south in the winter, he has the right to believe that

---

10. Particularly Alvin Plantinga, as he develops the argument in his *Warrant* trilogy (New York: Oxford University Press, 1993–2000).

on their say-so. He is not obligated to make on his own the scientific observations that would constitute proof in the academic community.

Belief in God, and in Jesus as lord and savior, was accepted as basic in Mt. Lebanon when I was a child. As I mentioned earlier, this was the belief of my church, and most of the people I knew outside the church seemed, at least, to give some level of acceptance to that belief.

Later I would encounter opposition to these beliefs, and, then (having chosen the vocation of apologist and theologian) I would have an obligation to respond to that opposition. But as a young teenager, there was no need for me to do that.

3. Another consideration is also important. When I came to Christ, I was not only accepting a set of beliefs. I was accepting a way of life. In Scripture, Jesus' lordship covers all of life: "So whether you eat or drink or whatever you do, do all to the glory of God" (1 Cor 10:31). The intellectual sphere is part of this. When Jesus calls disciples to follow him, he calls them to a lifestyle that includes virtues like love, gentleness, and self-control, and also to a way of thinking that supports these. The "all" in "do *all* to the glory of God" includes thinking.

Thus, a Christian is not one who sets up a group of intellectual criteria and then decides whether Jesus measures up to them. Rather, he or she is first loyal to Jesus and *then* tests all intellectual criteria to find which of them measure up to Jesus.

This account of the rationality of the faith fits the nature of my conversion. For the issue in my conversion was not whether the Bible was true or whether Jesus could be believed. The issue was moral and volitional: was I ready to follow him, to obey him, to acknowledge his lordship?

Most people in my environment said they believed in Jesus. But there were only a few who were utterly devoted to him. But if Jesus was who he claimed to be, God in the flesh (John 1:1–14), the only appropriate attitude for a disciple was utter devotion. And, indeed, if he is God in the flesh, then he has the right to tell us how to think, as well as how to behave.

In Mt. Lebanon in the early 1950s, most everyone approved of Jesus. But hardly anyone was utterly devoted to him.[11] The student who preached to us in the Pioneer meeting might not have put it that way, but he was challenging us to nothing less than that level of discipleship: service to Christ by the mind and heart. So from the very beginning of my life as a disciple I was convinced of the utter centrality of the *lordship* of Christ over all of life.

---

11. I am reminded of Søren Kierkegaard who, writing in nominally Christian Denmark in the nineteenth century, asked how it was possible to become a Christian within Christendom.

I offended people, not by my beliefs as such, but by my "fanaticism." Later I would write a series of four big books called *The Theology of Lordship*.¹² It all began in my early teens.

---

12. *The Doctrine of the Knowledge of God* (Phillipsburg: P&R, 1987), *The Doctrine of God* (Phillipsburg, NJ: P&R, 2002), *The Doctrine of the Christian Life* (Phillipsburg, NJ: P&R, 2008), and *The Doctrine of the Word of God* (Phillipsburg, NJ: P&R, 2010).

2

I Was a Teenage Theologian

ONCE I WAS A disciple of Jesus, it didn't take long for me to get the idea that God was calling me to some kind of full-time ministry. In addition to my work on piano and organ, I was invited to lead youth meetings and to speak for children's church (where I had once terrorized the teachers). The Bible fascinated me as no other book did. I took every opportunity to study it, both in groups and by myself. Later Bob Frisbee, one of the seminary interns at Beverly Heights, suggested that the young people go through the Navigators' Topical Memory System. I used that system to memorize verses, through high school and college, and over that time I learned about 700 verses. These are the passages that I first turn to today when I am seeking the Bible's teaching on various subjects.

Again there was a symbiosis between my Bible study and my music. Mrs. M. left Beverly Heights around 1953, but took me and another organ student to meet Russell Wichmann, a brilliant young organist and student of Marcel Dupré. Wichmann took us on as organ students, and I had lessons on the wonderful Möller pipe organ[1] in the chapel of the Pennsylvania College for Women, today known as Chatham University, where Wichmann was chairman of the music department. Wichmann took me through a large portion of the classical organ repertoire: over half the organ works of Bach, the complete organ works of Mendelssohn, Franck, and Brahms, pieces of Widor, Mulet, and Dupré. He led me through service music by the likes of Helmut Walcha, Seth Bingham, and Richard Purvis.

---

1. Four manuals, eight divisions, with two of the divisions in the back of the chapel. Occasionally Wichmann asked us to meet him at the Shadyside Presbyterian Church, where he was organist. The organ there was of the same caliber, though older.

Improvising

I loved it all. It lodged in my heart, and it came out of me in a variety of ways. For one thing, I learned how to improvise, to create music spontaneously. Jazz (which I love, but have never been able to play) is built on improvisation, but improvisation is rare among classical musicians.[2] Organists do it more often than others, because they are frequently called to "fill in" during parts of the service when nothing much is happening—seating of latecomers and so on. Both Mrs. M. and her successor at Beverly Heights, Ted Ripper, were excellent improvisers, the former using a more romantic style, the latter a somewhat severe neo-classicism. In one of my first lessons, Mrs. M. told me that it was possible to turn a hymn into a symphony. Noting my astonishment at that idea, she gave me an example. I think she began with the tune "Still, Still With Thee," to Mendelssohn's *Consolation*. She began softly, then added stops, inserted additional themes and obbligati, and eventually concluded with a swell of triumphant chords. I was quite amazed and was determined to learn how to do this. I watched and listened carefully to Mrs. M's improvisations, and later to those of Ted Ripper. When I was tired of practicing, I frequently improvised. It was therapeutic.

I remember one occasion where I was playing the little chapel organ for some youth meeting. Ted Ripper was the speaker, and he sat next to the organ, watching me as I played. Someone (without giving me any notice) announced the taking of an offering, and I began ruffling furiously through my music to find something I could play during the collection, especially frustrated that Ripper was watching. Then Ripper smiled, looked kindly at me, and said, "Johnny, just diddle." I diddled, and I've been diddling ever since.

Wichmann also gathered that I liked to improvise, so he shared with me the text that he had used himself to learn that skill: Marcel Dupré's book on the subject, in French. I had been studying French in high school, and so the language (actually fairly easy French) was actually an additional encouragement for me to study the book. French organists had the reputation of being the best improvisers, and I enjoyed getting some idea of what they were taught when they were my age.

As it turned out, in God's providence, I acquired that skill just in time. Wichmann recommended me for several organist positions in churches, and I looked forward to doing that as my first job. One of those was a position in a Christian Science church, and I've sometimes wondered what would have happened to the course of my life if I had gone there. Bob Kelley, always on

---

2. In learning to improvise in the classical style, I acquired a skill that is of absolutely no commercial value.

top of things, cautioned my parents against my taking that position. But neither my parents nor I had the discernment at the time to investigate the teachings of Christian Science and to turn down that opportunity. But again God stepped in. The Christian Scientists hired somebody else.

I was ready, however, to put my musical training to work. Sometime later, Mr. Esposito told me that George Estevez was seeking to hire an organist for the Beechview Presbyterian Church. George was a music student at Carnegie Tech, now Carnegie-Mellon University. I had remembered him as the bass soloist in a performance of Handel's *Messiah* at Beverly Heights. Now he was the choir director at Beechview Presbyterian, maybe a half hour's drive from my house. I visited there, then accepted the position.

Beechview was not as upscale a place as Mt. Lebanon. The members of the church were working people, middle class as we say. The church did have an organ, but it was a tiny Estey electrified reed organ with one manual and no pedalboard. The manual was divided into two sections, so that you could use one set of stops for the lower notes and a different set for the higher ones. That simulated the manual/pedal division typical of larger organs. However, there was almost nothing in my own organ repertoire that I could play on it. I could play some Bach pieces that were written for keyboard alone and a few by other composers. But I didn't know nearly enough pieces of that kind. What to do? I followed Ripper's advice: I diddled.

George Estevez understood my predicament, and he didn't seem to mind my improvising, but he occasionally asked me to play something more grand, which I was willing to do.

The choir music he selected was essentially the same repertoire that we used at Beverly Heights. So God continued to plant his word in my heart by the songs of the church. The difference between the two churches was that at Beechview nobody would have dreamed of asking young people to make decisions for Christ. The Beechview Church was not evangelical in that respect. I never heard anything there that seemed to me to be against Scripture, but I was not a keen listener in those days. And I did feel that although the Beechview people were wonderfully gracious, there was a lack of spiritual vitality in their fellowship. There didn't seem to be any sense that God's Holy Spirit could revolutionize a person's life. If my whole spiritual nurture had been transferred to Beechview Presbyterian, I would have been hurt. But in fact I never really left Beverly Heights during the three years that I worked at Beechview. I went to Beechview on Sunday mornings, but most always I was at Beverly Heights for the Sunday night youth meetings and evening services, and also for the Wednesday night Bible studies.

Theology en Route to Beechview

And something happened during my Beechview years that profoundly increased my theological understanding. As I got up early and drove to Beechview and back, I listened to the radio. When I woke up on Sunday to KDKA, there was first a program of religious music, including African-American (as we now say) spirituals. Then came a Bible dialogue between (as I would later describe them) a liberal Baptist minister and a neo-orthodox professor from Pittsburgh Theological Seminary. For the most part, they made no impression on me.

But then was *The Bible Study Hour*, with the teaching of Dr. Donald Grey Barnhouse, pastor of the Tenth Presbyterian Church of Philadelphia. I was fascinated by his every word. Barnhouse was a Californian who had evidently cultivated a kind of radio voice that cut through every other kind of sound. Trying to ignore him was like trying to ignore a buzz saw in the next room. But eventually it was his message that got through to me. He was in the midst of a series of messages from the Letter to the Romans that would eventually take something like ten years to complete. He was a remarkably intelligent and knowledgeable man who spoke with great clarity and who seemed to have answers to all biblical and theological problems. Doctrinally he was a dispensationalist with a Calvinistic understanding of God's sovereignty. I would later reject the distinctive teachings of dispensationalism, but I would often remember Barnhouse's treatment of problematic Bible passages.

On the way home from the Beechview service, I listened to *The Back to God Hour*, with sermons by Dr. Peter Eldersveld of the Christian Reformed Church. The CRC was Calvinistic, a Dutch-American body. Choirs from Calvin College, the CRC institution, sang on the program. I had not heard of the CRC before; this was my first contact with Dutch Calvinism, the first of many. Eldersveld was less flamboyant than Barnhouse, but he spoke clearly and helpfully. He was particularly gifted at relating Bible passages to cultural and political affairs.

Some might have thought that my attending Beechview rather than Beverly Heights on Sunday morning would have retarded my progress in Bible study. On the contrary, between Barnhouse and Eldersveld, my theological education took some giant steps. God used the radio, of all things.

He also used live teachers, of course. I heard many sermons by the senior pastor of Beverly Heights, William McLeister. McLeister was clearly evangelical, but did not put the emphasis on doctrine that Barnhouse and Eldersveld did. Essentially McLeister treated the congregation as people who had already made a commitment to Christ and who needed practical help in following Jesus. I was also helped by the assistant ministers and seminary interns at the church. Bob Kelley left the staff around 1955 to teach at the seminary and to begin a program of graduate study. But Bob continued to attend Beverly Heights with his wife and children, giving me a continuing opportunity to pepper him with questions. The seminary archaeologist, James Leon Kelso, also attended the church and taught a long-running men's Bible class. He visited the youth groups from time to time to show slides of his "digs" in Palestine.

John H. Gerstner

Another seminary professor who had great influence at Beverly Heights, though he did not attend there, was John H. Gerstner. Gerstner had attended Westminster Seminary in Philadelphia, which I would later attend. Then he earned a doctorate in Harvard's program in History, Philosophy, and Religion, writing a dissertation on Jonathan Edwards. He was a professor of church history at Pittsburgh Seminary, and was a strong defender of confessional Reformed orthodoxy.

Gerstner's level of scholarship was as intimidating as his orthodoxy to his seminary colleagues and to his audiences. The seminary was called Pittsburgh-Xenia Theological Seminary when I first was aware of it, later Pittsburgh Theological Seminary after it merged with Western Theological Seminary, the seminary of the PCUSA.[3] After the merger, Gerstner had few conservative colleagues, but he had a great number of disciples. A number of them took their internships at Beverly Heights and later took pastoral positions in Western Pennsylvania.[4]

I heard Gerstner speak and preach many times, at youth rallies, camps and conferences, and in church services. His clarity and cogency excelled any other speaker I knew. I don't think I have ever completely forgotten anything I heard him say. And when he dealt with a question that was in my mind, he dealt with that question fully and finally. Even today, as I write theology books and articles, Gerstner's voice resounds in my ear, reminding me of how he dealt with each subject.

3. This merger was the consequence of the larger merger between the United Presbyterian denomination and the larger (and more liberal) Presbyterian Church, USA.

4. I was amused that so many of these men actually *sounded* like Gerstner, even to this extent: Gerstner had an asthmatic condition, and he sometimes struggled to finish a sentence before taking a breath. But he turned even that condition into an asset. Struggling through, gasping to the end of the sentence, became a brilliant rhetorical device. Gerstner's disciples, though their lungs were for the most part entirely healthy, often imitated Gerstner's gasp simply to make rhetorical points.

A High School Satirist

If you have read this far, you might be wondering if I actually went to school during my teenage years. Indeed I did, at Andrew Mellon Junior High School and Mt. Lebanon High School. The first priority in high school was preparing for college, so I took all the science and math courses I could,[5] plus Latin, French, and honors English. I enjoyed the languages and English most, though I had some wonderful times in history classes. My honors English teacher for three years was Miss Virginia Elliott, and although I never developed a real taste for novels and poetry, she taught me how to write and thus laid the foundation of my eventual career. Miss Elliott was a Presbyterian Christian, member of First Presbyterian Church in downtown Pittsburgh, but she also taught a long-running Sunday School teacher training class for girls and women at Beverly Heights.

In my first year in her class, my sophomore year in high school, I wrote for Miss Elliott a long satire on Tennyson's *Idylls of the King* in blank verse. She thought it was very funny and showed it to other teachers. That satire established my reputation in high school as a writer, a humorist, a smart kid, and a hard worker. I wrote other satirical pieces and published them in the *Mounty*, the high school's literary magazine, of which Miss Elliott was the faculty sponsor. Then in senior year, she appointed me as co-editor of the paper, with Cathy Lynch. We focused on comedy and satire of course, sold more copies than was usual for the stately *Mounty*, and had a great time in the "PUB," the Publications Office that we inherited. I was somewhat devastated, however, when at Christmas time we had a visit from Gordon, a previous editor, then a student at, I believe, Harvard. Gordon told me that the 1956–57 *Mounty* was a terribly poor piece of work, inferior by far to the magazine he had edited two years before.

We tried to do better after that, but it was high school, after all. I also wrote some short comic pieces for the school Yearbook, the *Lebanon Log*, and edited for a while the French paper, *Potpourri*.

There was drama at Mt. Lebanon High School—not quite like the episodes that embroiled students in the following decade, but drama nonetheless. A good friend of mine named Eric, who wrote and drew cartoons for the *Mounty*, was a constant critic of the school administration. Eric didn't like rules, or forms, or being called in to see the assistant principal. Once he hung the principal and vice principal in effigy from a tree outside the school. On another occasion, we had one of those stuffy assemblies, in which students were called up to the stage to receive prestigious awards. During

---

5. This was the period in which the US raced the Russians to get to the moon.

the football awards, Eric (a very small kid) waited in the line of very large awardees. After the student ahead of him walked up on the stage, Eric went up on the stage and looked around with a bewildered expression, as if to say "where's my award?" We all laughed. It would have been good if an administrator had said "Touché" in thanks for the comic relief. But what happened next was hardly comic. The administration suspended Eric and announced that he would receive no recommendation to college. My friends and I did not sympathize at all with the administration's position. Their discipline did not come anywhere near to fitting the crime, if indeed there was a crime. I suppose their decision was a response, not to the assembly incident, but to Eric's whole "attitude" over three years. But this punishment did as much harm to the administration as to Eric; the administration sank very low in our esteem. The attitudes of many of us became very much like what the administration attributed to Eric. Eric stayed out of school one year, then matriculated at Amherst. He became a lawyer and "political activist."[6]

The last paper I wrote for Miss Elliott was a satire on Mt. Lebanon High School. A year or two before, a committee of our teachers visited New Trier High School north of Chicago and came back to Mt. Lebanon raving about how wonderfully well behaved the New Trier students were in comparison with us. In my satire, the narrator (yours truly) moves to New Trier and finds the school operating as a perfect mechanism. Eventually (probably this plot reflected something in the *Twilight Zone* or *Outer Limits*) the narrator discovers that the students are all controlled by electrodes planted in their heads directed by a monstrous machine in the furnace room. He heroically disconnects everything and destroys the hideous regime. Parallels with Eric and the Mt. Lebanon administration abounded. Miss Elliott described it as a "bitter paper." Well, I didn't really feel bitter, but I did think something should be said that would state the students' case.

Religious Adventures

Meanwhile, I practiced my theological interests. Another good friend of mine, Louie, was a Roman Catholic. We agreed to conduct in writing a debate about our respective theological positions. He would write a comment and slip it to me (usually during a class or in the hall). I would write numbers within his comment, to which my own comments would correspond. Then he would reply to mine and I to him, etc. Eventually, our joint treatise totaled about eighty pages. In the document itself, neither of us wavered

---

6. https://www.amherst.edu/aboutamherst/magazine/in_memory/1962/elwalgren. He died of cancer in 1998.

from our original positions. But at the end of the summer, after I returned from a cross-country trip (see below), Louie called and said he had left the Catholic Church and was attending First Presbyterian Church downtown. I was dumbfounded and very surprised. He gave me some credit for motivating his change, but since we both were then Calvinists, we agreed that God had done this.

But I had other religious adventures in high school that did not bring much credit on the gospel. With a group of my friends, I wrote to cults and sects that advertised in various magazines—groups like the Rosicrucians, the Mayans, the Harvest Publishers, the Faithist spiritualists, Christian Scientists, and so on, that claimed supernatural knowledge and power and promised transport to new orders of being. We told them fanciful stories, sometimes implying that we were visitors from other planets and the like. We sent one group's literature to other groups, working at least some amount of confusion for them, merriment for us. Fun as it was, it involved a lot of lying, and I did not make any effort to teach these people about Jesus. I did not love the people I was writing to. Today I repudiate all of this, in heartfelt repentance.

My Lack of Romance

Readers of teenage memoirs often look for accounts of romance. Alas, they will not find it here. I never dated in high school; indeed I did not marry until age forty-five. The reader must wait quite a while to read even of a serious relationship. There were many young ladies that I admired from afar in those days. But I hated the whole idea of parties and dating, part of a social disability that afflicts me still. I wanted to have a girlfriend, but I imagined that it could happen as in the movies: boy meets girl in the course of a great adventure, and they fall in love before even sharing a meal. But that never happened in real life. There were a few young women that I remember often, some who (I was later told) would have gone out with me if I had asked them, and one whom I remember as a spiritual mentor, who shamed me by her maturity in Christ.

Visiting the West

On graduation in 1957, I received a remarkable gift. With three friends, Dave Burnham, Bob Long, and Clark Blaise, I took a summer-long tour of the United States. Our eight parents paid for us to take a recent year Oldsmobile and two pup tents to national parks around the country, visiting also some of our relatives in western cities. They gave each of us $500 to spend on food, gas, and car maintenance, and we each had money left over when we returned.

Me in 1957

Our first night in the pup tents was in a Missouri campground, during a ferocious rainstorm. When it wasn't raining, it was very hot and humid, and I promised myself I would never live in Missouri. But we had happier times in Colorado: Denver, Colorado Springs, Pike's Peak, Mesa Verde (with the fascinating cliff dwellings). In Utah, we visited Bryce and Zion National Parks, and got a lecture on Mormonism in the temple area of Salt Lake City from a high priest of their faith. Our experience with cults and sects had prepared us for the priest's arguments. We listened closer when a Bible institute student got into a debate with him. I searched in my heart for the "burning in the bosom," which supposedly brings conversion to the Mormon faith, but that never came. But I did buy an inexpensive copy of the Book of Mormon and read it during leisure moments.

In Arizona, we visited the Grand Canyon, an overwhelming experience. Then came California. A television broadcast in Los Angeles, a visit to the newly built Disneyland, a swing into Tijuana, then up to San Francisco Bay. Dinners at Fisherman's Wharf and Trader Vic's. Sequoia, King's Canyon, and Yosemite Parks. Of all the states we visited, I thought I would most enjoy living in California. And indeed, in God's providence, I did spend 1980–2000 in that state.

Then we went on to Crater Lake in Oregon, a special favorite of mine. We had good views of Mt. Hood and Mt. Rainier on our way to Canada, where we spent some time in Banff and Jasper parks. Then back to the US: Yellowstone Park, Glacier Park, the Black Hills and Mt. Rushmore, then home.

We four grads had great times together. We hiked, fished (though I spent our deep-sea fishing excursion leaning over the edge of the boat), and went to shows. And we engaged in conversation, often philosophical and religious. We mocked the culture of our day. But we were very well behaved by today's standards, or even by the standards of the fifties: no drugs, no sex, no altercations.

Of the four of us, Bob was fairly secular in his thinking, went on to study physics and engineering at Cal Tech. Clark was interested in everything, always with humor and insight. He later graduated from the Writers' Workshop at the University of Iowa, and became a celebrated writer of novels and stories.[7] Dave went with me to Princeton, where we became roommates. In the summer of 1960 he and I traveled in Africa, the Near East, and Europe, and had more adventures together, which I shall describe later.

The National Parks filled me with an overwhelming sense of God's reality and his providential care for the whole creation. But one major thing was lacking during the summer of 1957. In that whole trip, we only attended worship services once or twice. Once was an outdoor service in one of the national parks; the other I don't remember at all. I'm not sure why we were so delinquent in this area. We were all interested in religion, and it would not have taken much for one of us to say on a Sunday, "Hey, let's stop and visit this church." But it almost never happened. There was always something else to do. So we were far from remembering the Sabbath Day to keep it holy.

In my case, my spiritual life was at something of a low ebb, though I would have told anyone that I believed in God and in Jesus. The correspondence with cults did not persuade me that any of them were true, but they injected a level of relativism into my thinking. What if I had been born and raised a Mormon? I asked myself. Can I really say that those who refuse the biblical Jesus are damned to hell? And what Miss Elliott called the "bitterness" of my last high school paper, whether that term truly applied or not, evidenced a lack of confidence in the cultural, educational, and religious establishment.

Summary

Mt. Lebanon High School tried to teach us values. And, as I mentioned in chapter 1, these were values that did not directly contradict Scripture. But they were more secular than biblical, more cultural than covenantal, more humanist than theist. By August of 1957, I had lost confidence in the values of the school system, and I was confused. My head was going back and forth between the hard-edged Calvinism of John Gerstner and the "everyone-get-along" humanism of my school.

So I was an easy target for what I would later describe as theological liberalism. I wasn't sure what to think when Louie announced to me his theological change. God had done it, but was that a good thing or not? I found it easy, when people would ask me questions about problems in the Bible, to say things like "well, of course, the Bible is a set of symbols, not a

---

7. See http://en.wikipedia.org/wiki/Clark_Blaise and elsewhere. He is usually described as a "Canadian writer," but he spent many years in the US.

literal description of anything." Later, I would condemn that kind of statement without hesitation, but in August 1957 that sort of thinking deeply infected my own theology.

But I was spiritually hungry as at no other time in my life. I knew that I desperately needed to grow in my spiritual life. I deeply missed the fellowship of Beverly Heights, and as I prepared to go to college I longed to find something like it in my next location.

3

Evangelical at Princeton

I WAS A FAIRLY passive participant in planning for college. My parents, in consultation with Fern Horne, our high school guidance counselor, recommended that I apply to Princeton, Yale, and the smaller (but still elite) colleges of Williams and Amherst. In the summer of 1956 (a year before graduation, and before the trip described in the last chapter) I played the piano for the boys' meetings at the New Wilmington Missionary Conference, then came home exhausted and looking eagerly to a few weeks' rest before school started again. But the moment I got home, my parents announced that we were going on a family trip to visit the four colleges mentioned above. They had arranged for conferences with admissions personnel. I protested mightily, but the decision was made, and as a fairly submissive son I had no choice but to go along.

My body, at least, rebelled. For most of the trip I had a painful stomach virus. I managed to look at the campuses out the car window and to muster some appearance of normality for the admissions' interviews. But when possible, I was in bed, taking whatever medicines could be found over-the-counter in the various states.

Still, I did form some impressions. All the campuses were beautiful. Yale was a bit too citified for my taste, but its facilities were the most impressive of the four.

My Uncle Dick had gone to Yale, and many of the family thought I should follow in his footsteps. Dick and I looked alike: red hair, freckles, weight problems. I inherited a lot of his outgrown clothes. He studied law at the University of Virginia and was married in the Washington National Cathedral, with most all of the family present, including me. He practiced law, became a state senator from the Franklin area (1962–77), and eventually chairman of the Pennsylvania Republican Party.[1] Sadly, he died in a plane crash near Harrisburg, PA. A bridge in the Franklin area is named after him. But even in 1956 his accomplishments recommended Yale as a possible school for me to attend.

But I preferred not to walk that closely in my uncle's steps. Princeton was closer to home, and it had much to recommend it. It was a bit smaller than Yale, and it claimed to put a larger emphasis on undergraduate pedagogy. Woodrow Wilson, president of the university from 1902–10, instituted a "preceptorial system," in which students would normally attend two hours of lectures per week in a course and then gather for another hour (a "preceptorial") given to discussion of the course material, under the leadership of a faculty member. The leaders of the preceptorials were often, though not always, full professors: Wilson greatly expanded the faculty to bring in enough scholars to handle the system.[2]

The rumor was that the faculties of Yale and Harvard were mainly there for research and to direct doctoral students. At Princeton, however, they honored faculty members for excellence in teaching undergraduates.

Another rumor was that Princeton was Presbyterian. That was not true. The university had been founded by Presbyterians to prepare students for ministry. It was considered for a while a more orthodox alternative to Harvard and Yale. But by the turn of the twentieth century, Princeton was no longer a distinctively religious school.[3] What religion there was, in the

---

1. Dick was a "moderate Republican." I am not moderate at all, a member of the religious right.

2. Wilson also dismantled the fraternities and replaced them with "eating clubs." The difference was not great in my eyes, but I thought the club system would be more relaxed, and for the most part it was. After two years eating in the undergraduate commons, my classmates went into "Bicker" in which we were visited by clubs that wanted us as members. I was accepted with some Christian friends into Terrace Club—not high in the social hierarchy, but a friendly place with good food.

3. It maintains, however, traces of its Presbyterian history, including its original motto, *Dei sub numine viget*, "under the power of God she flourishes." Some irreverent students, when I was there, translated it "God went to Princeton."

religious studies department, in the churches nearby, in the University Chapel,[4] was mostly theological liberalism, as I would discover to my shock.[5]

So after some thinking and praying I was inclined to go to Princeton. One problem was that I had told Yale that they were my first choice, and the rumor was that if you said that to either Princeton or Yale, the other university would turn you down. So fairly late in the process I called the Princeton alumnus who interviewed me and told him Princeton was now my first choice. As it happened in God's providence, I was accepted to all four schools and chose Princeton.

Freshman Year

My Mt. Lebanon classmate Dave Burnham, one of the group that visited the west in the summer of 1957, became my roommate in Pyne Hall, the freshman dorm. He was interested mainly in physics, but loved classical music. He brought a "hi fi" system, as we called them then, and we listened to a lot of concerti and symphonies.

I took a standard liberal arts program: Shakespeare, with thespian Alan Downer, Politics, in which the lecturer was William Ebenstein. Ebenstein had some history in Germany, and he hated fascism and also the totalitarianism of the Soviet Union.[6] I also took French. Princeton gave me credit for my three years of high school French and allowed me to take the last course of their basic French sequence. That cleared the way for me to take two years of Attic Greek, which, as it turned out, prepared me well for seminary.[7]

---

4. But when I was there the university chaplain was Ernest Gordon, author of *Through the Valley of the Kwai*, a Scot who told stories of God's providence in the dark circumstances of the war. Gordon thought that Barth's view of Scripture was too loose, and in general the chaplain's preaching followed evangelical patterns. But he invited radical theologians and pastors, like William Sloane Coffin and Paul Tillich, to preach in chapel.

5. In the same town was located Princeton Theological Seminary, which was also fairly liberal in its theology, but deeply influenced by Karl Barth. The seminary and the university were separate organizations.

6. Students who go to Ivy League schools (indeed to most all secular colleges) often report that they are inundated by left-wing political propaganda. That was not true of my experience at Princeton.

7. Attic is more complicated than the *koiné* Greek in which the New Testament was written. So my courses in Attic enabled me to read the New Testament in the original language. Before long I was having my devotions in the Greek Bible, particularly Luke-Acts, Romans, and Hebrews, which seemed to be the most difficult books linguistically and also theologically central.

Princeton also required undergraduates to take one course in science. The alternatives were physics, chemistry, biology, and psychology. Given those alternatives, of course I became a student of psychology.[8] I never thought of psychology as an actual science, and still do not. But Princeton did, given that their philosophy of psychology was generally behaviorist. So we actually had "lab" sessions, in which we would, for example, test one another's sensations. For example, a student would take two (fairly blunt) compass pointers, place them some distance apart on the arm of another student. We would take statistics to determine how close together those needles would have to be for the subject to feel them as one sensation rather than two. I don't recall what psychological conclusions we were supposed to draw from this "experiment."

Finally, I took "Problems of Philosophy." Most beginning philosophy students took a course in Plato, but I was more interested, even then, in problems than in individual thinkers. The lecturer was Ledger Wood, who had rewritten Frank Thilly's *A History of Philosophy*. My preceptor was Ronald J. Butler. At the first precept, Butler pointed out the window, where the leaves of a green tree were in motion. Butler asked the likely reason for the movement of the leaves. The wind, was the predictable consensus. But Butler asked, what of the possibility that each leaf is being shaken by an angel? The students ridiculed the hypothesis, but no one actually refuted it. As it turned out, what Butler wanted us to see (or at least to say) was that the wind hypothesis could be tested by scientific evidence, but that the angel hypothesis could not be.

Princeton's philosophy department was a bit behind the times. The school of logical positivism had said that no hypothesis could be "cognitively meaningful" unless it could be "verified" by certain approved scientific means. By 1957, logical positivism had run its course at most universities. But at Princeton Carl Hempel, one of the founders of logical positivism, was the leading philosopher of science, and he was firmly committed to that school of thought. Hempel's views did not permeate the Princeton philosophy department, but they were taken seriously by all his colleagues. It was assumed that all Hempel's questions, at least, were good questions.

Memorable as that preceptorial was, I did not become a logical positivist. Rather, I entertained seriously the possibility of angels in the tree, shaking the leaves. Does not the author of Hebrews cite Ps 104:4, "He makes his angels winds, and his ministers a flame of fire" (Heb 1:7)? The net effect

---

8. Then there was the physical education requirement, in which each student could choose to learn sports in various categories, including "combative." That is why I gained a tiny bit of knowledge about fencing, but fell somewhat short of the requirements to become a swashbuckler.

of that discussion was to encourage me to see God's providence in all the events of the natural world, what I would later call "concurrence."

My freshman year put me in a very new and strange intellectual atmosphere. Among other things, my grades did not measure up to my expectations. At the end of the first semester I had a B average. I knew some things had to change. In high school, grades were something of an afterthought; they seemed to come naturally. But at Princeton, we were expected to achieve a higher level of mastery in our courses. So in the second semester I quit studying in the dorm room and went every night to spread my books and notes out at a table in Firestone library. I learned that much as I loved Dave's classical music I could not listen to that and study for Princeton courses at the same time. My grades increased into the A range (with some exceptions: see below) and never declined again.

Seeking Christianity in Princeton Christendom

But I could not be content with my own reflections on philosophical and religious subjects. I needed someone to teach me about God. In the last chapter I spoke of my trip around the country in the summer of 1957, in which we talked much about religion, but went to church only twice. Now in the fall of 1957 I was spiritually hungry as I have never been before or since.

I visited a number of Princeton churches, first of all the University Chapel, then First Presbyterian, then Second Presbyterian. Second Presbyterian seemed more serious about God than the others, but it did not have the vitality that I remembered from Beverly Heights. It was not a church where a kid could get saved through the blood of Christ and learn the Bible from people who loved it. I accepted an invitation from David Gay, a friend in Pyne Hall, to visit his Episcopal church, a small church in the country named St. Barnabas. For several months, David and I alternated there as organists, and we were at least on the brink of getting a choir started. The liturgy was strange to me. I tried to get the hang of it, but never really understood what it was supposed to be about. I loved some things, like the hymn "I Sing a Song of the Saints of God," which jumps into my head whenever I think of anything Anglican.

My time there ended near Christmas, when Father Eddy, the rector, explained to the congregation that the carols about angels singing at Jesus' birth were not telling the literal truth. The praise of Jesus by angels, he said, was post-Resurrection. Well, at least he believed in the resurrection—or did he? If he felt free to take issue with the Gospel accounts of Christmas, I thought, how could he be so sure that the events of Easter really happened? And yet he sang the carols lustily, almost as if he really believed them.

Occasionally I visited the Westminster Foundation, the campus ministry of the Presbyterian Church, USA. The chaplain, Robert Montgomery, was up on all the latest theological writers and trends, and the latest in politics and culture. He wore clerical garb, the first Presbyterian I had met who adopted that costume. The burden of his message was that the church should be "in the world," which seemed to mean that we should not try to be too distinct from unbelief. We should seek solidarity with sinners, as Jesus did. Montgomery told a story about attending a cocktail party in his black coat and clerical collar, and how a fairly drunken lady said to him, "It means so much to us for you to be here with us." Certainly there was truth in this, but didn't Jesus attempt to lift sinners' eyes to higher things? And wasn't there also a biblical principle of separation from wickedness? Montgomery focused on only one side, and therefore he was not able to help me much. And what about all the other teachings of Christianity? Surely "church in the world" didn't exhaust the message of the Bible.

I also attended Wednesday night meetings sponsored by the campus Student Christian Association. The speakers at these meetings were local pastors, denominational chaplains, religion professors, and other professing Christian faculty. These meetings gave me a broader idea of the strains of religion at Princeton. Sometimes these were informative, but rarely inspiring. One minister on the SCA staff once told me, "I don't think that *anybody* believes anymore that Jesus is God."

The Princeton Evangelical Fellowship

I prayed that God would lead me into a fellowship that would help me toward maturity in Christ. In the course of that first semester I started noticing a sign that was erected near Murray-Dodge Hall, the same building where I went for the Wednesday night SCA meetings. The sign advertised a twice-weekly Bible study led by Donald B. Fullerton, D.D., of the Princeton class of 1913. I asked fellow students about the Princeton Evangelical Fellowship, which sponsored these Bible studies. The reply was that this organization was "fundamentalist." Well, I had given time and attention to maybe seventeen other religious viewpoints, why not fundamentalism?

Fullerton, after he graduated from Princeton, had sought opportunities for missionary service, and he had spent some time on the border of Afghanistan and India, bringing the gospel to the people there.[9] Health

---

9. For more on Fullerton's background and ministry, see http://www.

problems forced him back to the US, where he taught for a time at the National Bible Institute of New York, later Shelton College. But a friend of his called to say that his son was having a hard time spiritually at Princeton. He asked Fullerton to go and talk to him. Fullerton did, and started Bible classes on campus. Eventually these classes became known as PEF. Fullerton never married, and he evidently had independent financial means, though the group was also supported by donors, particularly PEF alumni. So eventually Fullerton moved to Princeton and gave the rest of his life to the PEF campus ministry.

Donald B. Fullerton, Bible teacher for the Princeton Evangelical Fellowship

At the time (early 1930s), there was no other evangelical Christian group on the campus. A few years later, Inter-Varsity Christian Fellowship would begin to establish chapters on American campuses. IVCF had a different approach to campus ministry from PEF: not formal Bible teaching, nor a single leader per campus, but rather student-led inductive studies and guest speakers. But Fullerton said that C. Stacey Woods, the first president of IVCF in the USA, agreed that he would not start an IVCF chapter at Princeton as long as PEF was there.

By nature, I probably would have preferred an IVCF type of ministry. I preferred more interactive Bible study, rather than just being lectured to. But I became aware of PEF before I learned of any alternative, and when I did learn of an alternative (see below), by that time I was sold on PEF.

Princeton Evangelical Fellowship, 1960.
I am in the second row

---

frame-poythress.org/remembering-donald-b-fullerton/, some of which I have excerpted here.

The Lord knew best, as always: PEF was exactly what I needed. Contrary to my inflated opinion of myself, I needed solid teaching. Fullerton supplied that need. Besides, the peer pressure within PEF encouraged the students to go deeper and deeper into Scripture, prayer, and evangelism. To discuss theological issues with PEFers, you had to know your Bible! Else, you would not be taken seriously. So PEF took me far deeper into Scripture than I had ever gone before, and, I think, much deeper than any IVCF group could have brought me. I continued on the Navigators' Topical Memory System that I had started at Beverly Heights, and studied thoroughly the new lessons I was learning through PEF.

When I arrived in 1957, PEF had two Bible studies a week in Murray-Dodge Hall. One was on Sunday afternoon, the other on either Wednesday or Thursday night, depending on everybody's schedules. Dr. Fullerton taught both classes. He was around sixty-five, thin, but somehow imposing, with snow-white hair. He usually spoke very softly, but he could rise to a roar when making a major point. He had a puckish, sometimes sarcastic, sense of humor.[10] I remember him being doubled up in laughter when describing pranks played by various undergrads. But when he spoke about God and the Bible he was deadly serious. He commented unfavorably about one talk we heard by Ralph Keiper, Barnhouse's assistant (on John 17 of all passages), who told too many jokes for Fullerton's comfort. (I, however, thought that Keiper's humor actually enhanced the quality of his teaching.)

Fullerton almost never missed a Bible class, though he had a number of ailments. He also attended, with the students, a daily afternoon prayer meeting held in a student dorm room. At those meetings, someone would read Scripture, the students would discuss the passage briefly, then we knelt and prayed for one another, for students we were seeking to evangelize, and for alumni, especially those laboring in mission fields. A number of PEF men visited a nearby institution in Jamestown, NJ, what we used to call "reform school," to teach Sunday School. I was a substitute teacher there on a couple occasions. Those boys were another topic of prayer, and God answered, bringing some conversions through this ministry.

Dr. Fullerton was constantly about his Father's business. When he met a new student, it usually did not take more than thirty seconds for him to

---

10. Some Princeton alumni from this period have complained about Fullerton using language about Jews and African-Americans that is now considered offensive. Those reports are true, and I offer no justification for them. But we should consider also that he was a man of his time, a time when ethnic humor dominated the airwaves, and long before sensitivities to the effect of such language were the subject of much reflection. I don't believe that Don Fullerton ever "hated" anyone, though often today such insensitive language is overinterpreted and condemned as hate speech.

get on the subject of Jesus and the gospel. Then Fullerton would talk with the student as long as possible and necessary, to discern his spiritual condition, to present the gospel, to answer questions, to urge a decision. When we students sought to lead others to Christ, our main strategy was usually to maneuver them into a situation where they could have a good talk with Dr. Fullerton. Not every student who talked with him was converted, but many were. It seemed to us that, humanly speaking, if anyone could get the gospel through to a Princeton student, it was Dr. Fullerton.

I can't recall my own first conversation with him. Most likely, I told him that I was already saved and trying to serve the Lord on the campus. He probably accepted that self-representation, but no doubt he looked at me as very immature spiritually. He made judgments of that sort often, and he was usually right, though occasionally too quick and too condemnatory. He often spoke of students past and present who suffered spiritual shipwreck because of this weakness and that. One didn't pray enough. Another didn't attend Bible studies regularly. Another got into a worldly group of friends. Still another started his decline by questioning the Scriptures, and often that questioning began when the student took a religion course. Another student thought he knew a lot, though in fact he knew very little. Often those that suffered shipwreck were Presbyterians of one sort or another.

The net conclusion of this emphasis, and the consensus among PEF members, was that a student could not hope to maintain his spiritual bearings at Princeton without regular attendance at PEF Bible studies and prayer meetings and devotion to campus evangelism. Most of the PEF students, as I myself, also accepted Dr. F's offer of a personal weekly Bible study at Dr. F's house on Alexander Street. When I arrived at his house, he would offer me a banana, or coffee, or a cookie. We'd sit opposite one another at the kitchen table. With me, he started at Genesis and worked through it verse by verse. He was concerned to emphasize the literal truth of the events described there. He had firm views on the controversies over evolution and the age of the earth and could argue them both exegetically and scientifically (according to the creation-science model). He wanted to ensure that I held orthodox positions in these areas.

Fullerton strongly emphasized the inerrancy of Scripture, the deity of Christ, the certainty of Jesus' resurrection, and in general the miraculous character of the Christian worldview. I had taken these things mostly for granted, but it was from Fullerton that I learned the divisions within the professing church over precisely these fundamental issues. Those who believed these teachings were biblical Christians, or "evangelicals," or "fundamental."[11] The others were "liberal," or, if followers of Barth or Brunner, "neo-orthodox."

At some point, the picture came together for me. Suddenly, I understood the mystery of why there was so little vitality in Princeton Christianity: most of the churches, chaplains, and denominations were liberal. Princeton Christians did not teach the Bible in depth, because they did not believe in the authority of the Bible. They did not lead people to trust in Christ alone, because they did not believe that Christ died to save sinners from the wrath of God.

Beverly Heights had given me a good background for life in college, except in this area. As a high school student at Beverly Heights, I received the impression that I could walk into any mainline church and hear the same gospel that had saved me in Pittsburgh. Beverly Heights was an evangelical church, but part of a liberal denomination, the PCUSA; and they did not want to make waves by telling their people the differences between the gospel of Scripture and the liberal message of humanism—even though these differences were differences of life and death. So they gave me almost no useful guidance on how to find a Christ-honoring fellowship in Princeton. That is my one critique of my home church, and a serious one.

Dr. Fullerton hated liberalism and neo-orthodoxy. He recommended Cornelius Van Til's writings on Barth. Like Van Til, he considered Barth and his followers to be liberals who conceal their liberalism under orthodox terminology. He admired J. Gresham Machen for his stand against the liberal heresy in the Presbyterian Church. I found Fullerton's critique of liberalism absolutely cogent. Though I had flirted with liberalism in my senior year of high school ("Well, it's all symbolic, after all"), I never went back to it, thanks largely to Fullerton's powerful argument. He simply showed us what Christ himself said about the Scriptures and the testimonies of other prophets and apostles, in other words, the Bible's witness to itself.

He also showed us—and I had never heard this before—that the Bible contains a very strong polemic against false teachers. Christians are to shun these: "from such turn away" (2 Tim 3:5).

Fullerton's theology was also dispensationalist and premillennial. At first, this teaching appealed to me somewhat. It was similar to that of Donald Grey Barnhouse, who I had listened to at home on the radio Sunday mornings. Like Barnhouse (DGB), Fullerton (DBF) knew dispensational theology thoroughly and had a great gift for expounding it and illustrating

---

11. In Fullerton's terminology, PEF people were "fundamental," never "fundamentalist."

it. But when I returned home, my most theologically knowledgeable friends, having imbibed the teaching of John Gerstner, told me that dispensationalism was a heresy. I never actually bought the dispensational system, but I could never bring myself to believe that it was as serious an error as the Gerstner disciples made it out to be.

On the issues of Calvinism and Arminianism, Fullerton straddled the fence. He loved the old Scottish covenanters. For a time, during his youth, he studied the theology of Abraham Kuyper with someone. His mother, however, whom he greatly revered, told him that the Kuyper lessons had dampened his missionary zeal. He recognized that was true, at least for him personally, so he left Kuyper behind. Fullerton admired a number of American Presbyterians, like Warfield, Machen, and Van Til. He had friends in the movement that had left Princeton Seminary to found Westminster Seminary, especially in the premillennial group that later left Westminster to found Faith Seminary. But I think he came to believe that Presbyterian theology, even at its most orthodox, was vulnerable to liberalism. Presbyterians (except for the Faith Seminary group) were a- or post-millennialists, and Fullerton saw those views as "spiritualizing" the Bible rather than taking it literally. Spiritualizing the Bible, in his mind, was the first step toward abandoning biblical authority altogether.

A couple years, before I arrived at Princeton, there was a division in PEF when someone began a "Baptist Student Fellowship" on campus. When I arrived, the Baptist group was not actually Baptist. It consisted of students who were mostly evangelicals from the PCUSA, who wanted to have an Inter-Varsity type group led by Princeton Seminary students. I attended a few meetings of the group and had some casual friends among them. As I mentioned earlier, their approach to Bible study had some appeal to me in my first days at Princeton. But by the time I was aware of the Baptist group I had determined that I could get better teaching and nurture through PEF.

Still the Baptist group was a thorn in Dr. Fullerton's side, and it doubtless made him even more suspicious of people from Presbyterian churches, even conservative ones, and people who leaned toward Reformed theology. He was a separatist: people in liberal denominations, in his view, should leave them immediately ("from such turn away"). Christians studying at Princeton Seminary (or other Presbyterian seminaries) should leave immediately. Fullerton told one Princeton Seminarian that he wanted to see nothing more of him but "a cloud of dust," as the student left the Seminary at full speed. Anyone who belonged to the PCUSA (even dispensational conservatives like Barnhouse and Keiper) were deeply suspect.

And, in Fullerton's judgment, people in conservative Presbyterian denominations like the Orthodox Presbyterian and Bible Presbyterian churches could not hope to achieve the spiritual depth of those in Baptist, Plymouth Brethren, or Independent Fundamental churches. He thought that Calvinists in general were like he was when he was studying Kuyper: unevangelistic, without passion for the Lord. The Orthodox Presbyterians, he said once, were "straight as an icicle, and just as cold."

When Fullerton addressed questions of the sovereignty of God and the free will of man, he typically told us to accept these as simply paradoxical. He was fond of the illustration of two parallel lines that never meet where we can see them, but which meet above the clouds, in Heaven. (Interestingly, Van Til used the same illustration, but for him the two lines were not divine sovereignty and human free will, but divine sovereignty and human responsibility. "Free will" in the Arminian sense received nothing but anathema from Van Til.) Fullerton also used the illustration of a sinner reading a sign that says, "Whosoever will, let him come" and following its direction. After coming to Jesus, he looks back at the other side of the sign, which reads, "Chosen in Christ, before the foundation of the world." So Fullerton may not have been a Calvinist, but he certainly was not Arminian either. He believed that by focusing on the incomprehensibility of God he had discovered a biblical balance that transcended those historic positions. So he had no particular allegiance to any historic tradition, though he was strongly opposed to the Roman Catholic and liberal Protestant movements. Although dispensationalism itself was a tradition going back to the early nineteenth century, Fullerton considered himself simply a student of the Bible, and he had a very low view of people who stressed Reformed, Lutheran, Anglican, or some other theological or ecclesiastical tradition.

He did have a strong (I am tempted to say Calvinistic) emphasis on the lordship of Christ, and that had a profound impact on the student who later authored *The Theology of Lordship*. Though some dispensational fundamentalists argued that you can trust Christ as savior without trusting him as Lord, Fullerton would have none of it. He insisted that if Jesus is not lord he cannot be savior, and he often quoted Rom 10:9-10—the confession of Jesus as lord—as the mark of the Christian.

He held the usual dispensational view of the OT law, that as law it no longer binds the NT believer. He was not Sabbatarian, but he thought it important to attend church and Bible studies on Sunday. But Fullerton had no prejudice against law as such. Commands given by Christ and the apostles are to be obeyed, Fullerton taught, and such obedience is the basic substance of the Christian life.

Some speakers at PEF conferences[12] advocated the "victorious life" emphasis of the Keswick movement. PEF had its annual fall retreat at the

12. Each year, PEF had a Bible conference and a missions conference, in alternate

America's Keswick conference ground. In this teaching the believer should cultivate passivity: let go and let God, quit striving for holiness. Striving, it was said, leads us into a works-oriented Christian life, at odds with the gospel of grace. Pastor Howard Burtner gave especially memorable expositions of this view at one PEF conference at Keswick. Fullerton never criticized this approach explicitly, and I think he admired Burtner and others who seemed to have achieved that "victorious life." But I never felt that Fullerton heartily embraced for himself this approach to sanctification. He had a view of spiritual warfare that was actually more typical of Reformed teaching: say no to sin and fight temptation by the grace of God and the power of the Holy Spirit. For Fullerton, and for PEF, this entailed separation from worldly practices like smoking and drinking. But these prohibitions were not at all central to the PEF ethic. The center, rather, was the lordship of Jesus. On sanctification, then, Fullerton was not entirely consistent. But the net impact of his teaching, on me at least, was Reformed.

Fullerton and the PEFers were somewhat suspicious of me. In several ways I didn't fit into the group very well. I belonged to a Presbyterian church and was more Calvinistic than dispensational in my theology. I majored in philosophy and took religion courses, strictly against PEF policy. When I was around Fullerton, I felt various barbs—such as stories about spiritual disasters among people who favored Presbyterianism, had ties to the PCUSA, took religion courses, and majored in philosophy.

But I attended most every PEF meeting and drank in the teaching with enthusiasm, as much of it as I agreed with, and I agreed with far more than I disagreed with. I loved the prayer meetings and tried on a number of occasions to bring non-Christians to the Bible studies (succeeding once or twice, as I recall). Like the other PEFers, I attended Westerly Road, an independent fundamental church (with, to be sure, a pastor, Ed Morgan, and some other leaders who were former Presbyterians).

PEF Bible studies began with the singing of a hymn or two, accompanied on the piano by Dr. Fullerton. When he found that I played the piano, he asked me to do it, and I became the regular pianist, and later the organist for Westerly Road Church.[13] So to some extent I became accepted in the

---

semesters. In addition was the opening retreat, usually held at the Keswick colony when I was a student. In general, the PEF conferences attracted impressive dispensational speakers from seminaries, churches, and missions. We heard S. Lewis Johnson, Charles Caldwell Ryrie, David Howard, Arthur Glasser, William Mahlow, John C. Whitcomb, Francis Steele, W. Cameron Townsend, Charles Seidenspinner, and many others. Francis Schaeffer came for an afternoon to speak to a group assembled in Fullerton's house. Attending these conferences was a highlight of my time at Princeton.

13. This was the extent of my musical activity at Princeton. I had expected to continue my organ lessons there, under the renowned organist of the University Chapel,

group. I was even elected treasurer for my last two years, even though I was a Presbyterian and a philosophy major.

Philosophy and Theology

So the major theological developments in my life at Princeton were through PEF and Westerly Road Church. But I believed that God wanted me also to become acquainted with the theology and philosophy offered at the University. I became a philosophy major and took other courses as well that were relevant to theology. PEF did not approve of this, but I wanted to experience liberalism in its most persuasive form, from its most learned advocates.

I took "Problems of Religious Thought," offered by the Religious Studies department. The lecturer was George Thomas, author of *Christian Ethics and Moral Philosophy*,[14] and the preceptor was Van Harvey, who later became famous as a Bultmann disciple and writer of *The Historian and the Believer*[15] and other books. Thomas assigned a number of things that interested me including C. S. Lewis's *The Problem of Pain*[16] and William Temple's Gifford Lectures, *Nature, Man and God*.[17] To summarize Temple's argument, "If mind emerged from nature, then nature must be grounded in mind." But Thomas, though grandfatherly in demeanor, had no sympathy with fundamentalism. In one discussion after class, he told some students, "Of course, this all assumes a critical view of the Bible."

Harvey had been raised a fundamentalist, the son of missionaries to China, but he had reacted sharply against the theology of his upbringing and regularly played the role of the skeptic. One student in the preceptorial, Mr. Coe, often responded to Harvey's questions by saying, "Well, of course that is a relative matter." Harvey regularly commended that answer and responded with ill-disguised contempt of anyone who expressed sympathy for orthodox Christianity. I was not myself convinced that Mr. Coe was the most profound thinker in the room.

The only other course I took that was deeply polemical against Christianity was the introductory sociology course with Melvin Tumin, "Cultural

---

Carl Weinrich. But for financial and other reasons that plan didn't work out, to the disappointment of Joseph Esposito and Russell Wichmann. I did practice my music for a while on the pipe organ in Alexander Hall, but for the most part my musical progress came to a halt at Princeton. I have, however, made use of my musical training in most every church that I have attended through my life.

14. New York: Scribner's, 1966.
15. New York: Macmillan, 1966.
16. London: Centenary, 1940.
17. London: Macmillan, 1953.

Anthropology." A recurring theme was "cultural relativism," and the villains of Tumin's lectures were usually Christian missionaries who brought about cultural change by preaching the gospel. Tumin thought they should have left the culture alone, however much they disapproved of it. And he never considered that the proclamation of the gospel might have brought any benefit at all to these tribes. The course seemed to me to be absurdly one-sided. Tumin never thought that any point of view other than his was worth discussing.

I took a couple history courses that focused on thinkers important to Christianity: "Medieval Thought" with Norman Cantor and "Renaissance and Reformation" with Edward Harbison. Though he was Jewish, Cantor presented a vivid and persuasive picture of Christian life in the middle ages. Even his hairstyle reminded me of a monk. At one point he asked why it was that Christianity became dominant in the Roman Empire while other religious movements such as the mystery religions faded away. His answer: of these, only Christianity made a historical claim. I have always considered that a very insightful answer and I lose few opportunities to present it to my own students.

Harbison had a gentle demeanor, but he carried much intellectual weight at Princeton. Because of its subject matter as well as its teacher, his "Ren and Ref" course provoked spiritual reflection among the students. One of his assignments was a good portion of Luther's *Bondage of the Will* together with *On Free Will* by Erasmus. In our preceptorial, moderated by Harbison himself, Luther won the debate hands down. I doubt that Harbison himself agreed entirely with Luther, but he seemed to take pleasure in watching his students beat Erasmus down.

I also took a couple courses in novels from English Professor Lawrence Thompson, who found symbols under every bed. He made us read a different novel every week, which was a chore for me. I prefer to read thoroughly, rather than fast. Thompson's discussions were amusing, but they almost sounded like medieval allegories. More satisfying as literary interpretation was a humanities course in which we read (in translation) Dante's *Inferno*, Goethe's *Faust*, and Cervantes' *Don Quixote*.

I also took a course on the History of Chinese Thought from the Oriental Studies Department. The professor was Frederick Mote, an excellent scholar and lecturer. For some reason, a number of PEF students took the course.

My major courses in philosophy were outstanding. The history of philosophy sequence was Gregory Vlastos on "Ancient and Medieval Philosophy" and George Pitcher on "Early Modern Philosophy" (ending with Kant). Sylvain Bromberger taught "Recent and Contemporary Empirical

Philosophy," but I did not get excited about Wittgenstein until some years later. Walter Kaufmann normally taught the course Hegel, Nietzsche, and Existentialism, but he was on leave when I took the course, and his replacement was Hans Jonas, who commuted to Princeton to teach it from the New School of Social Research in New York. Although I had not heard of him, Jonas was a very famous scholar in Gnosticism, existentialism, and bioethics. But he spoke in a very thick accent, scarcely intelligible to this Princeton undergraduate.

I also took courses in Elementary Logic, Advanced Logic, Philosophy of Religion, and Metaphysics, avoiding courses in Ethics and Aesthetics, which I thought would be too subjective.[18] The Elementary Logic course, taught by the old positivist Carl Hempel, was a breeze, and I expected Advanced Logic, taught by Hilary Putnam from Willard Quine's *Methods of Logic*, to be equally easy. It was not. It involved some mathematics that was well above my aptitude and achievement. I earned a D on the midterm and panicked as the final approached. Thanks to God, they distributed in advance a number of questions from which several would be on the exam. In taking the exam, we could choose two. Several of them required very complicated answers, the other two simple formulae. My roommate, who had taken the course before me, recommended that I memorize the two formulae. I did, earned a perfect score on the final exam and a B for the course.

In the Philosophy of Religion course, I finally got to study with Walter Kaufmann, who was probably the most famous member of the Princeton philosophy department, certainly one of its most lively teachers. Kaufmann had a quick and brilliant mind, and a wit that made philosophy into an enjoyable game. He regularly devastated other thinkers with a quick dash of sarcasm, and we students waited eagerly to find whom he would demolish next.

Kaufmann was a militant atheist, though he professed to be moved by religious literature "as poetry." As a teenager, he had a deconversion experience in which the problem of evil (he had lost relatives in the Holocaust) loomed large in his consciousness and displaced any inclinations to faith. The substance of his course can be found in his *Critique of Religion and Philosophy*[19] and *The Faith of a Heretic*.[20]

---

18. I believe they also offered a Philosophy of History course, taught by Ronald J. Butler, my first preceptor. I cannot remember why I didn't take it. I did take the Introduction to Social Philosophy course with Hugo Bedau, which introduced me to theories of government and punishment.

19. Princeton: Princeton University Press, 1979.

20. New York: Plume, 1978.

There was much in this course that fascinated me. Kaufmann criticized, not only orthodox Christians, but also liberals—he was an equal-opportunity offender. His *Critique* contains a devastating rebuttal of the Wellhausen Documentary Hypothesis, which divided the books of Moses into works of four or five different authors. I remember also a conference put together by the SCA in which Kaufmann debated the liberal theologian Julian Hartt of Yale (later one of my teachers there). Kaufmann asked Hartt two basic questions: Why be a theologian? And why be a Christian? Hartt hemmed and hawed, qualified and modified, talked as theologians talk. Kaufmann laughed, and the audience laughed with him.

Kaufmann also attacked the Bible, however, and orthodox Christian theology. I had no ready answer to all his arguments, but what he said was not strong enough to destroy my faith in Christ. I knew that if I did not have an answer, God did have one, and possibly a fellow Christian might have one. I went back to reading C. S. Lewis, whom I had read before, but now with greater interest and urgency. Lewis' *Mere Christianity*[21] seemed to me to make a powerful argument for God, more complex, perceptive, and profound than what Kaufmann proposed on the other side. Even more interesting to me was Lewis' book *Miracles: A Preliminary Study*,[22] in which he argues that opposition to miracles (as in Hume's philosophy) depends on the assumption of a naturalistic worldview that rules out miracles before the argument even begins.

At that point, Cornelius Van Til entered my life. Fullerton had referred to Van Til as a powerful critic of Barth, yet had criticized Van Til's approach as "too philosophical." But Christian philosophy was exactly what I needed at the time. Van Til was evidently an orthodox Christian who was able to reason at a sophisticated philosophical level, and so I tracked down his writings. Some of them were available in the University library. For more of them, I talked to Davis Young, a fellow student, who was the son of Edward J. Young who taught at Westminster Seminary and was a colleague of Van Til. From

Cornelius Van Til, my chief professor at Westminster

---

21. London: MacMillan, 1952.
22. London: Collins, 1947.

Dave I got the information I needed to purchase Van Til's writings for myself. First I read Van Til's pamphlet, "Why I Believe in God"[23] and then his book *The Defense of the Faith*.[24]

Van Til was not fond of C. S. Lewis. But in effect he broadened Lewis's argument in *Miracles*, arguing that *all* debates on *all* matters, not only debates about miracles, depended on assumed worldviews ("presuppositions"). I took Van Til to imply that Kaufmann's arguments, damaging as they sounded, were themselves based on presuppositions. Van Til thought it possible, furthermore, to show that non-Christian presuppositions make coherent thought impossible. And of course to think as Christians, we needed to think on the presupposition of Scripture. So God renewed my confidence in the Bible through Van Til's ministry to me.

James I. Packer's *Fundamentalism and the Word of God*[25] also played a major role in my thinking at this early point. It was the first scholarly defense of the authority of Scripture I had read. And, like Lewis and Van Til, it related that issue to a philosophical perspective. While Gabriel Hebert, whom Packer criticized, professed to represent "reason," Packer made the important distinction between Christian and non-Christian reasoning, a distinction that would influence all my own thinking and teaching on the subject. Like Van Til, Packer was saying that even our reasoning must be subject to the lordship of Christ.[26]

I did well in the Philosophy of Religion course, so, in a burst of overconfidence, I asked Kaufmann to be the advisor for my "Junior Paper," a long paper assigned as part of my philosophy major. Kaufmann graciously accepted my request. He suggested that I interact with some of the essays in Flew and McIntyre, *New Essays in Philosophical Theology*,[27] considered at the time a groundbreaking set of essays extremely damaging to Christianity (though some of the essays were written by liberal Christians). I hoped to write a paper that would make a difference, so I worked very hard, tried to show how several of the essays had common presuppositions, then developed a Van Tillian critique of those presuppositions. But Kaufmann would

23. http://www.reformed.org/apologetics/index.html?mainframe=/apologetics/why_I_believe_cvt.html.

24. 4th ed. Phillipsburg, NJ: P&R, 2008.

25. Grand Rapids: Eerdmans, 1958.

26. One of the happiest experiences of my later life has been Packer's willingness to write forewords to my *DWG* and my *ST*. He also, after meeting me in a restaurant, described my *DG* as "magisterial." Honor from one of my great heroes!

27. London: Macmillan, 1955. This book contains Antony Flew's "Gardener" parable, which I addressed later in "God and Biblical Language," now Appendix E in my *DWG*, 422–39.

have none of it. He gave me a C on the paper and told me that I had not given enough attention to clarity of writing and cogency of argument. I was too concerned, he said, with "bearing witness" and "taking on all comers." He also said that the Flew and McIntyre volume was of minor importance, not worth the time I had given to it. I might have reminded Kaufmann that he himself had recommended Flew and McIntyre to me, but I did not. I also thought my paper was better than Kaufmann had said, but I did not argue with him. Rather, I accepted the truth in his critique and decided to try harder, with God's help, to achieve high quality arguments.

The Metaphysics course, taught by G. Dennis O'Brien, renewed my self-confidence in some degree. O'Brien was a young Roman Catholic scholar, who had studied at the University of Chicago with Richard McKeon and John Wild, advocates of "classical realism." He was a preceptor in Kaufmann's Philosophy of Religion course, and Kaufmann invited him to lecture once. Kaufmann concluded his introduction of O'Brien by saying that he "could not vouch for his orthodoxy." Well, O'Brien was closer to being an orthodox Christian than anyone else on the philosophy faculty. He resembled Bing Crosby's character in "Going My Way" in his casual, friendly demeanor. And the substance of his thought deeply interested me theologically.

O'Brien agreed with the dominant positivists that metaphysics does not discover any facts not available to science. But he thought metaphysics was nevertheless a useful discipline, since we need to know, not only facts, but also "ways with the facts."[28] Different metaphysical systems offer us, he said, not new facts, but new ways with the facts.[29]

To validate this hypothesis, O'Brien dealt in some depth with three thinkers, Aristotle, Spinoza, and John Dewey. Aristotle defended a metaphysics of *things*, Spinoza a metaphysics of *facts*, and Dewey a metaphysics of *processes*. The positions of these men were in disagreement. But the disagreement was not over facts, O'Brien thought, but over ways with the facts. So O'Brien believed that so far as facts were concerned these three thinkers were not inconsistent with one another.

This approach was quite refreshing to this undergraduate philosophy major. The usual approach of Princeton philosophy professors (notably Kaufmann) was to focus on how various philosophers differ from one another and from us in their views of the world. O'Brien's approach was the reverse: to argue that there is far more agreement among the philosophers

---

28. A student jokingly suggested the exam question: "Distinguish between 'a way with the facts,' and 'away with the facts!'"

29. Today I am not sure how one can argue that a way with the facts (conceived as a method for dealing intelligibly with facts) cannot be itself a fact.

than they are generally understood to have. With a nuanced historical understanding, O'Brien argued that if we were to ask the same questions Aristotle did, in the intellectual context in which he wrote, we would come out with more or less the same answers he did. Same for Spinoza and Dewey. So it was almost as if Aristotle, Spinoza, and Dewey were saying the same thing from three different perspectives. At that point, "perspectivalism" entered my philosophical vocabulary. I came to see, not that all philosophers were saying the same thing by any means, but that *some* philosophical (and theological) disagreements can be seen as differences of perspective, rather than as differences over fact.

Special Program in the Humanities

I enrolled in Princeton's Special Program in the Humanities (SPH). Typically, liberal arts students at Princeton would take their major courses in junior and senior years and would write a thesis during their senior year, which usually came out to be less than 100 pages. SPH students, however, would take their major courses in sophomore and junior years. Then in their senior year they would be excused from classes, except for a special seminar, and spend the whole year writing a larger thesis.

My special seminar was, to my delight, a study of Pascal's *Pensées*, led by R. P. Blackmur of the English department. Blackmur, one of the few Princeton faculty who had no doctorate, was known as one of the "new critics," who (contrary to Lawrence Thompson) sought the meaning of a text *within the text*, rather than in the surrounding culture. In my view, he did not always get Pascal's theology right, but he tried hard to do it and gave me a good example of what can be made of great Christian writing in a secular academic setting.

As my thesis advisor, I was assigned Arthur Szathmary, who taught Aesthetic Philosophy. I had avoided taking that course, but I was curious about Szathmary and his approach to philosophy. I knew that he had some enthusiasm for Spinoza, and I did too, based on the course I had taken with O'Brien. O'Brien agreed to be the second reader for my paper.

So I was approved to write a thesis on "Spinoza, Ontological Proof, and Faith." I worked in a library carrel, which I shared with my Christian roommate, the physicist Raymond Chiao, and gathered everything I could find in the library about any of the three subjects in the title.[30] From there I sought to argue that the ontological argument for the existence of God

---

30. Including an early paper by Alvin Plantinga critiquing the argument (he later changed his position).

was really a way of declaring one's presuppositional values, and therefore of confessing one's faith. Anselm, Spinoza, Hartshorne, and others used the argument to prove different concepts of God, because they presupposed different concepts of perfection.

The paper ran to over 250 pages. Szathmary and O'Brien gave it a B+. O'Brien expressed some sympathy for my desire to function as a Christian in the secular world of Princeton, but he thought I had gone overboard in attempting "total scholarship." Many of the thinkers I cited and discussed made no contribution to my argument. He was right, of course. This was the same mistake I had made on my Junior Paper. I had tried to "take on all comers" and write something really *consequential*, something that would take those Princeton secularists by storm. But God had not called me to do that.

Summers in College

When school let out, what I most wanted to do was to get back to Beverly Heights. I wanted to see my friends there and see how they would respond to what I was learning at Princeton, especially at PEF. Summer was a busy time at Beverly Heights. The church partnered with a larger church, Mt. Lebanon United Presbyterian, for a college ministry, "Key Klub," the name based on Matt 16:19. Every Sunday night there was a speaker who made a college-level presentation of something theological. Naturally I played the piano for those meetings.

The main leader was Jerry Kirk, who a few years before had become locally famous as the head of Mt. Lebanon High School's Young Life chapter, a lively group through which many found Christ. Jerry was an assistant pastor at Mt. Lebanon U.P. then. Later he would become pastor of a church in Cincinnati and would be known as one of the nation's leading crusaders against pornography—even before the era of internet porn.

Sometimes, also, there were midweek meetings sponsored by Key Klub. One summer Jack Rogers, then a seminarian and intern at Mt. Lebanon U.P., conducted a Bible study, looking through one epistle of Paul each Wednesday night. Those studies were tremendously valuable to me, gave me a "big picture" understanding of Paul that I had never had before. I was disappointed in Rogers' later development as a critic of biblical inerrancy and a defender of the PCUSA denomination. But in the years 1957–61 he was a great help to me.

Another mentor was Jim Bailey, a seminarian who was an intern at Beverly Heights. Jim was involved in a group at seminary that arranged preachers for churches that needed them. Jim invited me to preach in a Brethren church what was my first sermon ever. Jim and I hung out together. He invited me to join him as he preached in a Pentecostal church on the Pittsburgh North Side. We discussed theology endlessly it seemed. He was as conservative as I was then, but after he left Beverly Heights he moved in other directions. His replacement, as I recall, was John Mehl, with whom I had a solid friendship.

One of those summers I was asked to work on the summer staff at Beverly Heights, which I was delighted to do. That involved leadership in the Key Club and youth ministries, and a few weeks as substitute organist. That summer I worked with John Evans, a grad of Harvard and a Pittsburgh Seminarian, who became a good friend, and some other folks from the church.

I could have spent all my summers hanging around the church, but my parents had other plans. They didn't think it was healthy for me to spend so much time in the church, and they thought my ultimate vocation would more likely be as a lawyer—like my uncle Dick. So Dad called a friend, labor lawyer Nick Uncovic, to see if he could get me a job at his large downtown Pittsburgh law firm, Reed, Smith, Shaw, and McClay. I resisted this idea fairly ferociously, but wanting to honor my parents I eventually gave in. For a summer, I became a legal messenger boy. Dad would drive me down there on his way to work. I would sit at a table in a corner of the hall with other messengers. Every now and then, one of the lawyers would call for one of us to hand-deliver a document to another lawyer or to an address somewhere in Pittsburgh. The addresses were all downtown, and we walked to each one. It was a good way to get to know the city. I presume the system has since been overridden by fax and email technology.

I was one of the better educated of the messengers, so I was sometimes asked to read a document aloud so that a secretary could type it up. In general I think I made a fairly good impression on them. But as I observed the lawyers at their work, I was pretty well convinced that the law was not God's calling to me. I could not get the least bit excited at the issues discussed in the documents I read aloud to the secretaries, or the activities of the lawyers as they ran here and there.

At the end of each summer, Key Klub sponsored a "College Briefing Conference" at one or another campground in the Pittsburgh area. I remember John Gerstner as the main speaker at one of them. At another was Tibor Chikes, a godly psychologist who had spent a year at Westminster Seminary. (He told me that Westminster was a great place, but urged me to watch out for the Orthodox Presbyterians.) Another speaker was Paul

Pulliam, from a journalist family, who helped us to relate our faith to the changing cultural scene.

The summer of 1960 was different from the other summers. That summer, I was absent from Key Klub and from the College Briefing Conference. My parents, together with the parents of my Princeton roommate Dave Burnham, thought that it was time for their sons to make a "grand tour"—to visit all the great tourist sites of Europe. Dave, you may recall, was also one of the guys whom I joined in a tour of America in 1957.

At first my response to the idea was negative. I was not (and am not) enthusiastic about the idea of travel, and I didn't relish the thought of another summer away from the church. But I had been considering whether God had called me to missionary service. I had been writing to missionaries—some supported by Beverly Heights and Westerly Road Church, some PEF alumni for whom we often prayed. Could I learn more about missions by visiting some of these fields? So I told my parents, fine, I'll visit Europe; but I'd very much like to visit Africa first. They were taken aback, but Dave (who had also been attending PEF) endorsed the idea and eventually both sets of parents agreed to support the trip. We wrote our missionary friends, developed an itinerary with the travel agent at the Princeton University Store, and took off.

From New York, we took BOAC to London, then to Kano in Northern Nigeria, a headquarters[31] for the Sudan Interior Mission. We observed the medical mission work of Dr. Arthur Barnett, then spent a week or so at Malumfashi, a smaller town, with Mel and Millie Dreesen, missionaries supported by Westerly Road. They were exceedingly gracious to us. We tried to pitch into the work as best we could, knowing of course that we could not fully avoid being a burden. Mel led us on a preaching tour in one of the outlying villages by bicycle. (My riding technique was pretty comical, but we made our destinations more or less on time.) I have often thought of the Dreesens and the village churches during recent reports of Muslim rampages against Christians in that region.

Our second stop was to be in what was then called the Belgian Congo. But this was the summer of 1960, in which the Congo and several other African countries became independent. We received a warning that the transition in the Congo could be dangerous for westerners, so we spent a night in Brazzaville (in the *French* Congo, across the river), and then caught a plane to Rwanda-Urundi. In 1994, this country would be the scene of horrible genocide, but in 1960 it was the very image of the peaceable kingdom. But we only stayed there overnight, then went to Kenya.

31. The main headquarters was in Jos.

In Kenya, we visited the Africa Inland Mission headquarters in Nairobi. They showed us the beautiful, impressive Rift Valley Academy, where sons and daughters of missionaries were educated. Our visit technically occurred during the Mau Mau uprising, but things were fairly quiet where we were. The country became fully independent in 1963. We visited the Sheldon Folk family in Mwingi for a week or so—very gracious people with great hearts to win people for Christ.

Then to Addis Ababa, where we visited first the Sudan Interior Mission headquarters, then Murray Russell and his wife in the small town of Dembi Dollo. Beverly Heights had supported the Russells, who, unlike many in the PCUSA mission force, were fervent evangelicals. Again, we tried to pitch in to the work around the mission. I recall that I made an attempt to tune the Russells' piano, which hadn't been serviced in a while.

Then we visited briefly with Presbyterian missionaries in Khartoum and Cairo, visits that became in my mind more like sightseeing than missions orientation. We visited the pyramids and went with a guide to Karnak to visit ancient temples.

This was the time of Gamal Abdel Nasser in Egypt, and the missionaries were quite restricted in what they could do. There was discussion of an edict to require the teaching of Islam in mission schools. But how could that be done without destroying their Christian character?

Dave and I visited a large, somewhat charismatic group of young Christians. They walked around Cairo, boldly singing Christian songs, such as "We Are Walking in the Light of God." At one point they asked Dave and I to exhort them and to report on our trip. The suggestion terrified me, but it turned out OK. The young Christians were most gracious. But from that and other experiences that summer, I discerned that God had not called me to be a cross-cultural communicator.

From Egypt, we flew to Jordan, which (before the 1967 war) was the location of most of the biblical sites. We actually went in and out of Israel for one overnight—which required us to play tricks with our passports and visas. Israel was a marvel of technology and freedom, compared to Jordan. But we spent more time in Jordan. Dr. James L. Kelso, who taught archaeology at Pittsburgh Seminary and Beverly Heights, was at an archaeological institute there, and he provided us with a guide who drove us from place to place. We stopped in at a "dig" with Harvard archaeologist G. Ernest Wright (whose "theology of the acts of God" I would later critique). We swam in the Dead Sea, marveling at how the solids in it held our bodies up virtually without our treading water.³² And we "walked where Jesus walked," at all the places where our guide said he might have been. Who knows? But certainly the general terrain and the type of buildings hadn't changed much since the first century.

The grand tour continued with Istanbul, Athens, Rome, Florence. We saw the same things everybody sees, without getting to know much of the actual culture. We had a much greater cultural awareness in Africa, where we stayed longer in several places and met actual local people, native to the areas. But we were, of course, properly amazed at the great artistic and cultural achievements of Western Europe.

We met another American—sadly I cannot remember his name. The three of us rented a car to drive through Italy and eventually to Switzerland. We hoped to visit L'Abri, the chalet at Huémoz sur Ollon, where Francis Schaeffer led a kind of Christian colony. Schaeffer had visited us once at PEF, and Dave and I had found him fascinating. Later, Schaeffer would become very famous, written up in *Time* as an apostle to the intellectual. But in the summer of 1960 he was known only to a few pockets of evangelicals. On our drive, we did find L'Abri, but, alas, Schaeffer was in the States. Others, however, were there, including Ran Macaulay, who I believe still works with the L'Abri ministry. Ran enabled us to stay overnight, have a meal or two there, and spend several hours listening to tapes of Schaeffer witnessing to non-Christians. I would meet and correspond with Schaeffer several times in my later life, but I still remember the spirit of the L'Abri ministry that we experienced in the summer of 1960. Schaeffer always intended to live in such a way as to demonstrate the reality of God, and his example had communicated much of this to Ran and the others we met at L'Abri.

From Switzerland we went to Paris, then London—possibly some other places intermediately. I do recall visiting Stratford in England, and possibly Oxford. Of all the places we visited, England was the place where I would have most enjoyed living someday. Then to New York, and home. I had sent back to Pittsburgh about 250 slides, which I still have, transferred to DVD.

---

32. We had swum in the Great Salt Lake in 1957, and the bouyancy of the Dead Sea was similar, but much greater.

4

Reformed at Westminster

Choosing a Seminary

My perception of God's calling developed so that at least by the middle of my college years I planned to take a seminary degree. Dr. Fullerton and the PEF men believed that the only two good seminaries were Dallas and Grace Theological Seminaries. Dallas was the largest seminary in the dispensational orbit, with the best-known faculty. Grace, in Winona Lake, Indiana, was the seminary of the Grace Brethren denomination.[1] Grace had given Donald Fullerton his honorary D.D., and Fullerton always said that Grace was more "balanced," less "intellectualist" than Dallas. He wanted me to have the opportunity to study with the senior theologian at Grace, Alva J. McClain. McClain was working on a major theological project on the kingdom of God, and volume 5, *The Greatness of the Kingdom*,[2] was already published.

Fullerton and the PEF respected Westminster as well, but they didn't recommend it. Westminster was founded in 1929, when the General Assembly of the PCUSA determined to reorganize Princeton Seminary so that the seminary would reflect "all points of view" within the denomination. This implied that Princeton would no longer maintain its traditional

---

1. They had broken with the Brethren Church (Ashland College and Seminary in Ohio) over the role of grace in the gospel message. Possibly that controversy was also over dispensationalism.
2. Chicago: Moody Press, 1968.

defense of Reformed orthodoxy, famous in the writings of Charles Hodge and B. B. Warfield. Rather than stay at Princeton under those conditions, J. Gresham Machen, the leader of the conservatives in the PCUSA, left the seminary and took with him some of the other orthodox professors[3] to start Westminster Seminary in Philadelphia.

Machen was the author of *Christianity and Liberalism*,[4] which maintained that biblical Christianity and liberalism were two different religions, opposed to one another at every point. This book made a profound impression on me. After reading it and after experiencing liberalism firsthand at Princeton I could never again have any sympathy for liberalism, though I had entertained such positions back in high school days. Certainly I could never give serious consideration to attending a liberal seminary. Fullerton was aware of the developments at Princeton Seminary, had known Machen, and had a deep sympathy for their cause. But unlike Dallas and Grace, Westminster was not dispensational and premillennial, and that prevented Fullerton from recommending it to Princeton students. He did give some lukewarm support to Faith Seminary, a premillennial seminary that broke away from Westminster in 1937, but that seminary, by 1961, had fallen under the dictatorial rule of Carl McIntire.

The original Westminster faculty, ca. 1936

But Westminster was my first choice. Van Til was on the faculty there, and he had already helped me immeasurably through his writings. I had also read E. J. Young's *Thy Word is Truth*,[5] a masterful defense of biblical authority and inerrancy, and the biography of Machen by Ned Stonehouse.[6] Both Young and Stonehouse were Westminster professors. And, as I mentioned in the last chapter, Davis Young, the son of E. J. Young, was a fellow student of mine at Princeton, and he occasionally answered my questions about Westminster.

---

3. Including Robert Dick Wilson, Oswald T. Allis, Cornelius Van Til, and R. B. Kuiper.
4. New York: Macmillan, 1923.
5. Edinburgh: Banner of Truth, 1963.
6. *J. Gresham Machen: A Biographical Memoir* (Grand Rapids: Eerdmans, 1955).

My Pittsburgh friends, however, had other ideas. Mostly, they wanted me to enroll at Pittsburgh Theological Seminary. This was the seminary from which most of the Beverly Heights interns had come, where among the teachers were Bob Kelley, James L. Kelso, and John Gerstner. But many of the other teachers there were liberal, and that was the predominant orientation of the school. Sometime in my decision year, I got a call from Clifford Smith, assistant pastor of Mt. Lebanon U.P., to meet him in his office. This was a fascinating visit. I knew that both Smith and his senior pastor, Cary Weisiger, were Westminster graduates. Both had opposed the merger of the United Presbyterian Church with the liberal Presbyterian Church, USA. Their preaching, indeed, was powerfully Reformed, and it was one of the factors that impelled me toward Westminster. But Smith did not recommend his alma mater.[7] He told me, rather, that he was seeking to get together a group of bright young evangelicals that could renew the evangelical witness in the PCUSA. He mentioned Jim Keller, a Key Klub friend, very smart, as another prospective member of the group. But to come into the PCUSA, I would have to come under care of a PCUSA presbytery and attend a PCUSA seminary. The presbytery would give me no credit for any work done at Westminster, which they rejected as a "separatist" school.

Certainly my meeting with Smith gave me much to pray about. But I wondered what kind of evangelical I would be if I spent my whole three years at seminary dealing with attacks on my position, and comparatively little of that time in the serious study of Scripture, understood as God's authoritative word. Later, I would get some confirmation of this line of thought when I discovered to my sadness that Jim Keller, during his years at Pittsburgh Seminary, had crossed over into process theology. I would meet him again when I did graduate work at Yale.[8]

---

7. Smith expressed respect for Westminster's theological and academic position, but he noted that the seminary was all too quick to enter into controversy, a comment I followed up in my "Machen's Warrior Children" http://www.frame-poythress.org/machens-warrior-children/. Smith had spent some years in the Orthodox Presbyterian Church (against which Chikes and Fullerton had warned me) following graduation and had supported Gordon H. Clark in the 1940s controversy between Clark and Van Til. Supporting Clark, who was perceived to be the loser in that controversy, Smith left the OPC and eventually found himself at Mt. Lebanon U.P.

8. In fairness, though, I should say that not everyone who attended Pittsburgh Seminary in those days lost their evangelical convictions. R. C. Sproul is the same age as I, and he went to Pittsburgh Seminary in the same years in which I went to Westminster. He has nevertheless become one of the most eloquent and clear communicators of Reformed theology anywhere. At seminary and afterward, R. C. stuck pretty close to Gerstner. Of course, the best possible reason for going to Pittsburgh Seminary was to study with Gerstner. If I had gone there, that would have been my chief motivation. But in the end I went to Westminster—to study with Gerstner's teachers.

John Gerstner also wanted me to come to Pittsburgh Seminary. His presence there was the best argument in favor of that choice. Gerstner was, indeed, a graduate of Westminster, so he was in an excellent position to compare the two. But the argument he presented when we had lunch together was not strong in my eyes. He said that Westminster was the best seminary in the world in setting forth Reformed orthodoxy,[9] but that I nevertheless ought to go to Pittsburgh instead in order to gain entry into the PCUSA.[10] Whatever interest I had, however, in joining the ministry of the PCUSA was dwarfed by my desire to have a theological education governed by Scripture as God's word.

My parents, however, also had their own ideas. They were not entirely reconciled to my desire to attend seminary, but if I were to do that, they wanted me to choose a seminary with some prestige, like the colleges to which I was accepted in 1957. From talking to various people, they had ascertained that the most prestigious seminaries were Princeton, Yale, and Union Seminary in New York. These were, however, the very last places I wanted to consider, because they were known for their liberalism.

I actually went for an interview with one of the Deans at Princeton Seminary. I asked him whether the students ever read books that advocated orthodox theology. The Dean replied, oh, certainly; Princeton students are exposed to all points of view. "Do they read Van Til?" Oh, yes, certainly.[11] I checked this out with some of the Princeton Seminary students I knew, and they told me these answers were not true. The students were *never* assigned to read anything that was written from an orthodox point of view, anything that accepted biblical authority and inerrancy. Even making maximum allowance for definitional differences, these conversations[12] did not convince me of the seminary's theological honesty or transparency.

9. However, like Smith, he opposed Van Til's apologetics.

10. Bob Kelley made the same argument when we talked about it.

11. I also asked him about the relationship between Princeton and Westminster. He replied that the two schools were "95 percent agreed." Years later, a Muslim cleric would tell some of my students that Islam and Christianity were 95 percent agreed on Jesus. Remember that sometimes the 5 percent disagreements are about the things that are most important.

12. There were others. I once visited the seminary bookstore, since I heard they were offering some orthodox Reformed books at bargain prices. I took a copy of Boettner's *Reformed Doctrine of Predestination* up to the student cashier. He looked at me, evidently gathered that I was a college student, and therefore assumed that I was a theological idiot. He worked up a wise expression and said, "You know, Prof. Dowey (i.e., Edward A. Dowey, Jr.) does not think that Boettner is a good guide to Reformed theology." I asked where specifically Dowey disagreed with Boettner. The student said, "Well, do you know where Calvin puts predestination?" "No," I replied. "Where does Calvin 'put' predestination?" With an air of triumph, the cashier replied,

For a while, I offered to my parents Fuller Seminary as a compromise. Fuller had been started relatively recently in California, where (after my 1957 trip) I had hoped to live some day. Many of the professors there were well known; indeed, some had studied at Westminster, such as Edward J. Carnell and Paul K. Jewett. I was enthused about the work of Carl Henry and Harold Ockenga, who was then the president of the Seminary. I had the impression from reading the catalogue that Fuller modeled its curriculum somewhat after Westminster's. The difference was that Fuller's faculty included some Baptists, even some dispensationalists, and it was perceived to represent the new evangelical movement, men the likes of as Carl Henry, E. J. Carnell, and Billy Graham.[13] I would have preferred Westminster, but Fuller, I thought, would provide good training for the pastorate and good preparation for doctoral studies if the Lord were to lead me in that direction.

My parents presented that question to one of their mentors, Harry McDonald. Harry was Jerry Kirk's successor as the leader of the Mt. Lebanon High School Young Life club, and he taught an adult Sunday School class at Beverly Heights, which my parents attended. Harry was a very sharp young evangelical, my parents respected him a great deal, and I felt sure that he would be favorable to Fuller. But when my Dad asked Harry whether he thought I should go to Fuller, or to a place like Yale or Union, Harry responded, to my profound disappointment, "these are all good schools." Since my Dad was already persuaded that Yale and Union (he would also have accepted Princeton) were more "prestigious," he took Harry's comments as a validation of his own point of view. He doubled down, indeed, and said that unless I chose a prestigious seminary I could not count on any parental support.

I hope I have given evidence already in this book that I was a compliant son, trying seriously to honor my parents. But at this point I had to assert my manhood. My parents had done great things for me and had

---

"under Christian faith and life!!!" I could not for the life of me see how the cashier's argument was supposed to discourage me from buying Boettner's book. (The whole book was about predestination, so in the book there was no place to "put" predestination; the question was pointless.) But I didn't venture a reply. I just put my head down, pretending to be the ignorant rube the cashier thought me to be, then gave him some money and took the book out of the store. But conversations like these left me with a strong impression that Princeton Seminary was not a place where one could discuss theology in a serious way.

13. At the time I regarded this amount of diversity as a point in favor of Fuller. But later I came to appreciate Westminster's greater homogeneity. Better to study one theological tradition thoroughly than to get a snippet of Calvinism here, a bit of Arminianism there, an occasional dispensational advocacy. That is advantageous even for a student who graduates from Westminster without accepting its theological position. At least the curriculum has raised all the issues and has fully presented the alternatives.

often given me good advice. But neither was a theologian, and neither had any idea of the differences between evangelical and liberal theology, even though I had tried to help them understand these issues. I would have gone to Fuller if that would have made them happy, but not to Yale or Union or even Princeton. My purpose in going to seminary was to immerse myself in the word of God, our only weapon against Satan (Eph 6:10–18). I considered even then that it might be useful to go later to a place like Yale for graduate study, to learn first-hand the prevailing liberal points of view. I told my parents that. But I could not entrust to Yale or Princeton my basic training for ministry. So I dropped the compromise and planned to go to Westminster, one way or another.

I would have worked my way through Westminster if I had needed to, but as happened so often in my life God provided me a soft landing. My parents' own generosity defeated their plan to cut me off financially. Through the years, they had given me stocks that would have yielded large amounts of money if I had sold them. And in any case, studying at Westminster was very inexpensive at the time. There was no actual tuition, and the charges for room and board were easily manageable. So I did not need to work to pay the expenses of seminary study. My parents' ultimatum, therefore, did not hinder my purposes at all. And when they saw that, Mom and Dad decided that it would be better for them to continue their involvement in my education and to make some contributions to my seminary studies. For that, and for so much more, they have my unending thanks.

Learning the Reformed Faith

Westminster (hence WTS) was a great theological feast. The senior faculty consisted of the "boys" that J. Gresham Machen brought with him from Princeton in the early 1930s. Ned Stonehouse taught New Testament, Paul Woolley church history, Cornelius Van Til apologetics, John Murray systematics. Edward J. Young (Old Testament) joined the faculty in 1936, and John H. Skilton (New Testament) in 1939, the year I was born. Then there were a couple of young guys, who in time made outstanding contributions to Reformed theology: Edmund Clowney (practical theology) and Meredith G. Kline (Old Testament). Assisting Van Til in apologetics was Robert D. Knudsen; assisting Murray in systematics was Edwin H. Palmer; and assisting Clowney in practical theology was John W. Sanderson.

I tested out of Greek because of my courses at Princeton, and that left me with a class schedule that was a bit more flexible than many of my fellow students. I did take Beginning Hebrew, from Edward J. Young. Young had a unique system of teaching, which made much use of transliteration and only gradually introduced the Hebrew alphabet, a few characters each week. Young kept saying "don't bother to memorize," advice that probably was good for students who had Young's own linguistic aptitude. Rumor had it that he had learned something like thirty languages, and every year he tried to learn one or two more. ("What are you doing this summer, Dr. Young?" "Oh, I'm thinking that this year I will learn a little Russian.")

But when we left Beginning Hebrew to take Kline's Advanced Hebrew, Kline announced that at WTS there were two theories about teaching Hebrew and that we were now about to experience the other one. Kline's lessons had us constantly drilling away at vocabulary, forms, and syntax. If you didn't memorize, you'd be dead on the exam.

Young and Kline also clashed in courses dealing with Old Testament content. Kline adopted the "framework hypothesis" in which the "six days" of Gen 1 are a literary device and the text makes no assertion about the chronology of events. Young, however, held to a day-age view in which the days are not twenty-four hour days, but the passage presents a general chronology of what came before what. We heard the framework view in Kline's OT Introduction course, the day-age view in Young's OT Exegesis. And after class some of us stood outside a door where the faculty was gathered, and Kline was describing his view to his colleagues: "Day One . . . ; Day Two . . . ."

The general consensus, however, was that it would not hurt for both views to be taught at the seminary. Neither contradicted any of the essentials of the Reformed confessions. Coming from Princeton, I was happy that WTS allowed this level of flexibility. Princeton philosophy professors often disagreed with one another, and those disagreements enriched the education of the students. And to some extent that was true even among Christians there. In PEF, we prayed, studied, and worked together despite considerable differences of theology and practice. Of course, you have to draw the line somewhere; else you have no way to resist liberalism. But believers will never agree with one another 100 percent. In general, the differences between Young and Kline enriched our study at WTS, rather than detracted from it. Kline developed a number of other original theories as well, some of which I agreed with, some of which I did not. But he became a hero of mine for his willingness to think creatively and to oppose traditions, within the bounds of Reformed orthodoxy. My view of Kline changed somewhat, however, in later years.

My PEF friends had given me the impression that WTS was in bondage to a theological tradition, and that WTS simply imposed that tradition on their students in mechanical fashion, rather than actually digging into the word of God. The relation of Young and Kline at WTS showed me that wasn't so. Both men subscribed to the Westminster Standards. But they saw their work, not as simply reciting those standards and insisting on them, but as helping students to interact with the word of God directly. WTS reinforced the training in critical thinking that Princeton had given me.

The same was true of the courses in biblical content: OT courses in Pentateuch, Poets, and Prophets, NT courses in the Gospels, Paul, Acts, Catholic Epistles, and Revelation. WTS understood itself to specialize in "biblical theology," a discipline defined by the orthodox Princeton theologian Geerhardus Vos. Biblical theology seeks to understand Scripture as a narrative of the history of redemption, and therefore to show how every part of Scripture advances this history. This emphasis carried into our preaching classes as well. Edmund Clowney[14] taught that a sermon should be mainly devoted to showing how its text advances the redemptive narrative. The preacher should not use Bible characters as moral examples (what Clowney called "moralism") but should show how they anticipate or reflect Christ in his redemptive work. I did not agree entirely with Clowney's critique of "moralism." It seemed to me then, and still does, that the Bible itself presents characters in its stories as examples of faithful or unfaithful living. Certainly there is no contradiction between advancing the redemptive-historical narrative and presenting characters as moral examples. Jesus is certainly our chief example, and if, say, David anticipates Jesus, to that extent he serves as an example as well.[15] But during Clowney's lifetime, his sermons typically moved me more than any others, because they remarkably directed my attention to Christ, the lord of the word.

The biblical-theological emphasis did not lead to any conclusions inconsistent with the Reformed confessions, so far as I could see. But, like Kline's creative theological positions, it reinforced my impression that WTS was not just interested in transmitting a tradition. It was mainly interested in teaching us how to read, understand, and treasure the Bible for ourselves.

The church history courses of Paul Woolley were more like Princeton courses than any others I had at WTS. Woolley was himself a Princeton alumnus. His teaching method was mostly lecture, from a rough outline, but he often gave opportunities for discussion. When students asked questions, he demonstrated remarkable erudition. Woolley was quite up to date on the literature, and on most issues he had a carefully developed opinion. Although Woolley clearly supported the seminary's general theological position, people often commented that nobody could predict where Paul

---

14. See his *Preaching and Biblical Theology* (Grand Rapids: Eerdmans, 1961).
15. Thanks to Rich Pratt for this insight.

Woolley would come down on any specific issue. He opposed prayer in the public schools, denied that government should play any role in education. He believed that abortion could be justified in some cases, a view on which we came to disagree profoundly. Like Machen before him,[16] he straddled libertarianism and new deal liberalism.[17]

At last I had the opportunity to study with Cornelius Van Til. Though he was sixty-five when I first met him, he would become the chief intellectual influence on me. I have written much about him, including a hefty book[18] and a number of articles.[19] His main message became mine: that God is lord over human thought as he is lord over every other area of human life. Van Til argued (1) that God intended human beings to think his thoughts after him, (2) that in the fall, human beings chose the opposite of God's thoughts, asserting their own autonomy against God's revelation. So in apologetics our goal (under the power of the Holy Spirit) should be to overturn that assertion of autonomy and to demand that every thought be brought captive to Christ. In this project there is no room for Christian apologists to claim neutrality. We are not neutral but, even in dealing with unbelievers, especially there, we presuppose the lordship of Christ.

---

16. Though Machen had died in 1937, he was a great, looming presence over the seminary during my student years, and in many ways still is. At WTS and in the OPC, there has been a constant stream of biographies of Machen as the "captain with a mighty heart." Certainly Machen was a brilliant scholar and a courageous leader in the battle between Christianity and liberalism, and his death was devastating to the seminary and the church. Even from 1961–64, we heard about him constantly. John Skilton, for example, taught NT Introduction using Machen's notes on Galatians. Nobody on the faculty reproduced all of Machen's qualities, but they seem to have taken after him in various ways. I've sometimes thought that E. J. Young best represented Machen's pleasant, conversational writing style; Ned Stonehouse replicated his careful academic research; Woolley reproduced his social and cultural stances; Van Til best resembled Machen's courageous, antithetical approach to theological error—and his sense of humor; and John Murray best expressed the theological position Machen wanted to inculcate in his students.

17. Woolley was also the closest thing Westminster had to a Dean in those days. Westminster had no president or cabinet of officers, doubtless because of worries about the role of administrators in the destruction of Princeton. But faculty members and others managed to take over the administrative functions that seemed to be really necessary. Woolley received all the applications for admission, and he became famous for returning most of them the same day.

18. *Cornelius Van Til: An Analysis of His Thought* (Phillipsburg, NJ: P&R, 1995).

19. Such as "Van Til the Theologian" (http://www.frame-poythress.org/van-til-the-theologian/) and "Van Til: A Reassessment" (http://www.frame-poythress.org/van-til-a-reassessment/).

So supposed objections to the Bible are based on false presuppositions. The work of the apologist is to expose those and to show that those presuppositions lead to the destruction of meaning and knowledge.

After this, Van Til's apologetics got complicated. I had no problems with the basic thrust, but I had a number of problems with the complications. For example, Van Til sometimes thought he could predict how non-Christians would respond to each apologetic move. I thought no, because (1) if, as Van Til says, unbelieving thought is incoherent, then there is no predicting where it will go in a given dialogue, and (2) we cannot predict definitively the work of the Holy Spirit, which certainly can do surprising things in the course of an apologetic encounter (John 3:8).

Van Til was an exciting teacher. He did not lecture, usually, but had us read "unpublished syllabi" he had written on different subjects. Then he would lead a directed discussion, based on that reading material (or not based on it, as he saw fit). He wrote on the board a lot—words and diagrams. He used a lot of homely illustrations: the nonbeliever is like a little girl he saw on a train, slapping her father, but all the time supported on his lap. Aristotle is like a man who is trying to put beads (material facts) on a string (forms); but the string is infinitely long, and the beads have no holes in them. The unbeliever is like a man made out of water, trying to get himself out of the water on a ladder made of water.

Students would learn these illustrations and think they understood Van Til. Too often, they acquired a very basic knowledge of Van Til's approach, thinking too highly of themselves. The illustrations made Van Til out to be a very simple thinker, and in some ways he was. But he expected us to go beyond the simple level. One goal of his courses was to give us students an understanding of the history of philosophy and modern theology. Although Machen had died in 1937, Van Til wanted to impress on us anew Machen's belief that Christianity and liberalism were two different religions, separate and opposed. The little girl slapping her daddy's face was a picture, not only of the neighborhood atheist, but also of Plato, Aristotle, Spinoza, Kant, and Hegel. And, for that matter, of Schleiermacher, Ritschl, Barth, Brunner, Bultmann, and Tillich.

Van Til's arguments at this point became fairly technical. It was hard to follow his reasoning, because he spoke two technical languages that almost nobody in the US was (or is) able to speak: (1) the philosophical language of idealism, and (2) the language of Dutch theology and philosophy. So his discourses carried the students far beyond his homely illustrations. Those who thought they understood Van Til on the basis of the illustrations often were humbled when they encountered Van Til's more technical teaching.

Knowing that only so much of this could be covered in class, Van Til sent his students out to do research. We had two apologetics courses (each two credit hours) taught by Van Til in the first year. In each of these, Van Til tested us with a midterm and a final exam. And for each of these courses he asked us to write *two* term papers. When one student asked how long the papers should be, Van Til replied, "Oh, longer than anything you've ever written before." The joke among the students was that Van Til graded papers by weight: he would throw them down the stairs and give A grades to the ones that fell the farthest. A friend advised me that if a student desired an A he would have to write at least thirty-five pages.

Since I didn't have to take Greek and didn't have family or work responsibilities, I had more free time than other students, and I decided to put much of that time into my first apologetics term paper, which Van Til said was to be written on the proofs of God's existence. The high school satirist popped up inside me and I decided that, given all this talk of the *length* of papers, I would make mine *super*-long. So I took fifty pages from my Princeton thesis (acknowledging that of course) and added seventy-five pages of original material. So what I turned in to Van Til was 125 pages long. It was the longest term paper I had ever written or ever would write, and it was most likely the longest term paper Van Til had ever received. Van Til lived up to his caricature by giving me the highest possible grade, and that paper established my reputation on the Westminster Campus as a young scholar to be reckoned with. Ultimately I have that paper to thank for my own career as a theologian and apologist. Its title: "Our Proof of God and God's Proof of Us."

I also took some Th.M.-level courses from Van Til, within the B.D.-level program. These were seminar-type courses with a lot of back-and-forth discussion. Van Til and I did not always communicate well. The philosophical language I learned at Princeton was that of Anglo-American language analysis, which was not easily translatable into Van Til's language derived from philosophical idealism.[20] And even in theology our wires crossed. I spoke the language of American evangelicalism, while Van Til spoke the language of German and Dutch thought. In my analysis, Van Til and I agreed closely on the essentials. But our discussions often did not always seem that way. Often comments I made in class, intended as analytical questions, came across to Van Til as criticisms of his position. So he was always somewhat reluctant to accept me as an ally.

---

20. Though, interestingly, Van Til had earned his doctorate at Princeton University in the mid-1920s, under the direction of A. A. Bowman.

I also took an upper-class required apologetics course from Van Til's associate Robert D. Knudsen. The course was called "Christian-Theistic Evidences," and Knudsen (not implausibly, given our presuppositional orientation) taught it as a philosophy of science course. Knudsen was very learned in phenomenology and existentialism, and he was committed to a Dooyeweerdian understanding of the nature of theoretical thought. Herman Dooyeweerd was a Dutch Christian philosopher with whom Van Til had had a close relationship into the 1950s. But by 1960, Van Til had become more critical of Dooyeweerd, while Knudsen remained loyal to the Dooyeweerdian approach. That caused some tension between Van Til and Knudsen, though Knudsen appeared to students to be almost slavishly Van Tillian.

During my student years, I wasn't very knowledgeable about Dooyeweerd, but neither was I willing to adopt Dooyeweerd's philosophical framework, granted Van Til's hesitations. And my training in Anglo-American language philosophy left me very critical of phenomenology and existentialism (among the sources of Dooyeweerd's approach), which my Princeton professors considered "muddled." I tried in Knudsen's class to get clarifications on such matters, but I was never satisfied. Usually Knudsen would answer by a long reply using the technical language of the philosophers I was asking about. Knudsen was quite skilled at this: when he taught about Heidegger, he *sounded* like Heidegger. But, I thought, there is a lot of difference between *imitating* Heidegger and *explaining* Heidegger. To explain a philosopher, you usually need to put his ideas into language intelligible to your students, or at least to define the philosopher's terminology. Knudsen failed to do that to my satisfaction.

But in the midst of all these debates, I hardly realized that I had become a smarty-pants kid theologian, the kind I later would criticize fervently. I did not show Knudsen proper respect, though he was a man of great erudition and Christian maturity. I was not a good student in Knudsen's class, and my debating mentality kept my fellow students from learning what they should have learned. And I was not a good colleague to Knudsen in later years. May God forgive me.

Students at WTS often said that they had come to the seminary to study with Van Til, but they had stayed to study with John Murray. Van Til was by far the more famous of the two, but the two were at least equal in the quality of their thought. Murray was to me a wonderful surprise. As I mentioned earlier, my PEF friends had warned me that WTS was more interested in teaching Reformed tradition than in teaching Bible. That warning had forearmed me with suspicions, especially of WTS systematics. If WTS had taught systematics as many Reformed seminaries have done, by expounding the confessions and the classic Reformed theologians, I would have resisted, and I could very easily have graduated an Arminian or dispensationalist. But John Murray's approach was to list the Bible proof-texts for each doctrine (and the problem texts emphasized by that doctrine's opponents) and exegete them meticulously in his deep Scottish brogue, so that there could be no question of what the Scriptures taught.[21] Unlike Van Til, Murray rarely permitted questions in class. He read from carefully written lecture manuscripts.[22] But the consensus among the students was that Murray's lectures themselves answered all the questions that could have legitimately been asked.

I took very detailed notes on Murray's lectures, since he did not provide even outlines for the students (except on the board), then took notes on my notes, reducing their content by about half the number of pages. Then I took these notes with me on long walks to memorize every point and subpoint.[23] The students knew that Murray meant business; there were no short cuts to success in his courses. But what Murray wanted from his students (with occasional exceptions) was mastery of his lectures. I was able to accomplish that, and certainly it was that effort that led to my being known today as a systematic theologian.

But for three courses in the systematics curriculum, Doctrine of Scripture, Doctrine of God, and Christian Ethics, I did not have Murray as a teacher. Rather, I studied with his assistant, Edwin Palmer. I remember that before I came to WTS I saw an ad for the seminary featuring Palmer. It showed a picture of him leading a discussion on the campus of the University of Michigan. That presented him as a man who knew what was going on with my generation, and I looked forward to his teaching. He was a tall, blond man, a Harvard graduate, who had earned a doctorate from the Free University of Amsterdam. He had been in the U.S. Marines, and had fought near Okinawa in the war. He also had published two books, popularizations of Reformed doctrine. He worked with organizations to promote Christian

---

21. One humorous comment that circulated about WTS contains much truth: at WTS you can learn all the theological disciplines, but not in their traditional locations. You learn apologetics in the biblical studies courses (which focused often on Bible problems and critics), systematics in Van Til's apologetics courses, Bible exegesis in John Murray's systematics courses, and biblical theology in Edmund Clowney's practical theology courses.

22. Most of that material, and much more, has been published in the *Collected Writings of John Murray* (4 vols. Edinburgh: Banner of Truth Trust, 1976–82). This collection is absolutely indispensable to anyone who wants to do serious theological work.

23. The route I took was sometimes itself called the "Murray Mile," because John Murray himself had taken long walks through that residential neighborhood during the years that he lived in a WTS dorm room.

schools and to discourage abortion. His big, broad smile reminded me of Bob Kelley. I expected to like him a lot, and I did.

In his classes, Palmer communicated his enthusiasm for theological study and made a good effort to know the students individually. For a while, he served as dean of students. But his substantive theological work suffered by comparison to that of John Murray. I sympathized with Palmer: Murray had developed his lectures over a period of thirty years or so. Writing an adequate series of lectures in systematics was a formidably difficult job.[24] But Palmer's time at WTS was over after four years. He went on to distinguished work as head of the NIV translation committee before he died of a heart attack in 1980.

But in God's providence, when I went back to WTS to teach in 1968, I was assigned the systematics courses that I had taken with Palmer, not any of those I had taken with Murray. Had I been asked to teach one of Murray's former courses, I would have started by following his lectures very closely. But my notes on Palmer's courses were far less detailed, and they left more room, therefore, for creativity.

The consensus around WTS was that the true successor to John Murray was Norman Shepherd. He was doing doctoral work at the Free University of Amsterdam when I became a WTS student, but many spoke of him as Murray's best student and a likely future faculty member. In the fall of 1962, I took the course in Gospels from Ned Stonehouse, who had recently returned from a study leave in the Netherlands. But Stonehouse got sick and died toward the end of that semester. The seminary arranged to complete the course with the help of doctoral students.[25] But they called on Shepherd to teach New Testament Biblical Theology, which Stonehouse had been scheduled to teach in the spring of 1963. Shepherd's natural field was systematic theology rather than New Testament. But he did a fine job with this assignment. We students saw him each day spreading books and notes around a library table, evidently trying to stay a week ahead of the students. Doubtless his notes on Stonehouse's lectures played a major role in his teaching. But we all felt that Shepherd's course was as good as any we had had at WTS. I studied very hard for the exam, using my Murray Mile method to memorize Shepherd's lectures. But perhaps I studied too hard. While I was taking the exam, my mind froze; I started drawing a blank. I improvised answers, and Shepherd gave me a B. He could justifiably have given me less than that. It was all my fault, and I confessed as much. But

---

24. I would later attempt the same task myself, but not without fear and trembling.
25. One of these was George Fuller, who later became president of the seminary.

nevertheless Shepherd remembered me when he actually did succeed Murray and sought an assistant to teach with him in systematics.

The practical theology teaching at WTS was excellent in some ways, but, well, problematic. As I said earlier, I had great respect for Edmund Clowney as a preacher, and I sought to follow his emphasis on redemptive history as the core of each sermon. But I was not entirely persuaded by Clowney's critique of "moralism," which seemed to me to go much too far. But Clowney also presented brilliant analyses of the doctrine of the church and Christian education, which I have followed closely ever since.

Clowney and I became good friends at a later point in my life. He seemed to be knowledgeable on almost every subject. Other faculty seemed formidably brilliant in their own fields. Nobody would dare to debate Meredith Kline on a point of Hebrew exegesis. But Kline was far less impressive, in my estimation, when he got outside of his own field. I thought that Clowney's *general* intelligence—on matters outside his own field, on matters of general culture, philosophy, the arts, and so on, was greater than that of any of his colleagues.

But, given my PEF background, I had hoped that seminary would provide me with the ability to share the gospel with unbelievers. I had hoped to become like Dr. Fullerton, able to direct a conversation to the subject of Christ and salvation. The theology and apologetics teaching at WTS certainly provided content for evangelistic conversations. But it left this introvert with no confidence in approaching people with the gospel. Further, although my Practical Theology courses gave me some good hints on how to nurture people in a pastoral role, including youth ministry, ministry to women, counseling, and such, the whole prospect of pastoral ministry left me feeling (and, I think, being) entirely inadequate.

I now think I could have gotten better training in these areas at Fuller, or even Pittsburgh Seminary. But I had thought that fundamental to any kind of ministry was a solid orthodox biblical theology. WTS certainly gave me that, as the others could not have done. But in many other areas it left me unprepared for ministry. WTS grads with natural gifts for relating to people did well in pastorates. But I needed more, as my summer experiences were to prove.

Summers in Seminary

My priorities in seeking God's calling were (1) foreign missions, (2) the American pastorate, and (3) academic theology. I thought that foreign missions was the area of the church's greatest need, but my 1960 trip convinced me that I was not called to foreign missions. A pastorate in America would have been my second choice: certainly a vocation in which one could meet a lot of needs and draw a lot of people to Christ. Then I thought that if I felt I could not do the work of either a missionary or a pastor, I could default to academics.

Summers at seminary were opportunities for the testing of gifts. The summer break at WTS was nearly four-months long, a good period for an internship.[26]

In the summer of 1962, I became a student pastor in Canada. There were two little Presbyterian churches, Mille Isles and Côte St. Gabriel, in a rural area forty miles north of Montreal. The area was generally French-speaking, but these congregations served a pocket of Irish Protestants who for the most part knew no French. The two churches had services only during the summer, with seminary student interns, supervised by pastors of larger churches in the area and by a missions committee of Montreal Presbytery. Two friends of mine at WTS, Don MacLeod and Kent Gordon, had performed this job in previous summers, and they recommended me to take it in the summer of 1962.

I was, for most intents and purposes,[27] the pastor of these churches during the summer. The whole time I had one phone call from my supervising pastor and one visit from Ron Rowat, a WTS alumnus who worked with presbytery's home missions program. The people were gracious and gentle, but my introversion and social awkwardness were evident to all, and I had virtually no success in ministry there.

It was a busy time. I preached every Sunday, set up Vacation Bible School, led a weekly youth group with several outings for the kids. I drove around to visit the people in a Chevrolet that required eleven tire repairs over the course of the summer. If God had equipped me with gifts for pastoral ministry, he had plenty of occasions to demonstrate that. I prayed to him a lot, but I did not see the summer as affirmation.

In the summer of 1963, I was a summer intern in the Covenant Orthodox Presbyterian Church of Pittsburgh. As the summer began, I was ready to give up on ever becoming a pastor, but I considered the possibility that my failings of 1962 came from a lack of adequate supervision. The Pittsburgh job offered more in that respect. The pastor was the founder of the church, the Rev. Calvin Knox Cummings. Growing up in Pittsburgh, I

---

26. It was also a great time for faculty research and writing; my student years were part of a golden age for Westminster faculty publications. Today, the summer break is much shorter. Part of it was removed to create the January term. And both the January term and the summer months have been cluttered with courses.

27. I did not have authority to administer communion or to call meetings of elders.

remember seeing his name in the Pittsburgh Press and thinking to myself that given his name and denomination he would be an interesting person for me to get to know. As it turned out, he was the secretary of Westminster's Board of Trustees, and he regularly sought a WTS student to work with him during the summer months.

Cummings had graduated from WTS in the early 1930s, when Machen was still alive. His Presbyterian USA presbytery refused to ordain him because he agreed to support the church's boards and agencies "only insofar as they agreed with the Scriptures." So he, like Machen, was forced out of the PCUSA and he became one of the first church planters of the OPC. He first established the church on the North Side of Pittsburgh, then put up a building in Wilkinsburg, to the east of the city. The local PCUSA church and presbytery did all they could to prevent the church from erecting a building, but the Orthodox Presbyterians won that battle, and Covenant Church began several decades of slow, steady growth. They had, particularly, a strong ministry to families with children, and in time began a K-12 Christian school.

I stayed with my parents in Mt. Lebanon that summer, but drove to Wilkinsburg every day to carry out my duties. Cummings asked me to preach for every Sunday evening service, and he supervised every step of my sermon preparation. He also asked me to teach the junior high class in the church's Vacation Bible School. I also led a number of youth meetings. Later in the summer, I became a camp counselor for the first and only time in my life.[28]

But perhaps most of my time was spent visiting homes in the community on behalf of the church. Every month, Cummings received a package of cards from a real estate company, with names and addresses of people who were moving into the area. Every afternoon, I took a packet of these cards to part of the church's target area. Most of the people were not at home when I called on them, but some of them were. In those days people did not resist visits from strangers as they do today, and I was quick to identify myself as a representative of the church. I'm sure that I made over 1,000 calls that summer. But I received no training in how to carry on such conversations—either from seminary or from Cummings. And in this area I was a failure. Of all of those calls, I could not cite one of the people I talked to who took an interest in the gospel or who visited the church.

---

28. In a baseball game, I was asked to pitch for both teams. But I couldn't get the ball over the plate even once. Eventually I was relieved. I was also asked to plan a skit for my campers to perform. Fortunately, another counselor gave me one of his ideas that he didn't need to use.

The summer of 1963, then, largely confirmed my self-evaluation after the summer of 1962. I did not feel that God had gifted me to be a pastor. My preaching was adequate, I think, but in every other area I fell far short.

But my experience at Covenant Church did prove a blessing in other ways. Cummings often invited me to have lunch with him and his family, and I delighted in getting to know them. His wife Mary was a wise, gentle, godly woman, selfless and always hospitable. His sons Wilson, Cal, and David became good friends of mine, and in later years all three would be students of mine at WTS. Their beautiful sisters were Gwen and Mary Grace. Gwen taught in the Kindergarten of the Christian School. She eventually married Noel Weeks, who studied at WTS and became professor of ancient history at the University of Sydney, Australia. Mary Grace was a high school student in 1963, but some twenty-one years later she would become my dear wife. For that story you must read ahead.

Student Life at Westminster

At Westminster, students obtained two theological educations: one in the classrooms, from the professors, and the other from their fellow students. The second education taught the student what it was like to live with people professing the Reformed faith. There were pleasant aspects of it, and others that were less so.

We all professed to be Reformed in our theology, with a very few exceptions.[29] The debate among us was about what *type* of Reformed theology one embraced, what *faction* one favored and which factions one disfavored. During my time at Westminster, there were mainly two factions, though later on I discovered that there were others. One faction was sometimes called the "truly Reformed." These toed the theological party line meticulously. They also observed a kind of lifestyle that was assumed to be authentically Reformed, which included smoking and drinking and avoided too many expressions of piety like chapel services, prayer meetings, evangelistic adventures, and such. They derided those whom they thought were too emotional about their faith. They were constantly critical of revivalism, mass evangelism, the giving of invitations to receive Christ, the use of testimonies in worship, and so on. In other words, they defined their "Reformed" position

---

29. Percy Crawford, a very Arminian evangelist, was a Westminster graduate. Van Til told us a number of stories about him. Jack Cottrell was at Westminster during my student years. A top student, Jack went on to be a leading (Arminian) theologian of the Church of Christ.

to a large extent by what they were not: they were not "broad evangelicals" or "American evangelicals."

The other faction was sometimes called "fundamentalist" or "evangelical," but did not differ much from the truly Reformed in theological formulation. The fundamentalists did not often smoke or drink, not from the belief that these were evil or wrong, but out of health considerations and/or desire not to offend broadly evangelical Christians. They were open to meeting for prayer, going to chapel, visiting homes in the neighborhood for evangelism, and so on.

The truly Reformed tended to be students who were raised in Reformed homes and Reformed churches. Often, but not always, they were of Dutch ancestry, members of the Christian Reformed Church, and graduates of Calvin College.[30] For this reason, the truly Reformed were sometimes called "the Dutchmen," whatever their actual ancestry. The fundamentalists came from a broader variety of homes and churches. Often they had come to faith in college. A number of them had come from secular colleges (as I came from Princeton) or from broader evangelical colleges (like Wheaton and Taylor). A significant number came from the South.

Scripture played a role in debates between students of these two factions, but to a large extent our differences were social and cultural. They had to do with national origin and denomination. From a Scriptural and even confessional point of view, there was no reason why these two groups couldn't be the best of friends, worshiping together, socializing together, working together. But in fact it rarely happened. The fundies thought the Dutchmen were not sufficiently spiritual, and the Dutchmen looked down on the fundies as uneducated,[31] without historical roots, and pietistic.[32] Rarely did the truly Reformed ever have fundie roommates. One of the truly Reformed staff members told me that in his opinion fundamentalism was a greater danger to the church than liberalism. Since opposition to liberalism was a large part of the reason for Westminster's existence, this was strong condemnation indeed!

I was early identified as a fundie, though I made a pretty high grade average in my courses, which fundies were not supposed to do. I didn't drink

---

30. Recall from chapter 2 that during my high school years I listened to the *Back to God Hour*, with the preaching of Peter Eldersveld, on the drive back from Beechview Church. Now during my seminary years, for the first time, I was getting to know fellow believers from that denomination.

31. Though some of us had graduated from good colleges, one of us even from Princeton.

32. The truly Reformed loved to line up their opponents with historical movements they didn't like.

or smoke,[33] attended chapel regularly. My roommate was also considered part of the faction, a brilliant Canadian linguist named John Austing, who to my disappointment left seminary after two years without a degree to become a Wycliffe Bible Translator.[34] John spent most of his life translating the Scriptures into the language of the Omie people in Papua New Guinea. John and Will Metzger set up a prayer meeting in the part of Machen Hall where we lived.[35] I attended when I could. Will was in seminary a Young Life leader, and later, for many years, the Inter-Varsity representative at the University of Delaware. He wrote *To Tell the Truth*,[36] an excellent book on evangelism, still in print and highly respected.

Blue Bell Church

Because I had been squeezed into the "fundamentalist" category by my WTS peers, and because of my PEF background, my search for a church to attend led me first to independent Bible churches of various kinds. I had no institutional loyalty to the PCUSA, the liberal body that had swallowed up the old UPNA to which Beverly Heights belonged. But eventually I decided that I really was a Presbyterian, and I tried to find a Presbyterian church in which I could find fellowship in Christ and test my gifts for teaching and music.

Most of the WTS faculty were ministerial members of the Orthodox Presbyterian Church, the denomination founded by J. Gresham Machen and others when they were forced to leave the PCUSA.[37] There were other conservative Presbyterian denominations as well, particularly the Evangelical Presbyterian Church, which by a complicated path descended from a body formed in 1937 when some premillennial pastors and churches left the OPC. The OPC was considered more "truly Reformed," the EPC more "fundamentalist." Temperamentally I was more suited to the EPC, but I did not sympathize with the 1937 split, and so I moved in the direction of the OPC.

---

33. My abstinence had more to do with personal aversion than with any theological principle. But I did take notice that even in the early 1960s reports on the effect of smoking on health were largely negative.

34. In my third year, I roomed by myself in the same dorm room.

35. It was called "Georgetown," originally a servants' quarters in the mansion that became Machen Hall. It was evidently named for somebody named George who lived there once.

36. Downers Grove, IL: IVP, 1981.

37. At its founding in 1936 the body was called "The Presbyterian Church of America." Threat of legal action from the PCUSA led them to change their name to "The Orthodox Presbyterian Church."

In time I began to attend regularly a tiny church in Blue Bell, PA, which was part of the OPC, but which seemed to me to have more of a fundamentalist atmosphere about it.

The church was called the Community Orthodox Presbyterian Church of Center Square. Center Square was one of the names associated with the area, but at the time the church's location wasn't a center of anything. The building sat on a narrow, largely deserted, rural road. It was a "historic" building, a tiny former Methodist station for circuit-riding ministers. The Methodists no longer used it, but they formed an association to maintain the cemetery in the back of the church. They rented the building to the OPC congregation for a small yearly sum, and required the OPC to maintain the cemetery, which we did.

"Blue Bell" was another name for the church's location, and in time that phrase supplanted "Center Square."

Only about fifty people worshiped there each Sunday, but when I first attended there was a lively spirit and signs of growth. The pastor was Henry Fikkert, a tall Dutchman from Brooklyn. They had to add about a foot to the height of the pulpit so that Henry could read his notes. Though Henry's ancestry was Dutch, his mentality was rather different from the "Dutchmen" described earlier. He worked hard to evangelize the area, and new people came frequently and stayed. When I arrived, I saw plans drawn up for a new building. Henry's sermons were very clear, full of the gospel, but also aware of world events and culture.

WTS was some distance from the Blue Bell Church, so we seminarians who went there would regularly be invited to Sunday lunch by members of the church. Usually this duty fell to Henry, his wife Doris, and their large family, which I believe eventually included seven kids. At Fikkerts' house, we talked about everything, it seemed, and developed a real sense of community.

One item sticks in my mind from the history of the church. Several years before my arrival, a long-time church family presented the church with a surprise. It was a painting on the front wall of an open Bible (reading "My word shall not return to me void," Isa 55:11) overlaid by a cross. Now many truly Reformed, of which there are many in the OPC, believe that the Second Commandment forbids any pictorial representation of God in the place of worship.[38] Arthur Kuschke, the very conservative seminary

---

38. See the Westminster Larger Catechism, Q and A 109. My own view is that the Second Commandment forbids making pictures to *worship* them. It does not generally forbid the use of pictures in the worship area (the temple of Israel made lavish use of pictures), and it does not forbid the use of pictures to *teach* the people. And it certainly does not forbid the use of pictures that might be thought to represent divine attributes: indeed a picture of *anything* might be taken to represent God's wisdom and power.

librarian, worshiped then at the Blue Bell Church, and he believed that the picture of Bible-and-cross violated that principle, since the Bible represented God's attribute of truth, and the cross represented God's attribute of grace. But the session of the church, even though they had not approved the picture, defended it against Kuschke's arguments, and refused to take the picture down. A large controversy followed. In the end, the Kuschkes' left the church, as did others on both sides of the debate. That left the church very small, but poised for the growth spurt that I had noticed when I first visited the church. In effect, the controversy had removed the truly Reformed faction, leaving mainly the fundamentalists to carry on.

That story fitted in with a lot of what I was hearing about WTS and the OPC. These organizations defended for the most part a biblically balanced theology, but for some reason they were constantly prone to controversy. In my paper "Machen's Warrior Children"[39] I enumerated around twenty controversies that had divided this movement between 1936 and 2000: controversies over eschatology, the use of alcohol, apologetics, philosophy, Sabbath, and so on. Most of these, in my judgment, were a waste of time, and they prevented the church from proclaiming the gospel effectively.

I only knew Henry as pastor for one year, after which he left for a pastorate at an OPC at Fawn Grove, PA, and then to pastor the largest church in the OPC (about 500 members) at Cedar Grove, WI. Henry's successor at Blue Bell was Ivan DeMaster, the church's youth worker, who graduated from WTS that year, two years ahead of me. Ivan was an admirable young man, friendly, earnest, humble, of great integrity. He was not, however, as winsome as Henry as a preacher, community evangelist, and visionary leader. The church's membership leveled off somewhere below fifty, and plans for a new building were set aside.

At that point, I became much more involved. I played the organ, an electrified reed organ powered by a blower in the basement. I have always prided myself in making good music with unlikely instruments. The organ had some keys that didn't sound at all, some stops that didn't work, some notes that sounded unexpectedly. But my improvisations and hymn accompaniments seemed to serve the congregation well. I also directed the choir. Ivan also frequently asked me to teach the adult Sunday School class, and occasionally I led the Sunday night young people's meetings as a substitute for other seminarians. I joined other men in the church in visiting homes in the vicinity of the church. So besides my summer pastorates in Mille Isles and Wilkinsburg, my work in the Blue Bell Church gave me practice in pastoral skills, and it illumined my deficiencies as a prospective pastor.

---

39. http://www.frame-poythress.org/machens-warrior-children/.

I had come to seminary for many reasons: to study Reformed theology, to explore Van Til's apologetics, to learn the Bible from godly teachers. But to a large extent I hoped most of all to be equipped to be a pastor, and my failure to achieve that goal was my greatest disappointment at WTS. Particularly, I had hoped that I could become an evangelist—to be able to talk to seekers like Don Fullerton did. For most of my life I have been unsuccessful whenever I have tried to share Christ with someone. Sometimes I blamed the problem on my introverted personality, sometimes on my sinful self-preoccupation. But I hoped that at seminary someone would have found a way to deal with that. But WTS was not the place. Their interest was in correct, intellectually sophisticated doctrine, and not much else, though of course they endorsed evangelism and missions. (Mostly what they said was that to be a good evangelist you need first to be clear on your doctrine—true, but not helpful in my case.) I think that WTS has improved in these areas since my student days, and I intend to indicate later in this book how those improvements have taken place. But they happened too late for me.

I could possibly have gotten better training in this respect at Dallas or Grace seminaries, or even at Fuller. But my desire to become an evangelist had been complicated by an equally strong desire to be *sound*—to be sure that I was teaching the right doctrine. I believe that WTS served well that second desire, but not the first. So I left WTS with a tension that I have never overcome: my passions are pastoral, but my abilities are academic. "Tension" is not a strong enough term to describe what I feel. Successful as I am in the academic field, I am often totally bored with academic theological study. And though I love above all working in the church, seeing up close the work of God, I frequently back away from ministry from fear that I will mess everything up.

Yes, I know. A mere human being cannot mess up the work of God. But there is a big difference between those whom God has gifted to work effectively in ministry, and those he has not. And to my sadness I have always been in the second category.

So I set aside all ambitions in the fields of missions and pastorate, and headed back to the one area in which God has generally given me success, hoping that I could avoid getting bored to tears. As time passed, I resolved that tension somewhat by developing academic theology in ways that would encourage the ministry of the church. I have never wanted to be one of those theologians who constantly criticizes evangelists and pastors. Although these groups sometimes deserve criticism, I have wanted to develop theological ideas that encourage those who are on the frontlines of the kingdom warfare.

5

The Most Tendentious Guy at Yale

MY PARENTS WERE RELIEVED: at last their son was going to a "respectable" seminary. For doctoral work I applied to Harvard (where Gerstner had studied in the program of history, philosophy, and religion), Yale (the philosophical theology program), and the joint program of Columbia University and Union Seminary in philosophy and theology. For having the highest grade average, I had won the Westminster Graduate Fellowship. They told me that the WGF was usually used by students who wanted to study abroad—often Scotland, England, or the Netherlands. But I was more impressed by the above American programs. I was more interested in learning content than in learning languages and trying to live cross-culturally. WTS gave me the money anyway. And for this respectable kind of study, my parents chipped in once more.

All three schools accepted me,[1] but Yale was my choice. So at last I was following in the footsteps of Uncle Dick (see chapter 3). I liked the Yale program because of people like Paul Holmer and William Christian, who specialized in Anglo-American language analysis. But I didn't want only that. Most Ph.D. programs with that emphasis specialized in mathematical logic and the minute analysis of very small issues (e.g., can I know another person's toothache?); I also wanted to work on big theological issues, and Yale had a lot of people who were able to do that, like Lindbeck, Hartt, and Calhoun.

I had also heard that Robert Clyde Johnson, author of *The Meaning of Christ*,[2] was leaving Pittsburgh Seminary to become academic dean at Yale.

---

1. I received strong recommendations from WTS professors, Young, Clowney, and Van Til.
2. Louisville, KY: Westminster John Knox, 1958.

The Pittsburgh students were in awe of Johnson.[3] And of course Yale had a great tradition of church historians, including Kenneth Scott Latourette and Roland Bainton.

When I arrived, there was no on-campus housing available, so I rented an inexpensive room in an apartment building called "The Fairchild" on, I think, Whitney Ave. (or was it Whalley?), not far from the campus. I found out later that many of the residents of the building were alcoholics, though a few were grad students at Yale like me. But (still seeking pastoral opportunities) I told God that I was ready to try to help my poor housemates. I did present the gospel to some of them and took some with me to church, but my efforts, as usual, were forlorn.

Something in the Yale rule-booklet suggested to me that I could get doctoral credit for my years at WTS, since many of my fellow doctoral students came without seminary at all. I applied for that credit, but waited and waited without any response. I assumed that my request was denied, and so I chose my courses with a full program in mind.

The philosophical theology program enabled me to take courses both at the Yale Divinity School and in the university Department of Philosophy. The first year I took courses that I hoped would prepare me for comprehensive exams, which had to be taken before writing the dissertation. I took History of Doctrine from the venerable Robert L. Calhoun, during his last of many years of teaching at Yale.[4] Calhoun was revered by the Yale community, but he had barely ever published anything.[5] Ed Clowney had studied with Calhoun back in the 1940s. He described Calhoun as a liberal, not reconstructed by Barth, Brunner, or by his colleague H. Richard Niebuhr. But Calhoun was, above all, a fair scholar. Clowney recalled a seminar led by Calhoun in which one student quoted Warfield, and another sneered, "Oh, that was Warfield." "And a very great scholar, young man, and don't you forget it!" snapped Calhoun.

When I studied with Calhoun, he had a number of ailments, but his lectures were impressively comprehensive, intelligent, and gracefully delivered. He knew Plato very well, which enabled him to skate easily through

---

3. I was not. At a youth conference, Johnson had said that we cannot be certain of Jesus' sinlessness, despite many biblical witnesses to it, because 2 Cor 5:21 says he was "made sin." But I thought it might be interesting to engage him and to see where this kind of reasoning came from.

4. Both Latourette and Bainton were retired, but one saw them from time to time walking across campus.

5. As with R. P. Blackmur at Princeton and Paul Woolley at WTS, I took notice that this was not impossible.

the medieval controversies about universals. So his account of the history of doctrine was philosophically informed.

I wrote a term paper on Athanasius' view of Scripture. I worked very hard at it, thought it was one of my best. There were original thoughts in it, but also a pretty comprehensive view of Athanasius' writings. But the papers were graded by a teaching assistant—not a historian, but a fellow a year ahead of me in the same program I was in, philosophical theology. My paper was never returned, but they recorded a B+. That was the only time I thought Yale did me an injustice.

I had several courses with George Lindbeck, who today is known as the father of postliberalism. He was a fairly liberal member of the Lutheran Church Missouri Synod, and he represented himself to students as one who was on the "right wing of the avant garde of the ecumenical movement." By "avant garde," I took Lindbeck to mean that he was willing to see denominational differences (including the Protestant/Catholic/Orthodox difference) disappear; but "right wing" seemed to mean that the confessions all presented important truths that should not be lost. That left his teaching in some tension.

From Lindbeck, I took a course in Paul Tillich (with which he seemed, on the whole, unsatisfied), a course on Aquinas (which was more at the core of his specialization), and I audited his course in "Comparative Dogmatics," in which we looked closely at confessions from various branches of the church and heard his argument that these should be seen primarily as compatible with one another and as perspectives on the whole Christian message. The Aquinas course was very valuable, and the Comparative Dogmatics course was a major influence on my own perspectivalism, though also a caution to me against letting perspectivalism go too far. Some doctrinal differences, I concluded, do not represent merely differences of perspective, but differences between truth and falsity.

From the university philosophy department, I took William Christian's course, "Meaning and Truth in Religion," which followed his book of that title. I don't recall too much of it. Christian's burden was to reconstruct the language of religion into something that could be intelligible to contemporary analytic and process thinkers. I also took a course from H. D. Lewis, who visited from England. His course was mostly an argument for libertarian free will. I wrote a paper for him opposing that position, and my paper has been the core of my critiques ever since. Lewis was personally a very gracious man.

Also in the philosophy department, I took a course from Paul Weiss, a disciple of Alfred North Whitehead, in which he expounded his book *The*

God We Seek.⁶ In his earlier book *Modes of Being*,⁷ he had made some modifications in Whitehead's process philosophy. I have never had much patience with the constant twists and turns in the process movement, but Weiss was a colorful teacher, very skillful at cross-examination.

In the Divinity School, I took "Theology of Culture" from Julian Hartt, who, I recalled, had stumbled badly in his debate with Walter Kaufmann (see chapter 3). Frankly, I had very little idea of what Hartt was saying in the course. We read Eliade and various other authors.

I missed studying with Hans Frei, who would later electrify the theological world with *The Eclipse of Biblical Narrative*,⁸ or with Brevard Childs,⁹ who developed Frei's concept of narrative for biblical theology. Childs taught OT, and it would have been a stretch for me as a philosophical theologian, to study with him. I did not have such an excuse for missing Frei, only that when I was at Yale, Frei taught mostly courses in nineteenth-century German liberal theology—in German. I read German well enough to pass my language exams, but I didn't feel competent to think or read theology in German, and that is what I was told Frei required.

I wrote pretty good papers in all the courses I did take, but I was very poor in seminar participation. The other students seemed very excited about the seminar topics, eager to get things right and to impress the profs and fellow students. Often they would read beyond the assignments and raise problems they thought the rest of us had not considered. That's the way seminars were meant to be. But not for me. I could do what I was asked to do, but honestly I did not care about it very much. So when the seminar met, I generally had very little to say, except on those occasions when I had to read and defend my own paper before the group. On those occasions, I think I did pretty well, but I did not gain a good reputation with fellow students.

The only friend I knew at Yale was Jim Keller, from Pittsburgh and Key Klub (chapter 3). He had gone to Pittsburgh Seminary and emerged as a process thinker. We took Calhoun's course together at Yale, and he borrowed my notes once when he had to be away (or did I borrow his?). He and his wife had me to dinner once and we chatted about old times. But at that point in our lives we had little in common. Jim later taught for many years at Wofford College in Spartanburg, SC.

---

6. Carbondale, IL: Southern Illinois University Press, 1964.
7. Carbondale, IL: Southern Illinois University Press, 1958.
8. New Haven, CT: Yale University Press, 1980.
9. Childs had some evangelical connections, I was told, and that might have made him especially interesting to me.

Westminster OPC

I thought to continue my involvement in the OPC, so when I arrived at Yale I called Bill Moreau, pastor of Westminster OPC in Hamden, CT, the nearest conservative Presbyterian church to downtown New Haven, where I lived. I had known Bill slightly at WTS; he knew who I was, and he offered to pick me up for services. The church was maybe twenty minutes from where I lived, in a pleasant rural/suburban setting. Like most OP churches, this one was very small, thirty-to-fifty members. As with the Blue Bell Church, the members were very hospitable. I spent most Sunday afternoons with Bill and his wife Jackie, or with another family in the church. Often several of us students would have dinner with the Bacon family who had maybe seven children, and a very nice rural estate in central CT, maybe forty-five minutes from the church. In time I started a choir and taught some adult classes. Everyone was very kind and sweet, but I quickly became disappointed with the church. It was not evangelistic at all, just a haven for people with Reformed backgrounds. Bill's sermons eventually seemed to me to follow a predictable pattern: very negative. In my parody, the first point was against Arminianism, the second against dispensationalism, and the third against the civil rights movement.

Back to Beverly Heights

By April of 1965 I was in a malaise about my Yale experience. For one thing, I had no idea how well I was doing. My professors still had not turned in my fall term grades or returned my term papers. My only measure of success at Yale had been my performance in seminars, which was in my estimation a total failure. I had no real friends in the student body. The church people were very kind and generous, but there was nobody there with whom I could discuss my life and my ideas on a peer basis. And the study of theology had become very dull to me. I forced myself to do it, but I really didn't care much what Aquinas or Tillich thought about this or that.

But about that time I got a surprising letter from Bill Taylor, then the assistant pastor of Beverly Heights. He told me that Bill McLeister, my childhood pastor, was accepting a call to a church in Jackson, MI. Also, Larry Brown, one of the assistant pastors, and Mary Louise Wright, the organist/choir director, were leaving, amid some criticism that was in part theological. Bill invited me to come back to Beverly Heights for a year and serve as a sort of Jack of all trades: doing some teaching and preaching, helping with children's and youth ministry, and taking over organ and choir duties. I greeted that invitation with the trepidation appropriate to a bolt out of the blue. But after a few days of prayer and consideration, it seemed to be God's answer to my malaise.

I asked Julian Hartt (who was managing the doctoral program) if I could have a year's leave of absence from the program. He said that I could apply for one, but he urged me to reconsider. He even suggested that Yale could help me some if the problem was money. Apparently he knew some things about my performance that I did not know. Before I left Yale that year, I learned that my grade average was in the highest category (A grades, which were called "High Honors" in the program), and that my papers were also in the A range. Had I known that, I might have chosen to stay at Yale, but God evidently arranged things so that I would return to Beverly Heights for a while.

For that year of classes I was awarded an M.A. degree, so I stayed until graduation, then headed back to Pittsburgh. I stayed with my parents in Mt. Lebanon and drove a family car to the church each day. The Vietnam War was heating up then, and my mother was frightened that I could be drafted. I had always had a 2-S (student) classification, but I lost that when I left Yale, even though I told the draft board that was temporary. So Mom was right to be worried. I was 1-A through 1965–66. She urged me to enroll in officers' school so I would not be drafted as a "buck private." But that was not the reason I had come home, and I trusted God (some would say foolishly) to keep me out of the hands of the government. God did come through, of course.

At the church, I had an office in the middle-floor classroom space. I spent my time writing outlines for topical Bible studies (my first attempt at systematic theology), practicing the organ, and setting up schedules for choir songs, soloists, and so on. There were two services on Sunday morning. The choir morale was low after the loss of Mary Louise Wright, but they rallied to the support of the church. They were willing initially even to sing for both services, but in time I set things up so the choir rarely sang at the first service.

Remembering the exciting times we had on Wednesday nights when I was growing up, I asked Bill Taylor if I could resurrect the old "Youth Club" as a combination Bible Study and choir rehearsal for kids and teens. Others were helpful, but in time I felt terribly inadequate as the director of the operation, and we hired a dear lady from the church to handle the elementary student program.

I basically used the choir music from the church files that I remembered and liked from the old days. I made no effort catch up with new music being written. That would not have been adequate long term, but for my year it was accepted by the singers and the people. We provided music for all the special services. We even did a program of selections from *Messiah* near Easter. I think I did a fairly good job, but I could have done much better if I had actually studied choir directing and vocal production.

My teaching stressed the authority of the Bible and a solid overview of Reformed doctrine. The denomination was on the verge of approving the "Confession of 1967," with which I had a lot of problems. It was hard to identify specific problems in the new confession, but the purpose of it (and even more of the revisions to the subscription vows) was to legitimize Barthian theology in the church. I tried not to take a confrontationalist posture, given my age and lack of ordination,[10] but I did come across to some as a critic of the denomination, and that caused some tensions.

The people as a whole, however, were tremendously appreciative and sorry to see me go at the end of the year. I had enjoyed my time, but I still felt that God had not equipped me as a pastor. Again, I defaulted to my academic pursuits. I went back to Yale and regained my 2-S draft status.

A postscript: a couple years later, Bill Taylor invited me to preach at an evening service at Beverly Heights. I hesitated, warning him that it would be hard to prevent myself from going into a tirade about developments in the PCUSA. Bill (who was almost as radical as I in his heart of hearts) told me to go ahead and bring my tirade. I tried to be gentle, but I did say some critical things about the denomination. Certain people were listening, and I was never asked to do anything more at Beverly Heights—until 2010 (I think), when I was asked to speak for the twenty-fifth anniversary celebration of Rick Wolling's ministry there. That was a great time. I met again people I hadn't seen in fifty years.

Back to Yale

Yale told me that I could not simply take a year off from the program and then be reinstated; I needed to re-apply. But when I re-applied, they accepted me, quite easily, it seemed. Indeed, they gave me a full scholarship for the rest of my program, without my even applying for it. They also decided

---

10. I was accepted as a member of the church, which was actually a little questionable. Around 1964 I had decided that I could not any longer be a member of the PCUSA, so I asked to become a member of Westerly Road Church in Princeton, which they agreed to do, and I asked Beverly Heights to erase me from its rolls. Bill Taylor told me, however, that the church had never erased me. Perhaps the fact that my Dad was an elder had something to do with that. Anyhow, for several years I was a member of two churches: Westerly Road and Beverly Heights. I found that amusing, and not a violation of biblical church polity. The problem was finally settled when I joined Covenant OPC around 1967.

that I could receive a full year's credit in my doctoral program for the three years of study I had at WTS. Finally I had a reply to the inquiry I had made nearly two years earlier![11]

My second stay at Yale was different. My Mom and her sister Auntie Dean went up before I did to investigate the housing situation, and they signed me up for something nicer than I had before, a room in a private home on Lawrence St., right near the Divinity School. My parents let me drive a family car, a Pontiac convertible. (I never drove with the roof open, however.)

During my year away, the university had dropped their procedure of granting the M.A. degree to students on the basis of one year's grad courses. Instead, they had decided to grant the M.Phil. on the basis of two years of grad courses and completion of the comprehensive doctoral exams. Of course, I already had the M.A. and they couldn't take it away from me. Now recall that they had granted me a full year's credit for my work at WTS. So at that point they regarded me as having completed two years of Yale classes. The only requirement remaining for the M.Phil., therefore, was the comprehensive exams.

So I arrived early in the summer of 1966 and prepared for comps. Mine were in history of doctrine, history of philosophy, modern theology, and philosophical theology. I worked very hard on them and took the exams in the early fall. I got good marks, so I qualified for the M.Phil. in 1966, after only two or three months of study. Today it remains the easiest degree I have ever earned.

I had more or less planned to spend two more years at Yale, to finish the doctorate in 1968. Now I could spend all that time on my dissertation. Of course, I also wanted to audit some courses I had hoped to take. One was the Lindbeck Comparative Dogmatics course that I mentioned earlier. I also audited a course in the Authority of Scripture by a new young star on the faculty, David Kelsey. In Kelsey's course, the emphasis was, not on how theologians formulated the authority of Scripture, but how they actually *used* Scripture to warrant their theological proposals. I found this course tremendously helpful, like Kelsey's later book *The Uses of Scripture in Recent Theology*,[12] which I reviewed in *Westminster Theological Journal*.[13]

---

11. Later on I had asked Julian Hartt why the delay in answering my inquiry. He said that they didn't give this privilege to everybody. Some students, he said, had come from places that weren't as academically respectable as WTS. But the faculty had come to the conclusion that my preparation warranted this credit.

12. Philadelphia: Fortress, 1975.

13. See my review of *The Uses of Scripture in Recent Theology* (http://www.frame-poythress.org/review-of-kelseys-the-uses-of-scripture-in-recent-theology/ and in *DWG*, 466–89).

But the major new member of my cast of characters in 1966 was Paul Holmer, who had been on leave during my first year at Yale. Holmer was a kind of evangelical, though not doctrinally predictable. Raised an evangelical, he had played the piano for Mordecai Hamm, the evangelist who led Billy Graham to Christ. But Holmer had strayed somewhat from standard evangelicalism when he began to study philosophy. He became something of a "positivist" (as he described it) for a while, but came to be profoundly influenced by Søren Kierkegaard and by the later work of Ludwig Wittgenstein.[14] Gradually, Holmer came to find more and more sympathy with his evangelical upbringing.[15] When I was there, he was the campus advisor to Inter-Varsity Christian Fellowship (which was itself not always bound to the evangelical party line).

I audited Holmer's course in Contemporary Theology and found it quite fascinating. Eventually I asked him to be my dissertation advisor, which he was willing to do. He and I had some friends in common, including Ed Clowney, who once called him "the fountainhead of Kierkegaard scholarship." And Holmer seemed to be happy to have the opportunity to work with an evangelical student. He was not initially enthusiastic about my view of biblical inerrancy. (Somewhere in his writings he refers to infallibility and inerrancy as nonsensical claims.) But he was genuinely curious about what I would do with these ideas.

Since I was interested in questions of biblical authority, Holmer suggested first that I read and critique F. Gerald Downing's *Has Christianity a Revelation?*[16] Downing answers "no" to the titular question. He argues that the point of the Bible is not to unveil God, though it does at times present information claiming to come from him. Downing is, therefore, actually more favorable to "propositional" revelation than to "personal" revelation, though most modern theologians favor the second and condemn the first. I wrote a paper of about eighty pages that in my judgment destroyed Downing's basic argument while applauding some of the moves he makes against the liberal consensus. Holmer liked my work, I think, and he urged me to formulate a dissertation topic more precisely.

---

14. Some would find Kierkegaard and Wittgenstein to be an odd combination, but Wittgenstein, who read little of other philosophers, read Kierkegaard extensively before it became fashionable to read him. Wittgenstein considered Kierkegaard to be the most profound philosopher of the nineteenth century.

15. See my review of his *The Grammar of Faith* (http://www.frame-poythress.org/review-of-holmers-the-grammar-of-faith/).

16. London: SCM, 1964.

The Dissertation That Never Was

I remembered that in past large papers I had sometimes tried to do too much. That was especially true in my Princeton senior thesis, and I did not want to make that mistake again. At the same time, I wanted to write a dissertation that would make a difference. So many dissertations are on trivial topics, dull and easily forgotten. I wanted my dissertation to be the beginning of a new movement against the presuppositions of theological liberalism. Certainly that was a tall order for a Yale graduate student, but I was at a place in my life in which I was not really interested in anything less.

My mind increasingly turned to the concept of "propositional revelation." Both Gordon Clark and his student Carl Henry had regarded that as a matter of some importance in the theological dialogue about Scripture. And as I read modern theologians like Barth, Brunner, and Tillich, it seemed to me that many of their innovations in the doctrine of Scripture were developed as alternatives to, or arguments against, propositional revelation.

I didn't want to use the phrase "propositional revelation" in my dissertation. With Holmer reading my work, I thought he would want me to scour the analytic philosophers' definitions of "proposition" and the arguments about whether such things existed. So I wanted to describe the issue in a more common-sense way: Is God able to give us information? Is he able to communicate language that makes a truth claim? Does he desire to do that? Has he done it?

If God has in fact revealed information to us, then it would certainly seem that we are obligated to believe what he says. Now it seemed to me that much of the argument of liberal theologians on Scripture was essentially an attempt to escape that very possibility—the possibility that God places us under obligation to believe one thing rather than something else. To put that another way, the possibility is that God is sovereign over our minds, that he governs our beliefs just as he governs our "moral" and "religious" behavior. If that is the case, then the God of the Bible rejects the autonomy of human thought, the cornerstone of the "Enlightenment."

So I thought I would, in my dissertation, examine all the arguments used by liberal theologians to oppose propositional revelation, and refute them. That might turn out to be a masterful exercise in language analysis, something Holmer would find impressive.

Now liberal theology, in my view, is a movement that began in the mid-seventeenth century in the writings of pantheists and deists of the time, like Spinoza and Cherbury. To pinpoint all the arguments against propositional revelation from Spinoza to the present would require a lot of research and analysis. But I thought in my heart that these arguments could possibly be reduced to three or four. Once I had isolated those arguments, I could analyze them as arguments, rather than having to make a minute analysis of every thinker who used each argument.

So perhaps the first chapter would have dealt with Karl Barth's claim that God reveals *"himself"* rather than "information." There I could follow Downing to a large extent. I could show that God revealing "himself" was not at all incompatible with him revealing "information," and that if God did not reveal any information at all he could hardly be thought to have revealed himself at all. Further, according to Scripture, God most certainly does reveal information. Chapter 2 might have examined the argument of Brunner that propositional revelation detracted from the "personal" character of revelation. Chapter 3 might have discussed the supposed conflict between science and the propositions of the Bible.

Was this project too big for me to undertake? At first it did not seem so. And even when I look at it again today, it seems to me that some enterprising graduate student could make a significant contribution by developing these ideas.

When I first described this topic to Holmer, he did not tell me it was too broad or too difficult. He did warn me against determining my conclusion in advance. Faced with the liberal view and the Clark/Henry evangelical view, I should maintain some independence from both. Maybe I could find a third alternative, he said. Holmer would not have presented propositional revelation as a feature of his own view of Scripture, but he was open to my thinking and thought I might be able make something out of the idea. I always felt that Holmer was rooting for me. He liked students who were "at odds with their environment" (like Kierkegaard). Once someone asked him about some theological point held by evangelicals, and Holmer said, "Ask Frame; he's the most tendentious guy around here."

Sometime that fall, I met with Holmer and some other professors to gain approval for my topic. They asked good questions, and we discussed the literature for some time. Later, Holmer told me that I had done a great job, and my topic was officially approved.

My next job was to read everything I could read of liberal theology from 1650 to the present. My purpose was to isolate the arguments all of these thinkers had used to oppose propositional revelation. So I read Spinoza and Cherbury, Lessing, Kant, Schleiermacher, Ritschl, Kierkegaard, Barth, Brunner, Bultmann, Tillich, and many others. I accumulated a huge library of notes and quotes from all these thinkers.

And then I sat down to write. But for the first time in my life, the writing didn't come. I would try to formulate, say, Spinoza's fundamental argument against propositional revelation. I would write something down, but would then feel that it wasn't quite right. Although Spinoza says A in some places, he says not-A elsewhere; so that a lot more research in his works would have to be done. I could not formulate Spinoza's view, it seemed, without writing a whole thesis on Spinoza! This was Yale, after all. I could not ascribe views to a thinker without doing research worthy of Yale. But there were maybe fifty thinkers in all.

So I didn't finish the task. Even though I had virtually two years free to do nothing except write the dissertation, I didn't finish it: one of many reasons for my growing disappointment while at Yale.

The New Haven Evangelical Free Church

I prayed about where I should go to church this time. I could not get interested in making the long trek to Westminster OPC every Sunday, as I had in 1964–65. Bill's sermons were not helpful, and there was little for me to do in the congregation. They seemed happy with a maintenance model of church life. The church was not in a good position to evangelize the Yale campus. And, frankly, I was hoping to find a church with some marriageable women (at least one!) of my age.

I talked with Jackie Moreau about this. She said that in 1964–65 I had been too much of a taker, not enough of a giver. That was certainly right. I had made some contributions at WOPC, but I did not reach out much to the people, and with some exceptions I did not seek to bring non-Christians to worship there. I was reluctant to invite visitors, because I thought the preaching would not move them. Jackie also told me that the Bacon kids were very disappointed to hear that I wouldn't be returning. I felt sad about that, but couldn't allow that to determine my decision.

I remembered that a friend, John Guret, a literary scholar who had gone both to Yale and WTS, had recommended to me the New Haven Evangelical Free Church, where he had worshiped. This church was well within walking distance from the campus, and John recommended the preaching of Pastor Arnold Malmberg as Reformed and profound. I visited the church and discovered that Malmberg had retired, though he still preached there occasionally. The new pastor was Frank Harris, an Englishman who with his wife and children had spent some years on the mission field. Frank did not stress Reformed distinctives, though he told me once that he was Reformed in his theological position. His preaching was evangelical, clear, focused on Scripture, practical. I enjoyed his ministry.

I sang in the choir, directed by a member of the congregation who used as anthems mostly popular gospel songs arranged in Lorenz collections.

These weren't as "high class" as the choir music at Beverly Heights, but they suited me fine. I often found them deeply moving. Occasionally I played the organ, but only as a substitute for their regular organist.

For a while I was one of several Yale people who led an adult Bible study on Wednesday evenings. That study was divided into small groups, and the several teachers were expected to cover the same biblical material each week. I confess that I lagged behind the other teachers.

Some of the Yale grad students at the church would later be famous. I attended an InterVarsity[17] Bible study with Ron Sider, who later authored *Rich Christians in a World of Hunger*.[18] Ron and I debated a bit. I kept insisting that the prophets' advocacy of the poor was mainly in a covenant context, based on redemptive solidarity. Ron thought it was a more general concept, based more directly on economic need. Later we talked again when we were both teaching in Philadelphia.

Merold Westphal was a philosophy student and later became well known as a scholar and author of books about phenomenology, existentialism, modernity and postmodernity, and hermeneutics (the philosophical topics in which I am least comfortable). Like Sider, Westphal taught under the auspices of InterVarsity, and I occasionally attended meetings where he taught. As I recall, his emphasis then was to show us that Christians need not fear thinkers like Marx and Nietzsche. Indeed, we can benefit from thinking about the issues they raise.

The church reached quite a number of Yale students, undergraduate, graduate, and divinity. I am very thankful for its ministry to me, though I did not find there my future wife, and I didn't find anyone with whom I could work out the implications of Van Tillian apologetics. I was disappointed a few years later when the church left downtown New Haven and erected a new building in the suburb of Woodbridge. Few Yalies could easily get to Woodbridge, and the move represented to me a choice of comfort over ministry.

Sometime in the early 1970s I did receive an invitation to play a recital on their new organ, and I accepted the invitation if only to renew acquaintances and to observe their new building. My playing was, well, OK for an

---

17. Of the campus Christian groups, I was only involved with Inter-Varsity. Campus Crusade for Christ also had a ministry among Yale students, but when I arrived in 1964 I was told that they had been expelled from the campus because of someone who put gospel tracts in professors' mailboxes. I was never able to find the off-campus location of CC, and I figure that a "crusade" that couldn't be found was probably not a very effective crusade. Later, however, I would have good relationships with CC people.

18. Downers Grove, IL: IVP, 1977.

amateur. But I could not work up any enthusiasm for the type of ministry they had chosen.

My First Teaching Experience

In addition to my full-ride scholarship, Yale invited me to be a teaching assistant in the Department of Philosophy. Someone recommended my name to Prof. John Wild to work in one of his courses. Readers may recall that I mentioned Wild in chapter 3, as one influence on Dennis O'Brien, with whom I studied at Princeton. Between O'Brien's student days and mine, Wild had moved from the University of Chicago to Yale, and had also changed his philosophical stance. In the earlier period, Wild had been a champion of "classical realism," following Aristotle and Aquinas over against the prevailing schools of the 1950s. But by 1966, when I returned to Yale, Wild had published *Existence and the World of Freedom*[19] in which he advocated a version of existentialism, correlated with the pragmatism of William James. He and I had a very cordial lunch. He was interested in my background, for he had been reading Dooyeweerd! He appreciated what Dooyeweerd had to say about idolatry.

I attended Wild's lectures, then led a discussion group once a week. I tried to recapitulate the reading assignments and correlate them with the lectures. And I made some use of my Van Tillian resources to try and steer the discussions in a Christian direction. At first, the discussions were lively and fun. Then a self-styled radical student, son of a well-known anti-war leader, challenged me very directly and did what he could to make me look more foolish than I was. I tried to encourage him to think creatively, and I tried to use him as a foil for my own more controversial ideas. But in time the students sided with him over me. The result was that after the sixth or seventh class sessions, I had zero attendance. At first, I took this personally and worried that I had been a failure as a teacher. But eventually I learned what should have been obvious: typically discussion groups were occasions for "quizzes," and I hadn't given any. I had considered doing that, but I had never liked quizzes as an instructional method (still don't), and I hoped I could avoid using them. But in time nobody came, and I couldn't even locate the students to announce a quiz.

So my first teaching experience was a total flop. Wild was appalled when I told him what had happened. But he responded with gentleness and grace. Of course I still list on my résumé that I have been a teaching assistant at Yale University.

19. Englewood Cliffs, NJ: Prentice-Hall, 1963.

Malaise Redux

But the monster of disappointment came over me again, which had been temporarily relieved by my year at Beverly Heights. My teaching had flopped, my dissertation was going nowhere. Despite being part of a good church, I had virtually no personal friends, not even someone who could usefully discuss these problems with me.

I went to a lot of movies then, probably too many, becoming something of a movie buff. I went mostly by myself, and often without any sense that the film would do me good.

I came to lose interest in theology, at least the theology I was studying at Yale. I still loved to read the Bible and to hear it expounded, but it seemed to bear no fruit in my life. I seemed to have made a wrong turn, but I had no idea where to go next. But then I got a call from WTS.

6

Westminster Again: The Boy Wonder

DURING MY SEMINARY STUDENT years and after, I did give some thought to the possibility that I might one day be asked to teach at WTS. It was not a strong possibility. Van Til and I, as I mentioned, did not communicate well, and Knudsen (for good reason) was not enthusiastic about me. So I wasn't expecting an opportunity to teach apologetics. I had also done well in systematic theology at WTS, but I had neglected that field in favor of apologetics and philosophy.

But John Murray retired in 1966, and in 1967–68 Norman Shepherd taught all of the systematics courses at WTS. Shepherd needed help, and he engaged in a search to find an assistant. I am not sure why he settled on me. As I indicated in chapter 4, I had gotten one of my lowest seminary grades in the one course I had taken from him. But I had a good reputation for scholarship, and I think Norman was impressed with the fact that I did not challenge the low grade he gave me, but instead apologized for my own poor preparation.

Norman was himself a New Englander, so he visited me in New Haven on his way to visit his family. I took him to dinner at the restaurant once known as "the dear old Temple Bar we loved so well" in the Yale Whiffenpoofs' Song. Norman ascertained my allegiance to Reformed theology and to Van Til's apologetics. As it turned out we had a number of friends in common. Like me, he had grown up in the old United Presbyterian Church of North America. (Unlike me, he had maintained their pre-1925 view of exclusive Psalmody, a view that John Murray had also held.) Norman had gone to Westminster College in New Wilmington, PA, where I had gone every summer to play the piano for the New Wilmington Missionary Conference.

Some weeks later, I dined with the WTS faculty in Philadelphia and presented some remarks about the current state of liberal theology. I thought at the time that there were some positive things going on: more careful thought in the thinkers influenced by analytic philosophy, a more positive view of history in thinkers like Pannenberg. Most of the WTS faculty thought otherwise, but they encouraged me nonetheless.

I did not share with any of them the malaise of my last year at Yale. None of them were skilled at counseling, and I thought that God would rouse me from such feelings once I was able to do something of value to the church's ministry. It occurred to me that J. Gresham Machen, everyone's hero at WTS, had also been through a period of malaise in his earliest teaching years at Princeton. Indeed, Machen had profound doubts about the truth of Reformed doctrine, though he recovered from that condition to become one of the great modern defenders of the faith.

My First Teaching Load

So I received an invitation to teach as an instructor at Westminster in the field of systematic theology. Shepherd asked me to teach the Doctrine of Scripture, the Doctrine of God, and the Ethics classes. The first two were areas where I had worked extensively and had felt I had some things to share with the students. Ethics was something of a problem, however. I had avoided ethics courses both at Princeton and at Yale, though these schools had well-known thinkers teaching the subject. (At Princeton, Paul Ramsey, and at Yale, James Gustafson.) But I had thought that ethical reasoning at the university level was largely subjectivist and its arguments not even faintly plausible. I was not required to take ethics courses, and I didn't expect that anyone would ask me to teach them. So I kept the discipline at arm's length. At Westminster, the senior ethics course in earlier days had been divided into a philosophical unit (taught by Van Til[1]) and an exegetical unit (taught by John Murray[2]). Later, these were brought together into a two-credit course that I took from Edwin H. Palmer. Palmer's was the only ethics course I had taken in my academic career. Shepherd, however, thought the course was important, and he expanded the course to four credit hours, to be evenly divided between Christian (presuppositional, of course) philosophy and biblical exegesis (chiefly the Ten Commandments). Then for some

---

1. See his *Christian-Theistic Ethics* (Phillipsburg, NJ: P&R, 1980), also available at http://presupp101.files.wordpress.com/2011/08/van-til-christian-theistic-ethics.pdf.

2. See his *Principles of Conduct* (Grand Rapids: Eerdmans, 1957), and *Divorce* (Phillipsburg, NJ: P&R, 1987).

reason he assigned it to me. As a first-year teacher, I said yes to everything Shepherd suggested, and so I spent much of my early study time working on ethics, digesting the writings of Van Til, Murray, and others.

Although I did not begin as a member of the apologetics department, Van Til greeted me warmly. If he was suspicious of me because of past disagreements, he didn't express those suspicions when I returned to WTS. On the contrary, he arranged with Shepherd so that part of my time would be given to teaching apologetics electives at the B.D.[3] and Th.M. levels. Now Van Til had always tried to provide the students with teaching on all current philosophical movements. He wanted WTS apologetics to be directed not only to man-on-the-street conversations, but also to the great thinkers of philosophy. He himself specialized in older thinkers, Knudsen in phenomenology and existentialism. But neither of them was comfortable in British and American language analysis. So they invited me to develop courses in these areas. In the early years, then, I taught courses titled Theological Method, Theological Argument, The Concept of Theology, Christianity and Analytic Philosophy, and Wittgenstein.[4]

Later on, however, the seminary added apologetics to my title in an official way. In 1972, Van Til retired from teaching the first-year apologetics course. He did not ask me to take it over, which would have been easy for him and not difficult for me. So I assume that at that time he was still not convinced that I was a true Van Tillian. Instead, the seminary invited Harvie Conn, then an OPC missionary to Korea, to return to the States and teach courses in apologetics and missions. Harvie was a delightful person,[5] full of

---

[3]. The Bachelor of Divinity indicated basic ministerial preparation. Later it was called M.Div. In my view, that amounted to degree-inflation. It always seemed odd to me to call this degree a master's degree. A master's degree should indicate something beyond bachelor's-level study. But in the theological degree, students took Beginning Greek, Beginning Hebrew, Beginning History, Philosophy, Theology, Preaching, etc. I do think that by the time they reached their third year, the students were doing graduate-level work. Perhaps that entitled them to a master's degree. But I always sense a bit of academic pride in the notion that seminary study was a "graduate" program.

When the seminary changed from the B.D. to the M.Div. as their basic ministerial degree, they offered to us alumni the opportunity to replace our B.D.'s with M.Div.'s. But one requirement was to turn in our old diplomas so they could be replaced with new ones. That would mean that I would not have any more my diploma with the signatures of the old faculty: Young, Murray, et al. I declined the exchange. So I carry on with the disadvantage of no M.Div. and an antiquated B.D.

[4]. Much of the substantive material from these courses can be found in my *DKG*, and the historical material in my *HWPT*.

[5]. Harvie had a wild sense of humor. Some years earlier, he was a pastor in New Jersey and reported on home missions for the OPC committee. Harvie spoofed the traditional missions report, dressing up in the "native costumes" found among New

zeal to reach people with the gospel. In Korea, he had witnessed to prostitutes and others rejected by society. Under his stewardship, the apologetics course became essentially a course in evangelism. Harvie was not equipped to add new features to the Van Tillian epistemology, but he was true to that system, he was able to present it clearly, and he pressed the students to take it to the streets. He had the students work on multi-media presentations of how to present the gospel to different kinds of skeptics.

But by 1975, Harvie decided that he should work exclusively in the field of missions and pass the apologetics teaching on to someone else. That someone else turned out to be me. Evidently, Van Til did not voice an objection, for if he had, I would not have been invited to teach the course. Although Van Til was largely retired, his opinions held sway over all matters concerning apologetics.

I had a few preferences too. I had developed lecture material in biblical epistemology for the course in the doctrine of Scripture, and I wanted the students in the apologetics course to know that material too. I didn't want to give those lectures twice, in two different courses, especially since the students enrolled in those two courses would be largely the same. There were various ways of handling this, such as making the doctrine of Scripture course a required prerequisite to the apologetics course. But that would have required reworking the curriculum to teach the two courses in different semesters, and the administrators didn't want to do that. The solution I settled on was to combine the two courses (doctrine of Scripture, 2 credit hours, and apologetics, 3 credit hours) into a gigantic 5 credit hour course to be called Introduction to Theology and Apologetics. This was a rather odd curricular move, and it took a long time for me to persuade my colleagues to accept it. Eventually, Ed Clowney saw the point I was making, and he brought about the change. So the new course had three units: Doctrine of Scripture, Biblical Epistemology, and Apologetics.

Triperspectivalism

I took very seriously my new role as a lecturer[6] at WTS. I was daunted by the thought of trying to attain the quality of my own teachers at the school. WTS was not only an evangelical seminary, not only a Reformed

---

Jersey beach bums. Everyone was in stitches, and it was not easy to get the OPC General Assembly to laugh.

6. During my student years, lecturing was the predominant method of teaching at WTS. A few teachers distributed printed outlines of their lectures: this procedure was considered *avant-garde*. A very few classes, like Van Til's, were interactive.

institution, but much more. It was a highly creative academic community. Teachers at WTS not only passed on a tradition, but added to it. There was always something new going on. Van Til's apologetics, the Vossian emphasis on biblical theology, Kline's innovative theories, the fruits of Stonehouse's intensive research—none of these were mere repetitions of the work of older theologians. These were not to be found in an examination of the Reformed confessions. These ideas were certainly *compatible* with historic Reformed theology, and they *supported* the principles of that tradition. But they were not themselves traditions. They were creative ideas within the bounds of orthodoxy.

The creativity was continuing when I returned to WTS in 1968. Several new teachers had joined the faculty. One was Jay Adams. Jay was hired to teach preaching, but he had also studied counseling, and he began teaching courses in that subject. In 1970, he published *Competent to Counsel*,[7] which developed a distinctively biblical approach. Adams' critiques of secular psychology were reminiscent of Van Til's antithesis. Another was C. John ("Jack") Miller. Miller also taught practical theology and became himself a church planter in the area. His New Life Orthodox Presbyterian Church sought in many ways to reform church planting in a biblical direction. His church was strongly evangelistic and bathed in prayer, and had little regard for traditionalists who challenged his model as "evangelical" or "pietistic." New Life was one of the first churches in our area to adopt a contemporary style of music in worship. That was anathema to many of the Orthodox Presbyterians. But many who opposed Miller in the early days later joined New Life in order to expose themselves and their families to the quality of its ministry. New Life became the fastest growing church in the Orthodox Presbyterian denomination.[8] Miller's approach is documented in several of his books.[9] He founded World Harvest Mission and the Sonship Discipleship Course. Adams came later to be critical of Miller. My only point for the moment is that Adams and Miller both contributed to the stream of new thinking that had always energized the otherwise traditional Reformed theology of Westminster.

Another man who joined the faculty during my absence was D. Clair Davis, who after studying with Gordon H. Clark at Butler University had scored in the 99th percentile of the Graduate Record Exam in philosophy. But following the Van Til/Clark controversy in the 1940s, WTS was not

---

7. Grand Rapids: Zondervan, 1970.

8. Not a large achievement, to be sure. But New Life eventually had hundreds of members.

9. *Outgrowing the Ingrown Church* (Grand Rapids: Zondervan, 1986); *Repentance* (Philadelphia: Christian Literature Crusade, 2009).

hospitable to Clark's ideas, even in the 1960s. Still, they called Davis to teach, not philosophy, but church history, on the strength of his Dr. Theol. from Georg-August Universität, Göttingen. It was evident to me from the beginning that Clair's mind did not move in predictable steps. In time he began to attend New Life and to defend it against the criticisms of traditionalists. He appreciated Adams too, as a serious, innovative Christian thinker. Although Clair has not published many books and articles, he has blessed many of us with his acute, biblical, and often unexpected observations on the work of God in the Christian life. He has lately been concerned about revival in the Christian life.

All of this was highly congenial to me: creativity within the bounds of Reformed orthodoxy. As later chapters in this book will indicate, I have often found myself resisting fellow churchmen and theologians whom I have considered "traditionalist." In the late 1990s, I found myself in opposition to colleagues at Westminster in California who thought that the genius of Westminster was that of meticulously following historical traditions, the confessions, and the theologians of the sixteenth and seventeenth centuries.[10] I have thought of these colleagues as traditionalists, and they have thought of me as at least a borderline heretic. But from my earliest days at WTS, I have been convinced that the school at its heart was far from traditionalist, though some members of its constituency could be described that way.

But what could I add to the seminary's venerable tradition, particularly to its tradition of creativity? The experience of my years as a Westminster student prepared me for the worst, for Westminster students had high expectations. They expected Reformed theology, but they expected that Reformed theology to be taught in a way that was exciting, inspiring, and thought-provoking. In 1968, I did not think I was anywhere near up to the task.

Granted the need for both creativity and faithfulness to the tradition, I saw myself as facing a choice of two options: (1) What many expected of me was that I would bring to my courses an updating of the modern theological and philosophical scene: Wittgenstein, process thought, Bultmann, Tillich, Pannenberg, Moltmann, et al. WTS had a reputation for being up-to-date on these movements, and I was equipped to help them continue their updating. I would not, of course, recommend the views of these thinkers to my WTS audience. Rather, like Machen and Van Til before me I would critique these movements using the criteria of Scripture, Reformed theology, and my predecessors at WTS, especially Van Til. Had I chosen this course, I

---

10. See my *TET*.

could have done it competently, but to be honest I would not have done it with enthusiasm and zeal. My boredom with modern theologians continued strong from my Yale days.

(2) A second option was far more appealing to me. As a WTS student, I had been deeply moved by the approach of John Murray (and by others, like Clowney and Kline) who had developed their theology directly from the Scriptures, referring to the theological scene only rarely. To do this, I would have to bypass in some measure my Yale experience and revert to the teaching I had received at WTS. But for me this was the only option. I believed deeply that theology and apologetics had to be rooted deeply in Scripture, not extrapolated from tradition, nor developed as a negation of heretical ideas. WTS had taught me how to dig into Scripture for answers to any conceivable question, and my new colleagues like Miller, Adams, and Davis encouraged me in that course. Not that I could ignore past history or the contemporary scene, but these contexts would have to serve my understanding of Scripture rather than the other way around. The other way around (i.e., (1) above) would have been more academically respectable, but I had grown very suspicious of Christians who seek academic respectability.

So I dug into Scripture. For some reason, I remember talking to Dick Gaffin, who was about two years older than I and two years senior on the faculty. We stood outside the little room on the ground floor of the library that the seminary had given me for an office, as I was getting ready to write my first lecture on a little typewriter. Dick asked what I planned to do. I told him that I expected to develop a version of Reformed theology informed by language analysis philosophy. I may have misled Dick somewhat. If I was interested in bringing analytic philosophy into it, it was only to clarify by analysis the force of biblical language. In fact, I did teach the students a bit about analytic philosophy, but that was far from the heart of my approach. Anyhow, we shook hands, and Dick said to me, "Go to it." And I did.

For the students, I defined theology as "the application of Scripture by persons to every area of human life." That definition rises out of the uses of the *didasko* vocabulary, especially in the Pastoral Epistles, and from suggestions of Calvin and William Ames. That definition gave to theology a biblical focus, and it helped assuage the tension I felt between academic theology and church ministry. For on this basis theology deals with ministry questions, not just philosophical ones; practical questions, not just theoretical ones. I did not want to eliminate the theoretical questions that had traditionally been the subject matter of theology, but I wanted to deemphasize them so that the practical questions of ministry were given equal importance.

In a lecture course, the teacher needs to think about structure. It's like writing a book. You need to think about what comes first, what comes second, what motifs to echo through the course. The students need to have some hooks on which to string the facts, or as we say today, a "narrative." Sometimes the course structure gets in the way of the exposition of Scripture. So I wanted a structure that, as much as possible, could be derived from Scripture itself. I say "as much as possible," because Scripture itself doesn't give us an explicit structure by which to teach it. Wisely, God has left that to the teacher. The teacher has the responsibility to assess his audience, for different audiences must be taught differently.

In my two first-year courses, Doctrine of Scripture and Doctrine of God, I started with the traditional confessional teachings as elaborated and defended by traditional theologians like Hodge and Berkhof. In the Doctrine of Scripture course, I added some of the ideas I had learned from Kline, that would appear later in his brilliant books *Treaty of the Great King*[11] and *The Structure of Biblical Authority*.[12] I also brought in some thoughts from David Kelsey on the "uses" of Scripture. In the Doctrine of God course, my main emphasis was on the contrast between divine transcendence and divine immanence, trying to impress on students the implications of Van Til's two circle diagram: that God and man are distinct, and there is nothing between them. Man can never become God, and God can never lose his divinity.[13]

I wasn't entirely satisfied with the transcendence/immanence distinction as a major teaching structure. There are many notions of transcendence, like the "wholly other" of Karl Barth, and of immanence, like the panentheism of process theology. I tried to make it clear to the students that these were *not* biblical concepts. But how could I define the authentic *biblical* meaning of transcendence and immanence, when neither of these were biblical terms?

But when I worked through the ethics literature I started to get some help. The first half of the Ethics course, dealing with the basic structure of ethical decision-making, was based on Van Til's *Christian-Theistic Ethics*.[14] In that book, Van Til distinguishes between the goal, the motive, and the standard of Christian behavior. This trio of concepts came in turn from various Reformed confessions, such as WCF 16.7. It occurred to me, although

---

11. Grand Rapids: Eerdmans, 1963.
12. Grand Rapids: Eerdmans, 1972.
13. Though, of course, he took on a human nature in Christ and in that sense "became" man.
14. Philadelphia: Westminster Theological Seminary, 1958.

Van Til does not stress the point, that these concepts enable us to distinguish the three major kinds of secular ethics. Teleological, or utilitarian, ethics (as in Epicurus and John Stuart Mill) stresses the *goal* of ethics (usually happiness of some kind) and then seeks the means of obtaining that goal. Existential ethics (Greek Sophists, Heidegger, Sartre) stresses the *motive*, the "authenticity" of expressing one's own inner intentions. Deontological ethics (Plato, Kant, Prichard) stress *duty*, derived from objective standards.

Secular ethicists typically honor one or two of these factors, seeking to avoid any reliance on the third. But biblical ethics honors the intuition that any meaningful ethical choice involves *all three* factors: a goal to be achieved, a moral agent to do it (motive), and a rule to show us how to achieve the goal (standard).

Further, it occurred to me that each of these involves the other two. Every goal must follow the direction of our standard. The standard must be conducive to the goal. Both must be accessible and adapted to the moral agent, who in turn must be made in such a way as to live under the standard and direct his life toward the goal. So if you fully understand the standard (Scripture) you will understand the goal (the glory of God) and yourself as an ethical agent (the image of God). So by my second or third year of teaching at WTS, I started telling the students that these three elements of ethics were each "perspectives" on the whole ethical task, indeed perspectives on one another. The goal was the "situational" or "teleological" perspective; the motive was the "existential" perspective, and the standard was the "normative" perspective. Students started calling this "perspectivalism" and a new theological program was born.

From the Ethics course, perspectivalism migrated to the Doctrine of God course. For it occurred to me that we are able to speak of the *goal* of ethics, because God has structured all of nature and history so as to achieve that goal and to give human beings a role in achieving it. We have a goal, because God is in *control*. The *motives* of our inner subjectivity are ethically important, because God has made us in his image, to be his temples. That is, our inward life, our heart, is a dwelling place of God, a place for his *presence*. And the *standard* of ethics is nothing other than God's own word, especially that set forth in Scripture. That standard expresses his *authority*. So I had a second triad, based on three characteristics of God: his control, authority, and presence.

But this second triad was not just an extrapolation from the first. I began to study the concept of *lordship* in the Bible. *Lord* (representing the mysterious Hebrew name *Yahweh* and other Hebrew and Greek terms like *Adon* and *kurios*) occurs over 7,000 times in the English Bible, often referring to Jesus. The Bible nowhere provides a formal definition of lordship. But I studied passages in which Scripture seemed to be expounding what it means for God to be lord, such as Exod 3:12–15; 6:2–8; 20:2–17; 33:19; 34:5–6, and Ps 103:1–22. In these passages, the ideas of *control, authority,* and *presence* kept emerging. I verified this analysis by other studies, such as Kline's understanding of the suzerainty treaty structure of the Decalogue and Deuteronomy. In that structure, the Great King shows his *control* over past events (the "historical prologue"), his *authority* over the vassal (the "stipulations"), and his *presence* to bless and judge (the "sanctions").

From this point on, various threefold distinctions parallel to these began to startle me, popping out of many Bible passages and theological/philosophical concepts. So this "triperspectivalism" began to characterize all my teaching, and later my published books and articles. It occurred to me that this structure may be importantly related to the doctrine of the Trinity, as I later argued in my "Primer on Perspectivalism."[15] But I hesitated, and still do hesitate, to claim that this is a profound insight into the deep structure of Scripture and the divine nature. I'm content to regard it as a helpful pedagogical structure or narrative, a set of hooks on which the student can place various biblical doctrines. I think that it encourages balance in theological formulation, the balance in Scripture itself between the objective and the subjective, the power and love of God, his law and grace, and so on.

Pedagogy

Not much of this appeared in my various articles published in the 1970s. My first book, which mapped out the general structure of perspectivalism, was not published until 1987.[16] In the 1970s I published only a few articles in multi-author books and book reviews in *WTJ*.[17] The reason was that I had determined to spend the early years of my career focused on pedagogy. I was thankful that WTS at the time was not a "publish or perish" institution. From the example and words of my senior colleagues I got the advice that it is best not to publish until you had something really substantial to say.

---

15. http://www.frame-poythress.org/a-primer-on-perspectivalism-revised-2008/. Available also in my *SSW I*.

16. *DKG*.

17. For a bibliography that includes everything I published during that period, see http://www.frame-poythress.org/bibliographies/john-frame-bibliography/.

Cornelius Van Til, John Murray, and E. J. Young did not publish their first books until the late 1940s, though they had begun teaching a decade earlier.

I had no trouble following their example. I worked mainly on lectures and lecture outlines for my courses. The lecture outline, believe it or not, was considered high tech at the time. Murray and Young typically read the manuscripts of their lectures during the class hour. Woolley did the same, but he did pass out to students very skeletal outlines of the lectures' subject matter. Kline presented ideas in a whirlwind on the board, but gave students no notes to take home. Van Til did provide notes of a sort, his "unpublished syllabi." But although he assigned those, his class presentations often had nothing to do with them. In general, notes were considered to be the student's responsibility. It was Ed Clowney who first tried to present to students the outline of his whole argument in written form, including Scripture and other references.

After I had worked out the content of my lectures, I followed the example of Clowney and gave the students mimeographed outlines of my lectures. Like Clowney's, they were highly detailed, probably too much so. I put in on them the amount of work that I would have put in on a published book. Many of them outlined content that would eventually appear in my published writings.

What of my dissertation? It languished. Yale had given me a 1973 deadline to submit my dissertation. Holmer had said that this wasn't a strict deadline. If I finished the dissertation after the deadline, he said, he would get me reinstated in the program. (Of course, I knew that Holmer wouldn't be at Yale forever.) I had hoped to work on the dissertation during the summers. But every summer I would get out the material I had produced the year before, read it, and tear it up. It never saw the light of day. Parts of the argument I wanted to develop can be found in *DKG*, *DWG*, and in *HWPT*. But in my early years of teaching, I was far more interested in writing class materials than in writing a dissertation.

Today, no one can expect to keep, or even find, a teaching job in a respectable seminary without a Ph.D., but in those days, and in the recent past, there were many respected professors without earned doctorates. Machen himself was the chief example. But also B. B. Warfield, the revered theologian of Old Princeton.[18] Among my teachers at Westminster, Edmund Clowney, John Sanderson, Paul Woolley, and John Murray did not have earned doctorates, and they were among the most impressive teachers

---

18. This was not only true of evangelicals. Karl Barth, for example, never earned a doctorate.

at the school.[19] So I followed in their train—without a doctorate, a throwback to an older time.

I don't feel that I am any worse as a teacher, scholar, or writer, for lack of an earned doctorate. But the lack of a "credential" has reinforced my natural shyness, especially around professional academics. I have always felt that many such scholars do not take me seriously. And perhaps I have reacted too strongly in the other direction, being more critical than I would otherwise be of "academic theology," especially as a way of preparing students for ministry.

Students

When I started teaching in 1968, there were fewer than 100 students at WTS. The first year group, to whom I taught Doctrine of Scripture and Doctrine of God, were around thirty. The third year class numbered around twenty-five. From the beginning, the quality of the students deeply impressed me. They seemed to me, for the most part, to be godly people, and very intelligent.

Shortly before I began to teach, Ed Clowney invited me to dinner, where I met three Harvard grads, then students at WTS. These had all been converted through Francis Schaeffer's ministry at L'Abri in Switzerland. Bill Edgar would later teach apologetics at the French Reformed Seminary at Aix en Provence, France, and then at WTS itself. Jim Hurley would earn a D.Phil. degree in New Testament from Cambridge University, and a Ph.D. in Counseling from Florida State University. He now heads up the Marriage and Family Therapy program at RTS, on the Jackson, MS campus. The third guest was Dick Keyes, who later directed the Southboro, MA branch of L'Abri Fellowship. Ed told me that these men, though they had not long been believers, were among the spiritual leaders in the student body. I was rather overwhelmed by them, by the depth of their minds and hearts. That evening alerted to me that I had undertaken a large job, to think that I had anything much to teach people like these.

Bill, Jim, and Dick were in my third year Ethics class. Ethics happened to be one of Jim's special interests. He had been teaching sexual ethics at a local Christian high school, and his term paper, on the head covering of women in 1 Cor 11 was eventually published in *WTJ*. It led to a published book, *Man and Woman in Biblical Perspective*.[20]

---

19. Some others, who did have earned doctorates, were among my least effective teachers.

20. Grand Rapids: Zondervan, 1981.

But there were many others at WTS who would excel in theology and become well-known teachers and scholars. Ed's son, David Clowney, was a second year student at WTS, who later taught apologetics at WTS from 1980–88 and philosophy for many years at Rowan College.

I had a special affection for the students who started WTS in 1968, who arrived the same year as me. I seem to have startled them at first. One of them told me later that in his first class with me I was sitting in the front row before class. When the bell rang and I rose to lead in prayer, the students were shocked that I was a teacher rather than another student. The name "boy wonder" was heard from time to time.[21]

One of those 1968 students was Willem Van Gemeren, who attended the same church I did and became an Old Testament scholar. My memory at seventy-five fails as to who as at WTS in what year, but there were many in the late 1960s and early 1970s who accomplished much in the field of academic theology.[22] I recall Moises Silva, the NT scholar, Ray Dillard and Alan Groves, OT scholars who died much too young, the brilliant apologist and theologian Greg Bahnsen, Dennis Johnson, who later taught NT and practical theology at Westminster in California, Paul Wells, who has taught theology for many years at Aix en Provence, France. There was Tiina Allik, who doctored at Yale and later taught at Loyola University New Orleans. Wayne Grudem, another Harvard graduate, went on to earn a Cambridge doctorate and write a *Systematic Theology*.[23] Wayne taught for many years at Trinity Evangelical Divinity School and Phoenix Seminary. In that early group of my students was also John Hughes, who earned a doctorate in New Testament at Cambridge, taught at Westmont College, and then moved to Whitefish, MT to be a freelance editor and pioneering writer in the field of theological computing. John and I have worked together often in the intervening years.

---

21. I have always appeared younger than my true age. About this time I returned to Princeton for some reason, and someone asked me if I were a freshman.

22. Of course, many also graduated to become pastors, missionaries, campus workers, etc. That was the main purpose of the seminary. And many of these did great work for the kingdom. But my memory, alas, is selective, and I seem to have retained more vividly the names of those who followed me into theological scholarship. I would recall also what I said earlier, that WTS prepared me for academic work better than it taught me the skills requisite for pastoral work. I think that was true for other WTS grads as well. God seems to have led us to make more of a mark on the academic theological world than on the world of pastorates and missions. Among the students who went into pastorates and mission work were my friends from the Cummings household in Pittsburgh, the brothers Wilson, Cal, and David.

23. Grand Rapids: Zondervan, 1995.

Vern Poythress earned an M.Div. and Th.M. degree from WTS in the same year (1974), and he and I began a special friendship during his student years. He had already earned a Ph.D. in mathematics from Harvard and would go on to earn an M.Litt. in NT from Cambridge and a Th.D. in NT from the University of Stellenbosch in South Africa. He had also studied linguistics under Kenneth Pike's direction and had taught that subject in the Summer Institute of Linguistics.

Sometime around 1970 I remember a faculty meeting in which Ed Clowney asked if there was anything we could do to assist students who were extraordinarily gifted. It was Vern that he had in mind. So the faculty developed an "experimental honors program," in which the student would have freedom to attend lectures or not, in any order, and was responsible only to pass comprehensive exams in different areas and to write a thesis.

Vern was attracted to my perspectivalism and combined my three perspectives with the triadic linguistics of Kenneth Pike: contrast, variation, and distribution; particle, wave, and field.[24] In thinking this through, Vern performed a great service to me. Vern's thinking provided solid support for my theological structure. Without that I might well have abandoned the

Students and faculty at WTS in the early 1970s. I am standing in the back, in tie. Van Til is in the front row. Vern Poythress is leaning against the right wall.

triadic scheme in time and gone in a different direction. But Vern encouraged me to think that this was a solid idea, one that had potential applications to many issues in philosophy and theology.

I think both teacher and students were aware that 1968–74 was a special time. We were working together to develop, formulate, and share important ideas. We were the new generation of WTS scholars—committed to the historic Reformed faith, but rethinking everything, developing creative ideas within the bounds of orthodoxy.

I launched my big five-hour course in Introduction to Theology and Apologetics around 1975. About the same time there was an enormous

---

24. Poythress developed these correlations in his first book, *Philosophy, Science and the Sovereignty of God* (Phillipsburg, NJ: P&R, 1976), and in many books thereafter. His forthcoming *Redeeming Philosophy* (Wheaton, IL: Crossway) develops this in a comprehensive and clear fashion.

increase in the student body; the reason is a mystery to me.[25] The classes of entering students nearly tripled, so that I was teaching the five-hour course to over 100 students in the new Van Til Hall auditorium. Unfortunately, the faculty remained about the same size. So I tried many things. I reduced the written assignments, recruited teaching assistants, and set up preceptorials on the Princeton model. At one time, I had eight teaching assistants for that one course—like running my own seminary. Still, I tried to read all the term papers myself,[26] and once did not return the fall papers to the students until May of the next year. By the end of the decade I came to the conclusion that teaching under these conditions was more than I could handle. That was the main reason I took the opportunity to move to California.

So from the period 1975-80 I have fewer memories of specific students. But over the years it has become evident to me that during that period I was training as many future scholars then as I had taught in the early part of the decade. In the mid-1970s, there was Reggie Kidd, a really cool guitar player, a white guy with a gigantic afro. With a Ph.D. from Duke University, Reggie is now my colleague at RTS Orlando, teaching NT. Frank James III earned two doctorates—one at Westminster, and one at Oxford. He taught church history at RTS-Orlando, then became president of the school. Now he is president of Biblical Theological Seminary in Hatfield, PA.

From the later years of the decade: David Schuringa became a colleague of mine at WSC in practical theology. Mark Futato earned a doctorate at Catholic University and became my colleague at WSC and later at RTS. John Muether became the librarian at WTS and later at RTS (another colleague of mine in that school). Doug Gropp became a prominent OT scholar after earning his doctorate at Harvard. Tremper Longman doctored at Yale and became an OT professor at WTS and later at Westmont College. Esther Meek earned her doctorate at Temple University while taking courses at WTS. She became a philosopher, published important books on Christian epistemology, and currently works as a professor at Geneva College. David Powlison did his undergrad work at Harvard and his doctorate at the University of Pennsylvania. He is now a professor of counseling at WTS. Jim Jordan established an organization called Biblical Horizons to disseminate his very creative theological work. He has published numerous books, newsletters, and articles as well, and works with Peter Leithart at

---

25. Was it the end of the Vietnam War? Economic dislocations? A more vigorous recruiting effort? Certainly the prayers of God's people had something to do with it.

26. I have always read student papers meticulously, marking every error and making long comments on substantive issues. But that has taken a toll on me, so that today I cannot stand to look at a pile of student papers. I have lately consigned most of that work to teaching assistants.

the Trinity House Institute in Birmingham, AL. Michael Payne became a theologian and missiologist. He was a colleague of mine for some years at the Jackson campus of RTS, and has also served in pastorates and in other seminaries. Kevin Vanhoozer studied with me only one year, but he went on to earn a doctorate at Cambridge and has taught at the New College, Edinburgh, as well as at Trinity Evangelical Divinity School and at Wheaton. Of all my students, Kevin has probably had the greatest impact on mainstream theological scholarship.

Carl Ellis, with a L'Abri background, who later earned a D.Phil. from Oxford and has taught many places, including WTS, played a special role in my own development. I remember around 1976 or so making a fairly technical point in the Introduction to Theology and Apologetics course and hearing a loud "Amen" from somewhere in the large classroom. That was Carl, giving me my best introduction to date to the Black church. We had had African-American students before at WTS, but Carl made a special difference. Responding to my perspectivalism and his own background, he wrote a term paper called "Jazz Theology," in which he identified the theological method of Black preaching (distinguished, of course, from what was called "Black theology"). He described the improvisatory nature of Black preachers as a serious theological method. I do not long remember most student term papers, but Carl's has remained a presence in all my thinking about theology, race, the church, and ministry.

Richard Pratt, like Doug Gropp, doctored at Harvard and later was a colleague of mine at RTS in the OT field. But his work has been as much missionary as scholarly, as the founder of Third Millennium Ministries. He has developed my triperspectival program into an epistemology that embraces practical as well as intellectual dimensions of Christian decision-making.

Among those who did not choose to follow the academic path, I particularly remember Dick Kaufmann, who was my pastor in Escondido, CA for fourteen years, 1980–94. New Life Presbyterian Church under his pastorate was the best overall church experience I have ever had. Dick later planted Harbor Presbyterian Church, which includes over six locations in the San Diego area. And I would not forget Andrée Seu Peterson, certainly the best writer of all the theologians I know, now senior writer on "faith and inspiration" for *World Magazine*.

Back to Blue Bell

I moved from New Haven to Philadelphia in 1968 to begin my work at WTS. My first habitat there was a garage apartment at 126 Allison Rd. in Willow

Grove. A few days after I moved in, I received a call from Tony Van Brakel, who I remembered as a member of Community OP Church (see chapter 4). Tony was now a ruling elder at the church. He had been instructed in OP doctrine and government by several WTS students who attended the church during the years I was at Yale.[27] Tony had made great strides in theology and also in the use of the English language, his second language after Dutch. He wanted to know if I had decided on a church home. My actual plan was to return to his church, Community OPC of Blue Bell/Center Square, at least long enough to greet old friends and to determine what my own future might be with the congregation. I wanted, of course, to attend a church that was Reformed and orthodox in its theology, clear in its preaching, motivated to reach the community. And I wanted also to find a church where I could make some contribution to the ministry. Tony assured me that, as during my student years, there would be opportunities for me to teach and assist with music.

While I was at Yale, Pastor Ivan DeMaster left the pastorate of the church, and the congregation hired various men as "pulpit supply."[28] The man who supplied the pulpit for the longest time was Henry Krabbendam—a Dutchman like Tony, but a very different kind of Dutchman. For one thing, Tony was short, and Henry was very tall. The church had to use the pulpit extension they had used with Henry Fikkert. More important, Tony was like the "truly Reformed" I mentioned in chapter 4, typical of the "Dutchmen" I encountered at WTS. But Henry was often criticized as a pietist—passionate about evangelism and prayer. He believed in "heart religion," did not hesitate to ask people very directly about the personal quality of their relationship with God. In time Henry developed a close friendship with Jack Miller. When Tony learned what Henry was about, there were disagreements and clashes. But the church began to grow again, and many of us felt the Spirit's presence in a fresh way.

But Henry was in the Philadelphia area mainly to finish his Th.D. program at WTS. When that was completed, Henry left Community Church and pursued full-time pastorates elsewhere in the OPC.[29] When I returned in 1968, there was no pastor. I was brought in as an advisor to the session, which consisted of Tony and my good friend David Laverell. Dave later

---

27. One was Bob Malarkey, who years before had attended Mt. Lebanon High School. Another was Noel Weeks, who later would be my brother-in-law. Noel is Australian, and he later taught as a professor of ancient history at the University of Sydney.

28. That is, to preach every Sunday, but not to serve officially as the pastor of the congregation.

29. He later became a professor of theology at Covenant College and spent much time preaching and teaching in Uganda.

doctored in mathematics at Indiana University, then attended WTS. He was a pastor in the PCA for some time, then joined the Department of Mathematics at Calvin College.

The three of us constituted a pulpit committee, and we interviewed Ronald Jenkins, who had been an OPC pastor in North Dakota. The congregation later met to call Ron as the next pastor of the church. Ron was a very pleasant, intelligent man. He was thoroughly Reformed in his theology. He had worked in radio, and his pulpit presentation was smooth and clear. He and his wife Joyce had seven children, and Ron was a model husband and father.

They were a musical family, and when they heard that I was an organist and (amateur) choir director, they asked me to organize a choir. Often the choir consisted entirely of three or four members of the Jenkins family. But their singing made a positive contribution to our worship. I went back to playing the old Estey reed organ. In time, Tony (now a successful businessman) offered to buy us a more modern electronic one, and we purchased a two-manual Rodgers with a full pedalboard, capable of playing most of the organ repertoire—at least *my* organ repertoire. I got into the habit of practicing classical pieces on the organ on Wednesday nights before the congregational prayer meeting. Then I would play them as preludes before the Sunday service.

I sometimes led the prayer meeting as well, and taught the adult Sunday School class. Once or twice Ron asked me to teach the Shorter Catechism—mainly, of course, to Jenkins children. And from time to time I even played the role of youth leader. But more often than not there were other seminarians who taught in the church, so that Ron and I would not be burdened with everything.

The church again had its ups and downs. New people would join, others would leave. So our membership hovered around fifty. Some losses were especially traumatic. The Harvie Conn family attended for a while, but left us. We had not managed to engage Harvie's great evangelistic gifts. Professor Norman Shepherd and his wife Connie also attended the church, but they left when they concluded that the church wasn't making a mark on the community.

Ron was a good pastor in that he preached the truth, visited the people, and set a good example. But he did not have many good ideas on how to attract outsiders. We did visit homes in the neighborhood a couple of times. For several years, one of our members edited a four-page paper called *The New Community*, which we sent to homes in the vicinity. I and others wrote brief articles for it, applying Scripture to matters of ethical and cultural interest. We hoped that paper would attract people to the church, but that rarely if ever happened. When we discussed outreach in the session, Tony told us that when he was growing up in the Netherlands, the church bell was sufficient. It rang when the service was beginning, and it summoned everyone in the community to come. If they chose not to, that was on their heads.

After maybe six or seven years, Ron accepted another call—to be pastor of the Westminster OPC of Hamden, CT. Indeed, the OPC is a small world. This was the church I had attended as a Yale student in 1964–65. But after the move, Ron was diagnosed with cancer, and he died after a brave struggle. I went up there to preach at his funeral.

Ron's successor at Blue Bell was James R. Payton, who had completed both his M.Div. and his Th.M. degrees at WTS in 1975. Later he would serve as professor of history at Redeemer University College in Ancaster, Ontario. Jim was a younger man, intellectually sharp, and he seemed quite intent on leading the church to a new level of effectiveness. It was evident that Jim would not merely maintain the existing ministry of the church. There was an edge to Jim's sermons and his proposals. At the end of my time in Philadelphia (see below) his vision and mine clashed sharply. But in the beginning of Jim's leadership, I continued mostly the same work I had performed under Ron's. I supported him as best I could, until the break between us, which I will describe in time.

Romance?

The reader will recall that my relationships with the opposite sex had always been disappointing. I did not date in high school. Then I studied at three largely male institutions, Princeton, Westminster, and Yale.[30] The 1970s were therefore a kind of second adolescence for me. I sought a wife, but I had developed no skills or virtues suitable for attracting and courting women. There were in particular four young ladies with whom I was often seen during that decade. I will not use their names, because they would be embarrassed by publication of their relationships to me. They were all attractive, gracious, and intelligent women, and I was in love with each of them for some period of time. But something would always happen to prevent the relationship from advancing toward marriage. I confess that these roadblocks were always my own fault. As I look back, I am terribly sorry for my unkindnesses to these godly young women. But I'm thankful for that special person God was preparing for me. That story belongs to the 1980s.

---

30. All three became coeducational eventually, including WTS, which admitted women to its counseling and M.A. programs.

Controversies

For all the virtues of WTS, it has always had a striking weakness: for some reason it has always been prone to divisive controversy. Of course, it was conceived in controversy, when the PCUSA reorganized Princeton Seminary along liberal lines in 1929. But Westminster's separation from Princeton did not lead to peace. Rather the founders of WTS and the OPC seemed unable to suppress the tendency to argue among themselves, about matters both important and unimportant.[31] WTS endured divisive conflicts in the 1940s, in the controversy between Van Til and Clark,[32] the 1950's controversy over the Peniel Bible Conference, and many others. The 1970s, alas, were no exception to this tendency.

1. The Dooyeweerdians

When I returned to WTS in 1968, someone told me that there was a "cult" of Dooyeweerdians on campus. Herman Dooyeweerd was a Dutch Calvinist philosopher, a very substantial thinker.[33] In years past, Cornelius Van Til had been closely associated with Dooyeweerd's school of thought, but after Dooyeweerd's visit to the US in the late 1950s, Van Til had become critical of him. Robert Knudsen, however, though disagreeing with Dooyeweerd's doctrine of Scripture, was a staunch supporter of Dooyeweerdian philosophy.[34]

There was a group of students on the WTS campus that admired Dooyeweerd and his followers. These supported one another by reading and discussing one another's papers in various meetings, often at the Knudsen home. They called themselves "The Kuyper Club" and very much resented being called a cult, as I learned from a very foolish remark I made to one of them. They were very critical about what they called the "scholastic" and "dualistic" nature of traditional Reformed theology. Often in exams and

---

31. I have written a critical account of this history of controversy in my "Machen's Warrior Children" (http://www.frame-poythress.org/machens-warrior-children/).

32. See my *CVT*, 97–113.

33. His major work is *A New Critique of Theoretical Thought* (4 vols. Philadelphia: P&R, 1955). His shorter work *In the Twilight of Western Thought* (Philadelphia: P&R, 1960) expounds several of his characteristic themes, and is responsible for arousing some controversy about his work.

34. For my own description and evaluation of the controversy, see my *The Amsterdam Philosophy* (http://www.frame-poythress.org/wp-content/uploads/2012/08/FrameJohnAmsterdamPhilosophy1972.pdf) and my "Dooyeweerd and the Word of God" (*DWG*, Appendix D, 392–421).

papers, they would completely ignore the class lectures and assignments and answer questions using their own reading in the Dooyeweerd literature and employing Dooyeweerd's technical terms. This was, of course, the era of student rebellion in the US, when "radical" students demonstrated against college administrators and even occupied their offices. The Kuyper Club also described their position as radical, not Marxist, as in the general culture, but "Reformational," as an antidote to scholasticism and dualism. Naturally there were many other students and faculty who stood sharply against the Kuyper Club approach.

I tried at first to position myself as a mediator. It seemed to me that both parties needed to hear some careful analysis of the language and of the issues under consideration. I thought that my studies in Anglo-American language philosophy could be helpful in the situation. I made some tentative approaches at such an analysis in class lectures and discussion. But the Dooyeweerdians saw no value in it. They saw me as a follower of an alien, non-Reformed philosophical movement,[35] essentially scholastic and dualistic.

About this time, followers of Dooyeweerd founded the Institute for Christian Studies in Toronto, Canada, and their very young faculty scoured North America, seeking to radicalize young Reformed people to embrace their cause. In the Reformed movement (especially in Dutch denominations, but also in the OPC), many churches and organizations (especially Christian schools) came under this influence, and as I saw it they were not open to calm discussion. I was not willing to accept passively the assimilation of the Reformed movement to a group of young militants. Eventually I became myself a somewhat militant opponent of Dooyeweerdianism.

My presbytery (the Ohio Presbytery of the OPC, which included the Pittsburgh area) put me on a committee to write documents on the subject, and in that capacity, I wrote, together with the Rev. Leonard Coppes, *The Amsterdam Philosophy: A Preliminary Critique*, which I cited earlier.[36] I debated one of the leading Dooyeweerdians on the floor of presbytery. Later the Christian School of Wilkinsburg sent me to a conference of the National Union of Christian Schools in Langley, BC, which was to consider whether the Union should drop their commitment to "the Reformed confessions" and adopt in its place a commitment to an "educational creed" reflecting Dooyeweerdian ideas. I spoke at that meeting, and the conference reaffirmed the Reformed confessions.

---

35. Which, in their jargon, "absolutized the linguistic aspect."

36. Knudsen begged me not to publish it, referring to it as "dynamite." But his advice was too late, and not cogent to me.

By 1975 the controversy calmed down, after some peacemaking on both sides. Nobody was persuaded of the philosophical and theological points, but there was some maturing of the combatants, including myself. We agreed to disagree in Christian love. Students attracted to Dooyeweerd tended to attend the Institute for Christian Studies rather than WTS, and when they did come to WTS they sought to learn from us rather than to attack our position. The issues became matters of academic discussion rather than grounds for institutional warfare.

2. Abortion

In 1967 or '68 I resolved my complicated ecclesiastical alignment by leaving Westerly Road and Beverly Heights churches and joining Covenant OPC in Wilkinsburg, where I had worked in the summer of 1963. Shortly after, I was licensed in the Ohio Presbytery of the OPC and then ordained in consequence of my call to teach at WTS. I decided to stay in the Ohio Presbytery, which covered Western Pennsylvania, rather than moving to Philadelphia Presbytery where I lived most of the year, because the Ohio Presbytery only met twice a year, and I could attend the meetings while visiting my parents in Mt. Lebanon. That worked out pretty well until I got into some trouble. I served as counsel for Arnold Kress, defending him against charges that he approved speaking in tongues. (Arnold ended up moving to the Christian Reformed Church.) That destroyed whatever respect my fellow presbyters had for me, and I retreated to Philadelphia Presbytery.

But around 1970, the General Assembly of the denomination appointed me to the Committee to Study the Matter of Abortion. A veteran pastor, Robert Atwell, had given a powerful speech, calling the attention of the Assembly to the rapid acceptance of abortion throughout the country. This was before the Supreme Court decision Roe vs. Wade, which virtually legalized abortion on demand. But many states had liberalized their abortion laws. The most liberal was that of California, which was signed by Gov. Ronald Reagan.

Atwell asked that the church do something to discourage this development. In response, the Assembly did what Presbyterian Assemblies do: they appointed a committee. On the committee were Professor Paul Woolley, Joseph Memmelaar (a urologist and OPC elder), Tom DeMeester (another distinguished medical doctor who served as an elder), the Rev. Robert Malarkey (who had gone to Mt. Lebanon High School and who had attended Community OPC of Blue Bell during my years at Yale), and me.

Demeester was not able to attend the committee meetings, so practically there were four of us. Paul Woolley, given his years of service and committee experience, was the natural candidate to be the chairman, but he declined because his view of abortion was different from the OPC mainstream (see below). So they asked me to be chairman. Having never served before on a church committee I felt quite inadequate, but I accepted the arguments of the others.

At the first meeting, Malarkey was the most helpful. He brought with him documents from various pro-life sources, with medical and statistical information. With these and some other material, I put together a tentative report, taking a strong pro-life stance on the issue. Dr. Memmelaar corrected some of the medical references. Only Paul Woolley argued against the substantive positions of the report. He held that although abortion was a decision to be avoided, nevertheless in a number of cases (including the elusive "health of the mother") it was not necessarily a sinful choice.[37] He also argued that the Bible did not *explicitly* condemn abortion by name. He wrote a minority report to that effect.[38]

At the General Assembly of 1971, the Committee moved that the Assembly "adopt" the Majority Report as its teaching on the matter of abortion. I did not anticipate the furor this motion would cause. Besides the Woolley arguments, a number of commissioners argued that the OPC did not believe in making statements on "political and social issues." This was my first exposure to the doctrine of the "spirituality of the church," which said that the church should concern itself exclusively with "spiritual matters" and not at all with matters outside that sphere. This view is essentially the same as the "two kingdoms" view, which distinguished between the "spiritual" kingdom and the "secular" kingdom. In the 1990s, I would suffer the wrath of some defenders of this view.

But even the defenders of the two-kingdom view generally allowed for exceptions, as in WCF 31.5. Some, in the spirit of Atwell's original exhortation, regarded abortion as such a serious matter than the church could not remain silent, even if it was justified in silence regarding other civil evils.

---

37. In those days, there was greater latitude on this issue in the evangelical movement than there is today. Carl F. H. Henry held the same position as Woolley. So did Bruce Waltke, who later changed his position. Meredith Kline sent to the OPC elders an unpublished paper called "Moses and Abortion" in which he argued that the key text Exod 21:22–24 was a "miscarriage text" and implies that the life of the unborn child has less value than the life of his mother. But, like Waltke, Kline later changed his mind, in "*Lex Talionis* and the Human Fetus," *JETS* 20 (1977) 193–201.

38. The report is available on the OPC web site, and I have reprinted the Majority Report as Appendix B (83–122) of my *Medical Ethics: Principles, Persons, and Problems* (Phillipsburg, NJ: P&R, 1988).

That argument, and the biblical texts cited in the Report, evidently came to prevail.

Woolley continued to argue that since abortion was not specifically named in the Bible, we should have liberty to perform them. I replied with a fanciful story: Let's imagine that Woolley and Frame went on a trip together hunting for deer. (That brought chuckles from the assembly; the commissioners could not imagine two less-likely hunters.) He and I go on separate paths. Then I see a motion in the woods and raise my gun. But the thought crosses my mind: is that my deer, or is that Professor Woolley? What if I were to say to myself that no text of Scripture proves the identity of the creature in the woods. Does that fact give me the liberty to shoot? Certainly not. But in Woolley's view it would have allowed me to: Scripture is not perfectly specific, therefore I have liberty to abort.

Despite the seriousness of the issue, which everyone seemed to acknowledge, the debate went on for a long time, until some of the senior members proposed adjournment, in effect giving the Assembly a year to think about it. That motion prevailed. And so we all came back in 1972. There was more debate, but this time the Assembly made up its mind. The Report was published one year before Roe vs. Wade.

3. The Shepherd Controversy

By 1974 the Dooyeweerdian controversy had died down. But there was no peace at WTS, for another battle was brewing. You should recall that Norman Shepherd was the successor to John Murray in the systematic theology department. It was Norman who visited me at Yale and approached me to join the faculty. I was immensely grateful to him, and I was quite overwhelmed by his theological knowledge and understanding. In historical and exegetical matters, Norman has always run circles around me. And also in his spiritual maturity.

Norman in the beginning impressed everybody as unimpeachably orthodox. He was like John Murray in so many ways: Scottish ancestry, exclusive Psalm singing, gentle demeanor but deadly serious about the things of God, profoundly knowledgeable about the Scriptures and the theological literature. I, like many others, thought that of all the members of the WTS faculty, Norman was the least likely to ever be accused of heresy. But it happened, and with regard to the central Reformation doctrine of justification by faith alone.[39]

---

39. WLC Q. and A. 70 defines *justification* as follows: "Justification is an act of God's free grace unto sinners, in which he pardoneth all their sins, accepteth and accounteth

In 1974, I drove with several WTS students to the meeting of the Ohio Presbytery of the OPC. One of those students was the third Cummings brother, David, whom I was responsible to examine for licensure. David had mentioned to me that Norman had presented in class an unusual view of how to reconcile Paul's justification by faith with James' justification by works: we can say that we are justified either by faith or works, as long as we regard these as *instruments* but not as *grounds* of justification. The ground of justification is the righteousness of Christ alone.

I responded in academic detachment. This seemed to me to be an exercise in rethinking historical terminology. Neither *instrument* nor *ground* was a biblical term, but these terms had been used in the historical discussion. I always think it is a good thing when theological scholars rethink technical language. This sounded to me like another example of Westminster's creativity within the bounds of orthodoxy. It was probably not a final formulation on Norman's part, but certainly one that deserved further exploration.[40]

David's exam went very well, as I expected. I had no doubt that he would pass. So I thought I would give the presbyters a peek at some of the new stuff going on at WTS, the "creativity within the bounds of orthodoxy." I asked David how we should reconcile the apparently conflicting statements of Paul and James about justification, faith, and works. David responded with Norman's answer. Presbytery was stunned. It was as if the building had been shaken. During the discussion period, elder after elder asked David for clarification. The problem, of course, was the statement of the WCF, 11.2,

> Faith, thus receiving and resting on Christ and his righteousness, is the alone instrument of justification; yet it is not alone in the person justified, but is ever accompanied with all other saving graces, and is no dead faith, but worketh by love.

---

their persons righteous in his sight; not for any thing wrought in them, or done by them, but only for the perfect obedience and full satisfaction of Christ, by God imputed to them, and received by faith alone." The basic point (and this distinguishes justification from sanctification) is that in justification God *declares* people to be righteous as to their legal status. He does not, in justification, *make* people righteous or holy.

40. This is typical of the way I responded to new ideas. Later Gary North dedicated to me his book *Dominion and Common Grace* (Tyler: Institute for Christian Economics, 1987, http://www.garynorth.com/freebooks/docs/pdf/dominion_and_common_grace.pdf) with this caption: "This book is dedicated to John Frame, an uncommonly gracious man, who will no doubt conclude that portions of this book are good, other portions are questionable, but the topic warrants further study." Gary, though too kind in his commendation, had me nailed on that one.

The elders told us, therefore, that we could not assert the parallel between faith and works that David ascribed to Norman. In the most important respect, they were not parallel. Works is *not* an instrument of justification, for faith is the "alone" instrument.

I should have known better. The elders took more seriously than I the specific language of the Confession. They couldn't look at the term *instrument* with the kind of academic detachment I favored. Still, I was a bit disappointed in the elders' reaction, because I did not think the Confession's use of the term *instrument*, a non-biblical word, should be used as a test of orthodoxy. I thought that all such terms should be subject to theological scrutiny and reformulation. And it wasn't clear to me that any of these elders was capable of defining what *instrument* even meant. But they did have a point. Whatever else the Confession meant by *instrument* it does seem that they used the term to indicate the human disposition that reaches out to receive justification as a sheer gift of God, apart from any human merit. Norman was trying to say that we also receive justification by our good works as well; but the term *works*, as Norman himself was later to emphasize, suggests merit. So *works* is less suited than *faith* to describe the "empty hand" that renounces merit and receives God's righteousness as free grace.

The moderator adjourned the presbytery meeting for lunch, at which time various elders gathered around David to urge the right answer upon him. David, the son of Calvin Knox Cummings, was a familiar presence in the presbytery, well-liked, and most of the elders had confidence that he would see the problem in his original answer. After lunch, the examination resumed, and David repudiated Shepherd's proposal in unmistakable terms, embracing WCF 11.2 as his own confession. Thereupon, presbytery licensed him. I thanked God for averting a crisis, and I drove David back to Philadelphia.

When David got back, he was loaded for bear. Understandable, certainly. He had gone to the seminary that was approved by his family and denomination and had been called unorthodox for reproducing in that denominational presbytery meeting the view of one of his teachers. David thought that Norman's views of justification should be at the very least scrutinized by the seminary.

David's experience may have been the beginning of the "Shepherd controversy," or perhaps others had been raising the same issue already. At any rate, the discussion of Shepherd pervaded life at WTS until 1982, when Shepherd was asked to leave. (By then I too was gone, having left for California in 1980.) Eight years.

The first meeting on the subject I recall was in Ed Clowney's living room, shortly after David and I returned from Pittsburgh. Arthur Kuschke, the WTS librarian, was there, having been warned of the situation by David and perhaps by others. I mentioned Arthur in chapter 4, in connection with the Bible and cross controversy at the Blue Bell Church. He was indeed a man of many controversies, having played a role in most every doctrinal conflict in the OPC or WTS since the Clark/Van Til battle in the 1940s. He had been for many years the chairman of the formidable Candidates and Credentials Committee of the Presbytery of Philadelphia.

In the Clowneys' living room, Norman recanted the view that had caused trouble for David Cummings, the idea that works could be considered the instrument of justification, but not the ground. He presented his current view in terms of an exegesis of James 2:14–26. He rejected the popular theory that James takes *justified* in a very different sense from Paul. Rather, according to Norman, James understands justification as Paul does, as that which makes us right with God, justification in the "forensic" sense. The conclusion we should take from James, according to Norman, is that we are justified by *a faith that works*. A faith that doesn't work is a dead faith, that is, no faith at all. To this conception Paul agrees, for in Gal 5:6 he speaks of "faith working through love."

I was very pleased by this formulation. It seemed to me to be perfectly in accord with Scripture, and indeed with Reformed tradition. I could remember John Gerstner growling, "it's faith alone that saves, but the faith that saves is never alone." And I noted that in the WCF 11.2, the statement that was so prominent in the Pittsburgh discussion, that very point was made:

> Faith, thus receiving and resting on Christ and his righteousness, is the alone instrument of justification: yet it is not alone in the person justified, but is ever accompanied with all other saving graces, and is no dead faith, but worketh by love.

So far, then, I supported Shepherd's position. But Norman did not stop there. He also drew an inference: since works are a necessary element of saving faith, and since saving faith is necessary to justification, works are therefore necessary to justification. Now this seemed to me to be a straightforward logical argument: A is necessary to B, B is necessary to C, therefore A is necessary to C. So I could, and still can, defend Norman's inference.

But others could not. They did not like the term *necessary*. In that term they heard the idea of "cause," perhaps, so that if works are "necessary to" justification, then works are "the cause of" justification, even the merit by which we deserve justification. But in fact the term "necessary" does *not* have that meaning. To say that A is the necessary condition of C is not to say that A is the efficient cause of C, certainly not that A is the merit by which we earn C. This fact seemed simple enough to me. At a later meeting, I tried to explain it to my colleagues, however, and it had no impact at all on the discussion. I was young and did not want to try to dominate the debate. So that was the end of that.

But suspicions multiplied and studies proliferated. There were meetings of the faculty, the board, the presbytery. The presbytery held maybe twelve long Saturday meetings to discuss this issue alone.[41] Various individuals and groups produced papers, and Norman was asked to reply to this paper and that; essentially, he was asked to produce evidence against himself, which was then scrutinized, and the discussion became more complicated.

If I had been Norman, I would have simply apologized for using the term "necessity," with which many people wrongly or rightly took offense. But as the discussion progressed, it became evident why Norman couldn't take that course. He had an agenda. He believed that many evangelicals, and those who opposed him in the Reformed community, held views of "cheap grace" or "easy believism," the view that one can have genuinely saving faith, but without practical holiness. The word *necessity*, in Norman's mind, guarded against that degradation of Reformed theology, and no other word really could. Indeed, Norman thought, if one opposed the use of *necessity*, he could have no motive other than to maintain easy believism.

In chapter 4, I complained against the caricatures of American evangelicalism that I found at Westminster. Two of them are at issue here: Norman's opponents thought that American evangelicals were largely guilty of self-righteousness, because they did not understand the Reformation view of justification. Norman, on the contrary, thought that evangelicals were more prone to the error of easy believism. Both were trying to react as sharply as possible against evangelicalism as they understood it. I differed, and still differ, with both sides. Although self-righteousness and easy believism are twin errors that show up too often in Christian circles, I don't think either characterizes American evangelicalism generally, and I don't believe that either characterizes any segment of Reformed Christianity that I know. The problem as I see it is that we tend too often to misrepresent one another. We need to work much harder to understand one another's words in the best sense, rather than the worst sense. And we should not in any case formulate our doctrines with the intention of saying the opposite of whatever we think American evangelicals say. Shorn of such agendas, we

---

41. This was quite extraordinary. I never saw any OPC presbytery give this level of attention to, e.g., evangelism or church planting or missions. But the OPC saw itself as pre-eminently the defender of orthodox doctrine, and for that they would bear any burden.

can work together to analyze problematic terms like *necessity*, and agree on a vocabulary that doesn't mislead or irritate.

Norman and his opponents introduced other issues into the debate. In the late years of the decade, Norman published a series of articles in *The Banner*, the Christian Reformed Church magazine, analyzing the doctrine of election. In those articles he tried to draw together God's eternal election with the historical election of the Jewish people. I did not agree with his main thesis. It seemed to me that these two kinds of election, though deeply analogous, were different in ways that Norman did not sufficiently explore.[42] But when these articles were published, I was packing to leave for California and did not have the time or interest to participate in the discussion.

In 1982, Norman was asked to leave the WTS faculty. He then took two successive pastorates in the Christian Reformed Church. After retiring in 1998 he began to write again, again on justification.[43] During this later period he also emphasized his view that Jesus' active obedience is not imputed to those who are justified. I disagree with him on this point, but I don't consider it a test of orthodoxy.[44]

There did not seem to be any likely way to end the controversy. In every vote that was taken in faculty, in the board, and in the presbytery, Norman was vindicated or at least not condemned. But his opponents were never willing to be quiet. So the end of one phase of the controversy was the beginning of another. I believe the seminary's decision to fire him in 1982 was unjust. However, it's hard to imagine the controversy being resolved in any other way.

One of my major regrets about the controversy was that Shepherd was prevented from making further contributions to Reformed theology in areas *other* than justification. Before I left for California in 1980, Norman allowed me to audit his lectures in the doctrine of God and in the doctrine of the Holy Spirit. These lectures contained deep insight, and they contributed much to my own teaching and writing in these areas.

---

42. See my *DG*, 317–30.

43. See his *The Call of Grace* (Phillipsburg, NJ: P&R, 2000); "The Imputation of Active Obedience," in *A Faith That is Never Alone*, edited by P. Andrew Sandlin (La Grange, CA: Kerygma, 2007), 249–78; "Justification by Works in Reformed Theology," *Backbone of the Bible*, edited by in P. Andrew Sandlin, 103–20 (Nacodoches, TX: Covenant Media, 2004); *The Way of Righteousness* (La Grange, CA: Kerygma, 2009).

44. The reader will note that I agreed with Shepherd on some matters, but not on others. In the 1999 controversy, which I will narrate, some of my opponents accused me of "agreeing with Shepherd." The opponents had no idea as to what my specific position was in the 1970s.

But apart from harm done to Norman, the seminary itself suffered greatly. The controversy came to dominate life at WTS, a dark cloud over everything. Teachers and students alike were judged by which side they were on, so that you could not hope even to be friends with someone on the other side. Every theological topic had to be examined in detail for its bearing on the Shepherd issue. People like me who sought clarity by analyzing both positions were not well respected. All of this was oppressive to me, and it was another major reason for my wanting to move to California.

The Last Years

California hovered in my mind often during the 1970s. I remembered my favorable impression of the place when I visited there in 1957. At WTS I seemed to notice that the OPC students from California seemed to be more sensible, balanced, and forward-looking than the easterners.

And sometime in the early 1970s Ed Clowney announced plans to move the whole seminary to the San Francisco Bay area. Our largest donor had decided to support two seminaries, one on the West Coast and one on the East. Gordon-Conwell would be the eastern seminary, and WTS would move to become the western one. They even had a specific location picked out: the campus of a former Roman Catholic school in Los Gatos.

I was fairly excited about the plan. California was not a center of Presbyterianism, but was more like a mission field. The climate was mild, the academic resources plentiful. And I thought that in some way we might be freer in Los Gatos from the heavy hand of Reformed tradition, more open to address the culture in fresh ways. Again I disagreed with Paul Woolley, who thought we should not go, for the same reasons why I thought we should. To Woolley there were major dangers in moving far away from our historic roots.

But in any case the plan fell through. Our donor died, and his heirs were interested in other things than in financing seminaries. So I tried to be reconciled to a lifetime on the East Coast. But then something else came up. A group of pastors and donors from California—this time southern California—wanted to have a Reformed seminary on the West Coast. This time, the proposal was not to move the whole seminary, but to start a new seminary like it.

Originally, Jay Adams was put in charge of the project. He had some creative ideas that would enable the new seminary to focus as a laser on the specific work of the pastorate. When he asked if I would like to be part of it, I jumped at the opportunity. Jay was interested in my participation in part because of my article "Proposal for a New Seminary."[45] But the Board and other administrators were not fond of Jay's plans, which would have cost a lot of money and limited the size of the student body. So Jay resigned from the project and was replaced by Bob Strimple, my colleague in systematics, whose vision for the new seminary was a bit more conventional than Jay's. Although I preferred Jay's plans, I was happy to sign on with Bob.

As I have mentioned, working at WTS in Philadelphia had become difficult in several ways. I had never solved the problem of how to teach classes of over 100 students effectively. I had hoped to launch a writing ministry alongside my teaching, but that seemed to be impossible at WTS. The Shepherd controversy, too, had absorbed far too much of our energy. And there were other forms of unpleasantness as well that afflicted me in the late 1970s, particularly in the year 1979–80. To summarize, this was a year of death. My car died, my dog died, my father died, and my church died.

My parents had bought me a 1967 Olds Cutlass, and it had held up well, but the Pennsylvania winters, particularly the salt on the streets, were too much for it. Something rusted out in the steering mechanism, so that I could not turn the wheels without moving the steering wheel as far as it would go. For a few years, the Cutlass was the best-selling car in the country, and I bought a new one for my transcontinental journey.

My dear Welsh Corgi dog, Midget, got sick. I hoped she would get well, but failed to take her to the vet. But the illness was serious, parvo virus as it now seems to me. I found her dead on my floor and buried her in the back yard. She had been a good friend.

My Dad was diagnosed with acute leukemia in the fall of 1979. He received some quick treatment in Boca Raton, FL, where he and my mother had retired, and he was declared in remission for a short while. But in six months he was gone. In God's providence, his funeral, in Franklin, PA, was the first stop on my drive to California. Dad was not pleased that I became a theologian, and he was not a spiritual mentor to me. But he worked very hard to support his family, and put all his kids through college and grad school. We were the top priority in his life. He was well respected, both by his employer and by his opponents (the labor unions, with whom he negotiated on behalf of Westinghouse Electric). Our family reunions were always good times. I have missed him very much.

But the end of my relationship to the Blue Bell Church was, if possible, even more traumatic. I had attended there off and on for nineteen years, from 1961, my first year as a student at WTS. My closest friendships were

---

45. See http://www.frame-poythress.org/proposal-for-a-new-seminary/.

among the people there, and my most satisfying experiences in ministry, teaching, and music, were at that church.

What happened essentially was that our Dutch elder, Tony Van Brakel, began to reveal his true vision for the church's future, and he began to insist on implementing it.[46] That vision, essentially, was the vision of a church like those he knew growing up in the Netherlands.[47] As a session member, I was in a position to stop or at least retard this development, and looking back I wish I had.[48] But my attitude tended to be "let boys be boys." Most of the changes Tony wanted were, to me, individually of little consequence. But Tony saw each change as a brick in a new structure; and once the structure was completed, I was crushed by it.

First we bought Psalters, for Tony thought it would be a good idea if we could sing all 150 psalms in our worship. I thought, well, sure, why not? But shortly afterward, the pastor started using the Psalter for maybe three to five of the worship hymns. When I asked why so many, he assured me that he did not believe in principle that psalms should predominate, but the psalm selections just happened to fit his Scripture texts and sermon themes. But eventually we came to sing psalms almost exclusively, as in the churches of Tony's Dutch upbringing. Once the mother of one of our members came to visit, and the service included five imprecatory psalms, with no explanation of their meaning or their function in the service. The lady, a longtime

---

46. To be honest, I think a lot of us try, in adult life, to reproduce the churches in which we originally came to meet Jesus. I have, through my life, always wished that the churches I later attended could be more like Beverly Heights, except for its unwillingness to teach me about the scourge of liberal theology. But Tony's tactics, as I see them now, were strongarm. He made no attempt before the fact to convince us that a new type of church was biblically warranted or that it would be an effective way to apply the Great Commission.

47. Tony had a shelf of something like twelve books, all in Dutch, from past generations of Dutch theologians and preachers. Tony told me that whenever he read theology, he checked its teaching against those twelve books. If it differed from those books in any particular, he threw it out.

48. The pastor, Jim Payton, cooperated with Tony in all of this. But I saw him as being the follower, not the leader. I will not say much about him in this account, because Jim and I were later reconciled. I hold him blameless. My own failure to resist these developments was as blameworthy as anything done by anyone else. And my criticism of Tony, too, should not be taken as condemnation. Tony was not an evil man, but a mature, godly believer, who in his own mind was convinced that he was leading the church in a more biblical direction. I suppose that people who believed as Tony did have as much right to establish churches true to their principles as anyone else does. But what he did at Blue Bell was jarring to me, and it destroyed the possibility of the church having any influence in its surrounding population. In my mind, that amounted to renouncing the Great Commission. And how can a church be a church if the Great Commission is not its goal?

Christian, was quite mortified and did not want ever to come back. That was a major danger signal to me. I had hoped that at some point we might be able to attract people from our neighborhood. But this change indicated to me that we would attract no new members except those who had a deep acquaintance with and appreciation of Reformed history.

We also adopted a practice that any non-member who wanted to take communion would have to be interviewed before the service by a team of elders. This was another historic practice in the churches of Tony's background. I thought that was quite unnecessary. Scripture mandates self-examination, not examination by church leaders, for those preparing to take the Lord's Supper (1 Cor 11:28).

Of course it went without saying that the cross-and-Bible picture on the front wall would have to be painted over. And it was.

And the special music came under fire. Joyce Jenkins, the widow of our former pastor, returned to the area and resumed attending our church. She sang in the choir and took some voice lessons. At one point I asked her to sing a solo in the worship service. Tony was furious. As it turned out, he objected because (1) he didn't want to see a woman take such a prominent role in worship, (2) he didn't think there should be solos in worship, only congregational singing, and (3) he did not believe in choirs, though we had had a choir for most of my nineteen years in the church.

There was also a change in the church's policy regarding discipline. Dave and Ellen Dombek were my best friends during my time at WTS, and we visited one another often. Ellen's mother was the lady who had been traumatized by the imprecatory psalms. Eventually, the Dombeks decided that they were not being fed spiritually, and they began to look at other churches, particularly the New Life Church of which Jack Miller was pastor. So they stopped attending the Blue Bell Church and began to attend New Life. Over the years, many people had left our church in a similar way, and some have come to us in a similar way from other churches.[49] Now Tony's view, evidently common among the Dutch Reformed, was that a person should never leave a church unless (1) the church comes to teach false doctrine, or (2) the person leaves the area. Neither of those conditions applied to the Dombeks. So the elders accused the Dombeks publicly of sin, and, without any formal charges or due process, instructed the congregation to "shun" them, to have nothing to do with them (as 2 Thess 3:6, 14; Titus 3:10; 2 John 10). Eventually, meetings were held between Blue Bell elders

---

49. In general, I believe that church members have the right to do this, as I argue in ER (http://www.evangelicalreunion.org/). But I do think that members who decide to look at other churches should first share their concerns with the leaders of the church of which they are members.

and New Life elders and the matter was resolved peacefully, so that the Dombeks could become members of New Life.

Then there was a fateful Saturday, a few weeks before my departure for California, when two elders came to my home around 10 AM and talked with me into the afternoon. Their message to me was that because I did not support the church's positions in the above matters, and because my teaching in the church did not seem orthodox to them, I was in their view not truly Reformed. After I left for California, they would do what they could do to erase my influence from the congregation. There would no longer be a choir, and the people would be instructed that my teaching was of a non-Reformed character. I was devastated.

Shortly after that meeting, a friend from the church asked to see me. He took pains that nobody would observe our meeting. Although he would not explain what had happened, it appeared to me that I too was being "shunned," like the Dombeks.

The church had decided, in effect, to become a Dutch museum piece rather than to carry out the Great Commission in its neighborhood. I was deeply disappointed, as well as being personally hurt. When the congregation got wind of what was happening, about half of them left to attend other churches. But the session continued to direct the church in the same direction. In time, Tony himself departed; the church, even in its changed form, was not Reformed enough for him. He had begun to read the writings of Herman Hoeksema and Gordon Clark and had determined that the doctrine of "common grace," held by most OPC pastors, was a vile heresy. So Tony began a new church, part of the Protestant Reformed denomination, which initially met in his apartment. The Blue Bell Church itself eventually ran into some conflict with the OPC presbytery and it left the denomination to join the Canadian Reformed Churches.

PEF had taught me not to be a Reformed chauvinist. I opposed the battles between "Reformed" and "evangelical" that had become extreme in the Blue Bell context. But after the events at Blue Bell I could not again take delight in hearing that someone or some organization was Reformed. "Reformed," as it turns out, means different things to different people, and some of these are downright ugly. Any knowledgeable and fair-minded person will accept that my theology is rooted in the Reformed tradition. But I refuse to parade that, or take pride in it, or use it as a club to beat others over the head. I do not and never will deny being an evangelical.

And I certainly will never accept any idea or practice on the ground that it is part of some tradition. It is sometimes nice to think that we are doing something that our forebears have done for centuries past. But Scripture (and Reformed Christians are supposed to be supporters of *sola Scriptura*) never commands us to do anything because it is traditional. The Great Commission tells us to take the gospel into new places, new cultures, new times, and speak the word so that people can understand it. In this task we can sometimes learn from our ancestors; no need to "reinvent the wheel," as we say. But we have no *obligation* to follow the patterns of past churches, and we often need to oppose traditions in order to communicate with people of our own time. I had thought that for many years, but in 1979 I became far more self-conscious as an anti-traditionalist.[50]

---

50. This means, of course, not that I am opposed to tradition as such, but that I am opposed to tradional*ism*.

7

Collegiality in California

BOB DEN DULK AND Bob Strimple preceded my trip to Escondido by a year. During that year, they set up an Escondido office for the new seminary and arranged to rent our first classrooms in an office complex in San Marcos, the town next door to Escondido. They visited donors and did much to ensure that the Seminary would be on a sound financial footing. Bob Den Dulk was formerly the director of development at WTS/Philadelphia, and he was the most knowledgeable and experienced fundraiser we had. Our main donor base was Dutch Calvinists, chiefly in the Christian Reformed Church, though others supported us as well, particularly people in the OPC. Bob had been raised in the CRC, and he knew the Dutch Calvinist donor base very well. When I heard how many Dutch folk were on board, a few alarms buzzed in my head, but I restrained my prejudice. Judging from those I knew, these were godly men. Although they were preoccupied with Dutch theology and culture, they were willing to support a seminary in which most faculty members and students would be Anglo. That seemed significant to me. They were bending toward us; surely I could bend toward them as well.

New Life Church

My first Sunday in Escondido, I attended the Escondido Christian Reformed Church. When I identified myself, the people were quite friendly and welcoming. One of them invited me for Sunday dinner, which I enjoyed much. The ECRC was a larger church than I was used to, maybe 300 people or so. That felt good, after I had spent twenty years in a church that rarely exceeded fifty. The preaching, by James Howerzyl, was biblical and

Christ-centered. After church, Pastor Howerzyl assured me that the church's session was firmly behind the seminary. They had voted to welcome members of the seminary faculty to their communion services without the customary interview (see previous chapter). And they wanted me to do some preaching for them.

New Life Presbyterian Church, around 1980

In coming weeks I preached several times at ECRC. Once I was asked to preach at their daughter church, which met in Ramona, across a mountain range from Escondido. I regret that I did not ask the questions I should have asked about the Ramona congregation. I committed a major *faux pas*—preached at ECRC in the morning, then preached the same sermon in the evening at Ramona. What I had not asked, and what they had not told me, was that the Ramona people worshiped at ECRC on Sunday morning and in Ramona on Sunday night. So when I preached in Ramona, they had already heard the sermon I preached in the morning. I had to make a major apology.

The Escondidians were forgiving. I preached a number of times at ECRC and the Ramona church, and I played the organ at ECRC several times when the regular organist was away.

But the ECRC was not to be my church home. Bob Strimple had become part of an OPC church plant that began in Mira Mesa, half way between Escondido and San Diego. When I arrived, the church had moved to a Seventh-Day Adventist building in Poway, closer to Escondido. The people had sent out a call to Dick Kaufmann, a student at WTS/P to lead the church plant and eventually to become its pastor.

Dick was a graduate of Harvard Business School who came to Christ after a time of work in his father's business. At seminary, he was a teaching assistant of mine and, more significantly, a ruling elder in New Life Church where Jack Miller was pastor. Dick had absorbed much of the teaching and spirit of Miller, and he was eager to join in the work of planting a new church. The church in California wasn't entirely new, but it was still very small after two or three years of existence. Dick's Christian maturity, wisdom, evangelistic zeal, and winsome personality recommended him well for the work in California.

Before we left for California, a group of us met at the Philadelphia home of Dick, Liz, and their children, several times, to pray for the new work. With us were Doug and Lois Swagerty. Doug was a student at WTS whose plan was to complete his seminary work at the new Westminster and to work alongside Dick in the new church. We had a list of about twenty-five people who attended the California church, and we prayed for each person by name. Dick and I agreed to share a van in our move, and that worked out well.

So, although I accepted preaching and organ assignments at ECRC, I worshiped regularly in the new work in Poway. Later I discovered that some ECRC people were deeply disappointed that several of us faculty members had decided to attend another church. But there was no indication of that in 1980. Rather, all indications were that there would be good collegiality between Christians of the two churches and other churches as well.

I remember a congregational meeting in which Dick asked us our dreams about the future of the church. The consensus was that the people did not want to have a "megachurch." We also did not want merely to get people with Reformed backgrounds to come to our church. Rather, we wanted to reach out to the unchurched with the saving gospel. That would mean that we would not try to be a "historic" Reformed church like ECRC, but we would speak the language of local Californians and we would sing their music.

Worship was, of course, a significant issue. In the 1970s the "Jesus People" emerged in California, playing guitars and singing tunes that sounded a bit like pop songs. In these years, the music of Maranatha! and Integrity Publishers was common in evangelical churches. This music, combined with biblical words, made biblical content plain to people who were not accustomed to church. New Life Church in Philadelphia was one of the first among the conservative Presbyterian churches to pick up this trend, and we followed them in this as well as many other things. In time, we even adopted the name "New Life Presbyterian Church."[1]

A few weeks after I arrived, the Seventh Day Adventist congregation asked us to go elsewhere, since they planned to remodel the facilities. A search for a new location led us to the First Baptist Church of Escondido. First Baptist was a declining congregation, but they had a building in the center of town, and they wanted another congregation to share it with

---

1. The original name of the church plant was "Covenant of Grace Orthodox Presbyterian Church." The theological concept "covenant of grace" is a precious one. But Dick persuaded us that the purpose of a church name is not to nurture the congregation, but to attract visitors.

them.² But some in our church said that for us to meet there would be in effect to "compete" with the ECRC. So Dick Kaufmann and others went to ECRC and met with Pastor Howerzyl and other leaders there. The report I heard was that there was a good understanding all around.³ The conclusion was that there did not need to be any spirit of competition or rivalry. ECRC had done good work in ministering to Dutch immigrants and offering a traditional ministry to those who preferred to be anchored to their historical roots. NLPC, however, would focus on reaching the unchurched, on evangelism.

So we moved into the First Baptist building as New Life Presbyterian Church of Escondido. About half of the original twenty-five people on our prayer list dropped out of the group in those early weeks for various reasons. But Dick was not at all deterred. He and other leaders took a survey of the spiritual gifts in the congregation, and saw to it that everybody had a job, so that our list of coordinators and workers resembled that of a church ten times larger. There was a refreshment coordinator, a children's ministry coordinator, etc.

Gerard Merrill was the prayer coordinator. His was a particularly touching story. He had worked with the police force, but in time had to leave employment because of diabetic symptoms. He was part of the original group that had planted the church, and he was on the list of people we prayed for in Philadelphia. By the time we arrived in Escondido, Gerard was completely blind and somewhat in despair about his future. But he had no problem dialing the phone. Dick suggested that he could contact members of the congregation by phone to ask how the church could pray for them. He would then bring these prayer requests to the meetings of the church staff and other groups that engaged in prayer. Gerard became an elder in the church and was greatly loved and respected. God did take him after ten to fifteen years of this ministry.

Dick asked me to serve on the session. I refused at first, because I had done so poorly at that job in Blue Bell. My failure to lead had allowed the Blue Bell Church to turn into a historical artifact. But I prayed about the assignment. When Dick got more specific about my responsibilities, I came on board. He wanted me to be the "elder in charge of worship." I would be the person in charge of songs, hymns, instruments, and liturgy.

As I mentioned, we intended our worship to reflect the pattern established at New Life in Philadelphia. But I had not attended New Life regularly,

---

2. There was some talk about merging the two congregations, but of course that kind of ecumenism was as difficult then as it is today.

3. But in 1999 I heard again that some at ECRC had been disappointed in this arrangement, that it had violated our unity in Christ.

so I was not used to their liturgical pattern. I largely took my cue from Dick, and also from Doug and Lois Swagerty. Doug and Lois had worked at New Life/Philadelphia while Doug was attending WTS. Lois had experience accompanying Scripture songs and Jesus People hymns on the piano. So at the beginning of my tenure as elder in charge of worship, I was more or less a figurehead. Dick would give his text and sermon topic to Doug, and Doug would choose some appropriate songs. He would then give it to me, and I would give it my rubber stamp. Doug presided at worship, and Lois accompanied the contemporary songs. We usually had one or two traditional hymns in each service, and I accompanied those, especially after someone gave us a small electronic organ.

But in time I learned to play the contemporary songs as well—up to a point. I attended a Sunday evening small group in which Lois was sometimes asked to help care for the children. When she was not available, I was asked to play contemporary songs for the time of singing. I regularly made a total hash of it. So eventually I started practicing our contemporary repertoire, with much help from Lois.[4] After three years or so, Doug graduated from seminary and was called to plant a new church in Oceanside. That left me playing all the songs, including the contemporary ones. My Blue Bell friends would have been astonished. And appalled! Thus, I was brought kicking and screaming into the strange new world of contemporary worship.

After 1983 I chose the songs, both contemporary and traditional, and led worship from the piano. Eventually others presided from the pulpit and I played.

And there was more for me to do. Dick suggested that we have an adult course in worship that we hoped every member would take at some time. Since our worship was somewhat unusual for a Presbyterian church, Dick wanted everyone to understand what we were doing and why. So I designed some Bible studies to serve that purpose. The first one went for four weeks, the second for seven or eight. Once our adult Sunday School got on a regular quarterly schedule, the

Me around 1983

---

4. That is an understatement. I largely mimicked Lois's arrangements.

course went for thirteen weeks. Eventually, the material I taught in this course became my book, *Worship in Spirit and Truth*.[5]

I was also charged with answering critics. We received a letter from an OP minister who had heard a rumor that our church was following the contemporary worship of New Life in Philadelphia. He listed a number of reasons why this was irreverent, unbiblical, and unReformed. Dick asked me to reply to the letter. So my teaching on worship took account of the fact that our style of worship was controversial, and it tried to deal with the controversy. Eventually I was dealing with a rather large literature that attacked "contemporary worship" and urged adhering to traditions. As at Blue Bell, I found myself in the role of the anti-traditionalist, though actually my personal preference was slightly in favor of traditional hymns. Of my two books, *Worship in Spirit and Truth* attempted to set forth in summary the Bible's teaching about worship. *Contemporary Worship Music*[6] sought to answer objections.

In the mid-1980s sometime, I tried to organize a choir, but it didn't turn out well. Attendance at rehearsals was not reliable, and my lack of training as a choir director was all too evident. But around 1988 or '89, Ed and Jean Clowney moved to Escondido. They were largely retired, after Ed's years as president of WTS/Philadelphia and Jean's years as choral director at Philadelphia-Montgomery Christian High School. After their move, Ed did some teaching at the seminary,[7] and they attended New Life. I was delighted to find that Jean was willing to direct a choir for us. I was her accompanist. We rehearsed on Sunday nights. Jean was far better trained than I, and she was willing to do the hard work of making sure who was available on what Sundays. I enjoyed playing the music immensely. The rehearsals, I thought, were a bit too democratic. Everybody chimed in suggestions, and I thought that it would have gone better if the singers had been quieter and Jean had overruled more of the suggestions. But on the whole I think the choir was a great addition to our worship. The choir music, usually filling the offertory slot toward the end of the service, was generally classical in style, rather than contemporary. I felt that added some balance to our musical repertoire.

Beyond the worship course, I did other teaching in the church. One course was on Old Testament theology, which, of course, became entirely

---

5. Phillipsburg, NJ: P&R, 1996.
6. Phillipsburg, NJ: P&R, 1997.
7. Ed was a great fount of wisdom, in the church, seminary, and presbytery, though he and I did not always agree. Among churchmen, Ed was my chief role model. I dedicated to him my *DWG*, and I call readers' attention to my comments about Ed in the Preface to that book.

irrelevant after OT scholar Mark Futato began to worship with us. Another was a thirty-nine-week study of the Westminster Shorter Catechism.[8] We divided this into three thirteen-week segments, and I went through the sequence five or six times during the 1980s and 1990s.

The one thing I did not enjoy about being an elder was going to session meetings. I always try to avoid meetings when I can, remembering the adage "a meeting is an occasion in which minutes are kept and hours are lost." Session meetings are mostly about two things: pastoral problems in the congregation and budgets. Both these topics are of immense importance. But I have never sensed in myself any gifts that would enable me to deal with them. So I rarely spoke up at the meetings, and eventually I received a dispensation from the body to be absent unless something came up particularly relevant to me. For that indulgence, I am exceedingly grateful to Dick, and to my brothers on the session.

New Life grew rapidly, as Dick expected and as we regularly prayed. We were, for a time, the fastest growing church in the denomination, surpassing in this respect even our mother church, New Life in Philadelphia.[9] In time we outgrew the facility at First Baptist and moved to a gymnasium at Central Elementary School on Fourth Avenue. But almost immediately we began making plans to build our own facility on Citracado Parkway. The new building was fairly utilitarian, and we didn't have nearly enough classroom space. But there was a good amount of land, and the place served us well until after I left Escondido in 2000.

Our rapid growth came in answer to prayer, as I shall indicate. But God used human means as well. In New Life's ministry there was a great emphasis on evangelism. Dick taught us to give priority to visitors: we should talk to strangers rather than only to friends. He himself was an example to us: after church, he would chase new people into the parking lot, rather than shake hands in the back of the church. The church also offered courses in Evangelism Explosion, which our people practiced door-to-door, and hospitality evangelism as well. Dick believed, and he taught me to believe, that the best way to nurture believers was to get them active in practicing the Great Commission. So I never felt that this emphasis on evangelism detracted from the ministry to those who already believed. My own relation to Christ grew deeper at New Life than it has at any other church. So of course I was not pleased to hear the church despised as "non-Reformed" by its critics.

---

8. I hope this fact and others dispel the rumor that I don't like catechisms and confessions.
9. Of course, the OPC did not present a high bar for us to overcome.

One year we had "Net Nite" on Wednesdays. The congregation gathered for a meal, then broke into teams. One team, trained in Evangelism Explosion, would go to present the gospel to recent visitors. Another team (often including Dick himself) would counsel people in need. Another team would work with children and youth. And another group would gather for prayer for all the others. Net Nite continued only for one year, because the congregational meal proved too great a burden on a few. But I see it as a high point of the church's ministry.

The church's work was bathed in prayer. Gerard's ministry and the Net Nite team were part of that, but there was much more. There was prayer in the session, on the staff. Frequently after a teaching meeting Dick would ask us to break into small groups[10] and pray for the implementation of the teaching. Often Dick would invite a group of us to his home to pray about some upcoming development. Every New Year's Eve there would be special meetings for prayer at the church. And God answered us.

My Family, at Last

When I moved to Escondido in 1980, I was forty years old and rather despairing about the possibility of marriage and family. My general shyness in social settings, and toward women in particular, had not changed over the years. But in 1983 I renewed my friendship with the Cummings family (chapter 4), and especially with Calvin and Mary Cummings' younger daughter, Mary Grace.

Mary was seventeen in 1963, when I had worked for her father as a summer intern in Covenant OPC. I was twenty-four, much too old to have a relationship with a seventeen-year-old girl. But I certainly noticed Mary's great beauty and godly character. She went off to study at Dordt College, and on graduation she married Jerry O'Donnell. Jerry was a psychology major, a friend of Mary's brother Wilson Cummings at Geneva College, and he occasionally visited the Cummings home. After they were married, Jerry took courses at WTS-Philadelphia, at least one of them with me. He taught at Eastern College, then for a while at Gordon College in Massachusetts, then at Dordt in Iowa (Mary's alma mater). They had three children, Debbie, Doreen, and David (later nicknamed Skip).

---

10. I am not a small group person, because of my introversion, and because I always tend to dominate (if I perceive that my leadership is needed) or say nothing (if I perceive that it is not). But small groups at New Life were a major means of growth to many people, and Dick was greatly devoted to them. I would not dream of criticizing this model.

Our friendship continued. Jerry and Mary had me to their home for dinner once in Philadelphia, and I stayed in their house in Sioux Center, IA, during a speaking engagement at Dordt. This trip to Dordt was full of drama. It was during the time I described in chapter 6, when disciples of the Dutch philosopher Herman Dooyeweerd were vigorously pressing their philosophy upon many Reformed institutions, including Westminster. This influence was especially prevalent at Dordt. Dordt was determined to be a fully Christian college, integrating every discipline with the teaching of Scripture. But the Dooyeweerdians insisted this could not be done without a concurrent commitment to Dooyeweerdian philosophy. A number of the Dordt faculty were committed to Dooyeweerdianism, and others, including Jerry, were under pressure to conform. I was already known as a critic of Dooyeweerdianism, and a number of people on campus, on both sides of the controversy, spent time with me discussing the issue. The president of the college invited me into his office for a chat. Nobody changed their minds, but I spent a day or so with the O'Donnells and renewed old acquaintance.

Eventually the Dooyeweerdian position prevailed and a number of nonconforming faculty, including the O'Donnells, left. Jerry sent out a lot of résumés and landed a teaching job at Nyack Missionary College near New York City. During their time in New York, the family attended Trinity Baptist Church, where Al Martin was pastor.[11] Sometime in the early 1980s, Jerry took the family to Tallahassee, FL, where he enrolled in the doctoral program at Florida State University. Calvin Cummings, Mary's father, had in retirement planted an OP church in Tallahassee, but he had left to plant churches in Melbourne, FL, and in Chicago, IL. He still owned a home in Tallahassee, and he made that available for the O'Donnells.

Sadly, after this move the marriage broke apart. Jerry began living apart from his wife and children and did a number of things contrary to his marriage vows. This led to divorce in 1983. I judged that under the circumstances Mary was the innocent party and that she was biblically free to marry again.[12]

The Cummings family announced this event in their Christmas letter that year. I wrote to Mary originally with the purpose of expressing sadness and promising prayer. But it was a long letter, and by the end the topic changed. Completely out of character, I mentioned the possibility of further correspondence with courtship in view. After I mailed it I was convicted

11. I am an admirer of Martin's preaching. It was interesting to me, however, that Calvin Cummings' daughter could become a member of a Baptist church. That indicated to me that the family, though certainly Reformed in its theology, was not "truly" Reformed as I have used that term in this book. I perceived that as a good thing.

12. See my discussion in DCL, 769–81.

with the feeling that I had done something profoundly stupid, which was typical of my relationships with women. But something very strange occurred. It turned out that I had not put enough postage on the letter, and it was returned to me. I might have thrown it away with thanks that God had enabled me to reconsider. But I prayed over it again, added the necessary postage, and mailed it out again.

Because of some awkwardness in mail deliveries, Mary received the letter without any other mail to distract her from it. Her first reaction was negative. But her parents, who were staying with her at the time, agreed that she ought to take the letter seriously, answer it, and see where God would lead. I was really quite surprised that she did answer me, and that she took the possibility of courtship and marriage in a serious way.

So over the following weeks we corresponded, sharing everything. Mary visited me in Escondido, and I visited her in Tallahassee. During her Escondido visit, she and I attended a dinner at the seminary. Also there were a number of board members, faculty, and people from the community. She noticed that at that dinner there were people she had known in every location of her past life: Philadelphia, Boston, Sioux Center. Although she had done it often, she had never enjoyed moving to a new location, having to put down new roots, having to make new friends. But this dinner in Escondido showed her that if she moved to Escondido she would already have friends. That was a great reassurance. In God's providence, however, most of those people Mary knew from the dinner left the area shortly after we moved there. But the dinner at the seminary was God's way of easing the transition for her.

On another occasion, the three children joined us in Escondido as together we looked for a house. We bought the one they liked best, a large four bedroom, with three baths, a fruit grove, a pool, and lots of flowers and palm trees.

Mary and I married in Tallahassee on June 2, 1984, and we are looking forward to our 33rd anniversary in June 2017.

The ceremony was fairly simple, in the OPC founded by Mary's Dad. He participated in the service, but the current pastor presided, Bob Evans. Bob had to check out the literature on marriage and divorce to assure his conscience that we were eligible, and he made the right judgment. Mary and I sang during the service, the version of Ps 139 found in the *Trinity Hymnal*.

The reception was outdoors on the church grounds, catered by the ladies of the church. My mother, brothers, and sister attended, and we had a good time. Some rascals from the church decorated the Ford Fairmont, our getaway car, with shaving cream, cans tied to the back, and string. The string went all around the car, tying the steering wheel, the gearshift, the pedals, the doors, etc. To drive the car we needed scissors. Eventually we were able to pull away, but when we saw a sign for a car wash down the street (with kids loudly beckoning us) we quickly took advantage of the solicitation.

We drove first to Orlando. Somehow, Larry Mininger, pastor of the Lake Sherwood OPC, had heard that I would be in the area and had asked me to preach. He was a little embarrassed when he found that we were there on our honeymoon, but we had a nice time meeting some old friends there. Some time before or after that, we visited Epcot Center, the latest addition to Walt Disney World. Then to my mother's condo by the ocean in Boca Raton, which she had vacated for a week to accommodate us. We had a great time there. One highlight was watching a mother sea turtle lay her eggs in a roped-off area on the beach.

Then back to Tallahassee, where we rented a U-Haul trailer and loaded it with some of the O'Donnell's furniture and other possessions (with Jerry's permission). Debbie and David joined us on the trip to California. Doreen stayed with her Dad for a while and later flew to San Diego to be with us.

My plan was for a leisurely trip, like my national park trip in 1957, visiting sites in New Orleans, Texas, New Mexico, and Arizona. But the consensus of our group was to make time. We did visit Carlsbad Caverns in New Mexico, the one natural wonder I had hoped to see in 1957 but had missed then. Then on to our new home in Escondido.

New Life welcomed us with a chocolate reception. They knew I had a special taste for chocolate, but a number of other New Lifers did too. Everybody wore something reminiscent of chocolate, and Mary and I picked the winners: Elane Cross and her daughters who wore T-shirts that, when they stood beside one another, spelled out "Her She's Dutch Chocolate," celebrating both the delicacy and Elane's Dutch ancestry.

Then we set ourselves to making a home. We had thought that Debbie, Doreen, and David were fairly well reconciled to our new structure, after our several visits and our joint project in choosing a house. Mary and I thought that God would overcome the well-known problems of establishing stepfamilies. But it was not so easy, as it turned out. The kids had a lot of anger because of the divorce and the move, especially their loss of friends. Jerry had moved into our area, which was sometimes helpful, sometimes not. At one point, Mary was in some anguish and asked me to bring in someone to counsel us. So I called my colleague and good friend Jay Adams.[13] Both at WTS/Philadelphia and at Westminster/California, Jay and I

---

13. As I mentioned earlier, Jay was the original coordinator of Westminster's California extension, but he had bowed out in favor of Bob Strimple. But Strimple later arranged for him to come to the California campus as head of a D.Min. program in preaching. Jay's doctorate was in public speaking, though he had been better known for

had next-door offices. Jay took some time to talk to Mary and me in our new home, but it was not a typical Jay Adams counseling session. He reminded us that our stuff was still in boxes out in the carport. "When you haven't even unpacked," he asked, "how can you expect your kids to be peaceful and cooperative?" That was calming and empowering, one of the best experiences of counseling I had ever had.

But the unpacking of our boxes didn't solve our problems. We went through several difficult years. What was most helpful initially was the tripod of church (New Life), school (Santa Fe Christian School), and home.[14] God worked in our lives through the consistency between these three in the values they taught.

But what most decisively made us a family was Justin. When their Mom became pregnant, the three older kids had made suggestions about what name we should give the child, and we chose one of their nominations. He was born on March 28, 1986, and the older kids loved him immediately. We never needed to call a baby sitter. Justin was a very compliant child, and smiled broadly when anyone played with him, though he certainly had a mind of his own. Then on April 9, 1988 (a day after my birthday), baby Johnny joined us: less compliant, more adventurous. As Johnny was born, I identified him as a blond, like Justin. But under the light, we discovered that he was clearly redheaded like me, and like two of Mary's brothers. Doreen commented about the *shape* of his hair: "He has a Mohawk." Justin appreciated his brother too, using an initial "t" in place of a "c": "Baby toot."

The first new child, and the second, drew us together in a way we had not yet experienced. To Debbie, Doreen, and David, Justin and Johnny were their brothers. And at last, I was not an interloper. I was the father of their brothers. And that was enough to make us a real family, or as close as you can get to that with a divorce in your past.

---

his counseling theory. But he desired to give more focused attention to preaching and for that purpose welcomed the California appointment. His protégé George Scipione became the teacher of counseling at the school.

14. For perspective buffs, the church was normative, the school situational, and the home existential. At least we hoped it would be. As for the kids themselves, Debbie was primarily normative (concerned with rules and fairness), Doreen existential (concerned with feelings), and David situational (concerned with what was going on). As Justin and Johnny grew older, it became evident that Justin was primarily normative and Johnny combined the situational with the existential.

Ministry

When Mary grew up in the home of her father the pastor, she learned to be selfless. The Cummings had a small house, but they opened it freely. Church members and others (including the present writer) often shared meals, stayed overnight, came in to talk after church. There were often meetings there. And the hospitality was sometimes long-term. For several years, Mary shared her bedroom with a girl around her age whose parents had left her without care. When Mary complained, her parents told her that there was no place for selfishness in the Christian life. And she learned that lesson well.

By 1984, as I've indicated, she lived in a much larger house, and we used it to minister to other people. By nature, I am not a very hospitable person, indulging my incompetence at cooking, cleaning, and entertaining. But God gave me the gift of hospitality when he gave me my wife. We opened our swimming pool to everyone we knew, and there was a constant stream of visitors there. Our house was often the location for church socials and gatherings, and the kids often had parties with their friends. Eventually this pattern widened to include people whom we didn't know, but who had some need. Mary and Debbie visited homeless people in the local parks, sharing with them food and the gospel. Some seminarians opened a house for people with drug addiction and other problems. We served as an overflow facility for them. Like the halfway house, we sought to help the people staying with us to find medical treatment, official documents like birth certificates, and jobs. While they stayed with us, we asked them to have devotions with us (Bible reading and prayer) and to attend New Life. In some cases, at least, we thought that the power of the gospel had turned lives around.

Many of the street people needed counseling, and I was sure that of all Jay Adams' friends, I was the only one who was *not* "Competent to Counsel."[15] So I told my dear wife that she (and others from New Life) would have to counsel these folks. I would finance the operation, but others would have to do the real ministry. We kept to that division of labor for the most part, as long as we were in Escondido.

To a great extent, we did not know what we were doing. Neither Mary nor I had any training in social work or in ministry to the homeless. But we tried to learn from our mistakes and to bring in others to deal with matters beyond our competence. Our goal was simply to provide a place to stay for people who needed Christ, to demonstrate God's love, and to help these folks in practical ways. I regret the discomfort that this brought upon our

---

15. Quoting the title of Jay's book (Grand Rapids: Zondervan, 1986).

children, and for that reason we did not continue these practices after we moved to Orlando. But, despite occasional disasters, I believe that on the whole God blessed this work.

The Seminary

But of course my reason for traveling west was to teach theology at the new Westminster Theological Seminary in California (which I shall abbreviate WTSC). My general evaluation is that for the seminary the 1980s were a great decade, the 1990s far less so.

The faculty WTS/Philadelphia (WTS/P) sent to California was certainly not an expansion team. It was an extraordinary group, highly competent and well regarded. In the OT department we had Meredith G. Kline and his son, Meredith M. Kline. I disagreed with the elder Kline about some things and would disagree with him about many more. But he was one of the most inspiring and interesting teachers I had studied with in my own seminary years. He had moved from WTS to Gordon-Conwell during the years of my grad study. But he had returned occasionally in the late 1970s to teach courses at WTS on an adjunct basis. When he was there, he chose (unfortunately, in my view) to get involved in controversy. He reviewed Greg Bahnsen's *Theonomy in Christian Ethics* very negatively,[16] and he engaged the Shepherd controversy, opposing Shepherd very strongly. Although I disagreed somewhat with his positions on these issues, I was delighted when Bob Strimple said that Meredith would join us in California. I knew nobody who could do better than Meredith at getting students interested in biblical theology.

I knew the younger Meredith as well. He had taken a Th.M. at WTS/P in systematics. He was a poet as well as a theologian and a good friend.

In NT Dennis Johnson, a native Californian, taught for us. Dennis was one of our best students at WTS/P, and he completed his doctorate at Fuller after some years in the pastorate, both in New Jersey and in Los Angeles. Al Mawhinney was also in the NT department. Al specialized in teaching Greek and was known for his pedagogical excellence at Covenant College. He also became our academic dean and did an excellent job. Steve Baugh also joined the New Testament Department faculty in 1983, the first WTSC graduate to join the faculty. He earned his Ph.D. at the University of California, Irvine.

---

16. Bahnsen's book now carries the publication data in Nacodoches, TX: Covenant Media Foundation, 2002. In my judgment, Bahnsen's reply to Kline was more cogent than Kline's review.

W. Robert Godfrey, with a Ph.D. from Stanford, came to teach church history after some years at WTS/P. His lectures were always crisp and clear, with a lot of knowledge and wit.

I taught apologetics, and Bob Strimple and I shared the courses in systematics. Bob also had administrative responsibilities, and when the two Westminsters formally separated in 1982, Bob became our first president, while remaining a teacher.

Derke Bergsma, formerly of Trinity Christian College in the Chicago area, joined us in practical theology. Jay Adams also joined us to direct the Doctor of Ministry program in preaching, as I mentioned earlier. Teaching counseling was George Scipione, one of Jay's close disciples and a friend of mine. In the early years, Dick Kaufmann taught evangelism, and later in the decade, Ed Clowney taught about the use of biblical theology in preaching.

In our early planning for the seminary, we talked of having a sharper focus on the pastorate than our mother-seminary in Philadelphia. WTS/P had become more and more devoted to its Th.M. and Ph.D. programs. We Californians wanted to refocus on the specific needs of the pastorate. Despite that focus, a number of future academics studied with us in the early days. I remember particularly Bill Davis, who went on to earn a Ph.D. in philosophy at Notre Dame and has since taught philosophy at Covenant College. We got to know Bill also from his math teaching at Santa Fe Christian School, where our three older children were students. None of them were mathematically inclined, but they took advanced math courses just to have Bill as a teacher. More recently my youngest son attended Covenant College and had Bill as a teacher and advisor. Only my older son (Mary's fourth child) Justin did not have the influence of Bill in his life and education.

Charles E. ("Chuck") Hill also studied with us in those days. He later earned his Ph.D. at Cambridge University and became internationally known as a scholar in patristics, Johannine studies, and canon. He is the author of significant books and articles, including *Who Chose the Gospels?*[17] and is now a colleague of mine at Reformed Theological Seminary in Orlando.

I taught my five-credit monster course,[18] which in Philadelphia we called "Introduction to Theology and Apologetics." In California we

---

17. Oxford: Oxford University Press, 2010.

18. After a year or two of this, our accrediting agency told us that we were teaching too many hours. So we subtracted one credit hour from Christian Mind. But with Strimple's concurrence, I managed to give the students the same assignments they had done in the five-hour course. The only difference between the two courses was that the four-hour version permitted less time for explanation and discussion of the concepts. Is that really what the accreditors considered to be an improvement? Frankly, I have never known accreditors to provide any educational wisdom.

streamlined that title to "The Christian Mind." Then we coupled that with a second year apologetics course called "The Modern Mind," replacing Knudsen's course in the Dooyeweerdian philosophy of science. That course dealt with philosophical, theological, scientific, and cultural trends in the contemporary period, and their roots in ancient thought. Much of the material of that course can now be read in my book *History of Western Philosophy and Theology*.[19] In systematics, I taught the doctrine of the word of God (part of "Christian Mind") and the doctrine of God (part of the course "God and Man" shared between me and Bob Strimple). I also taught some electives, though I cannot remember any of them at this moment. That's the way it is with me and electives.

For me the major change from Philadelphia was that at WTSC the classes were much smaller, and that at last gave me the opportunity to write books and articles. My first project was an expansion of my lecture outline, *Doctrine of the Knowledge of God*. My first plan was to publish precisely that: an expanded lecture outline—with I, A, 1, a, i, etc. I had felt for a long time that Reformed theology was weakest in developing argumentation—in showing how one assertion is grounded in another. Wittgenstein had published his first book, the *Tractatus Logico-Philosophicus*[20] using a decimal outlining system: 1, 1.1, 1.11, etc., and Vern Poythress had done something similar in his first book, *Philosophy, Science and the Sovereignty of God*.[21] So I put the first part of *DKG* together in that way and sent it off to P&R Publishers.[22] Their editors, however, thought it would be better if I rewrote *DKG* as a regular book, with parts, chapters, and a few subheadings. John Hughes, a former student who did some editing for them, wrote up a sample of what that might look like. That seemed good to me, and I certainly didn't want to launch an argument in the course of my first publishing project. So *DKG* became a regular book.

---

19. Phillipsburg: P&R, 2014.
20. London: Kegan Paul, 1922 (from the 1921 German edition).
21. Phillipsburg, NJ: P&R, 1976.
22. I chose P&R, because (1) For many years they had been part of the Machen movement and therefore they understood the nuances of Reformed theology and Van Tillian apologetics. They also exhibited in their publishing line the principle that I loved at Westminster: creativity within the bounds of orthodoxy. (2) Both the owner of the company, Bryce Craig, and the chief editor, Thom Notaro, had been students of mine at WTSP. I had reason to think they wanted to see their old professor in print. Other publishers had more marketing power and more academic prestige. But what I wanted most was a publisher who would let me write my own books, with as few editorial changes as possible. In that respect, and in others, P&R has always satisfied me.

The first draft took some time to write out, because I was still using the conventional typewriter I had used at Princeton. A major change came into my life in 1983, when I bought my first computer. It was a Columbia MPC, or, as we said then, an "IBM Clone." The Columbia could do most everything the IBM could do, and it was slightly cheaper. The computer increased my writing speed and made me far more productive as a writer.

DKG was published in 1987. Hardly anybody reviewed it, except Mark Karlberg, who was absurdly negative.[23] But Richard Pratt, who had been my student at WTSP, used *DKG* as a text in a class he was teaching at Reformed Theological Seminary in Jackson, MS. One day I got a package of letters from his students thanking me for writing the book. That was, frankly, a greater encouragement than any favorable academic review could have been.

Also in 1987, Vern Poythress published his *Symphonic Theology*.[24] I have noticed that Vern and I tend to publish books in tandem. He gets an idea, and I get the same one. That happened first with our 1987 books. Both books advocate a multi-perspectival approach to theology.

Collegiality

During the 1980s I was very enthusiastic about the new seminary. I was proud to be one of such an excellent group of colleagues, respected as scholars and teachers. We did not agree on everything, but we respected one another as brothers in Christ, and we upheld one another's right to work independently and creatively within the bounds of orthodoxy. It was significant to me that Bob Strimple had chosen Godfrey and Kline, who strongly opposed Shepherd, Clowney, who voted for the compromise that led to Shepherd's dismissal, and me, who voted to uphold Shepherd's orthodoxy, while disagreeing with Shepherd on some points. The Shepherd controversy, which had terribly divided the WTSP community, was not transplanted to California. Rather, people who had different opinions worked together to advance the Reformed faith in this part of the country. We rarely mentioned the controversy.

The seminary was a missionary effort. Orthodox Reformed and Presbyterian churches had been rare in California. Now our students and friends were planting new Reformed churches. People were coming to Christ through the Reformed gospel. And as happens with other missions efforts,

---

23. See my reply to him in *DG*, Appendix B (751–58).
24. Phillipsburg: P&R, 1987.

the differences between the missionaries became less important than the joint ministry we had embarked upon. Evidently God's sovereign hand had been at work, to extend his kingdom and to nurture our hearts. So I often boasted to people outside the seminary about our collegiality.

8

Confessionalism in California

For me the '80s were largely idyllic, with of course some indications of our fallenness. The '90s were the opposite, a relatively difficult time in my life, but one in which God gave us many reasons to give thanks.

The OPC and the PCA

I had been in the Orthodox Presbyterian Church since 1967, and Mary grew up in it. She came from one of the most distinguished OPC families (her father Cal a longtime pastor, her three brothers in OPC ministries). New Life/Escondido was planted by the OPC.

The denomination played an important role in the history of American Presbyterianism. Although it was not the only theologically orthodox Presbyterian denomination, it seemed for some years after its founding in 1936 to be the main alternative to the liberal PCUSA. But after 1973, there was a new option. As the OPC had left the northern Presbyterian Church, the PCUSA, over its theological liberalism, the PCA, Presbyterian Church in America, had left the southern Presbyterian (PCUS) for the same reason. The PCA was somewhat less focused on tradition than the OPC, more focused on evangelism, missions, and church planting. In time their membership and mission force was one of the fastest growing in American evangelicalism.

That was important to us at New Life, for we saw ourselves as outward-facing, evangelistic. And we saw ourselves as a church that would plant other churches. People from New Life had planted Coastal Community Church in Oceanside, pastored by Doug Swagerty. We also planted a congregation in San Marcos, the town west of Escondido. Dick became chairman of the Home Missions Committee of our presbytery, which oversaw church planting efforts. He developed a plan for the San Diego area, which he called "20 by the 21st" (i.e., twenty new churches by the twenty-first century). Several new churches were born from this planning, including one in Mira Mesa, and one in Rancho Bernardo, south of Escondido.

This plan of course required our presbytery to appoint and support church planters. But there were obstacles. Often we brought prospective church planters to meetings of presbytery. But this was not a good period in the history of the OPC presbytery of Southern California. The presbytery was highly factionalized, mainly in three segments: (1) OPC traditionalists, (2) Christian reconstructionists (of whom Greg Bahnsen was chief),[1] and (3) New Life sympathizers. The first group wanted to do everything the way Presbyterian and Reformed churches had always done it. To them the example of J. Gresham Machen was often decisive, though it was fifty years since Machen's death. The second group wanted the presbytery to be part of the theonomic movement, and they protested any action that did not conform closely to their particular orientation. The New Lifers wanted more emphasis on evangelism and church planting. Every presbytery meeting, therefore, presented a dramatic conflict, either between two of these factions, with the third standing aside, or between a de facto alliance of two factions seeking to defeat the third.

This was not a good atmosphere in which to develop a church-planting program. When prospective church planters visited us, they were discouraged by all the battles. More than once, we heard, "it's hard enough to plant a church, without having to fight battles in presbytery." Despite this atmosphere, occasionally a church planter would seek to join our presbytery, but he would get tripped up by the credentialing process. Most church planters came from denominations other than the OPC (especially the PCA) and they would fail examinations because they didn't know the OPC buzzwords, the details of presuppositional apologetics, the arguments for and against theonomy, etc. So often when we sought to bring church planters to our presbytery, either the church planter or the presbytery would reject the other.

When a church planter turned away from the OPC, or was turned away, the PCA was often ready to help. So several of our prospective church planters went into the PCA. That suggested to a number of us that we could

---

1. Theonomy, or Christian reconstructionism, is the view that the Mosaic law, for the most part, was applicable to contemporary civil government and that Christians ought to seek its implementation in all areas of politics and culture.

not compete with the PCA in church planting and should not try to. We began to ponder the maxim, "if you can't beat them, join them."

The best way to join the PCA, of course, would have been for the two denominations to become one. There were proposals to do that in the 1980s, but in one case the PCA rejected the OPC, and in another the OPC rejected the PCA. The OPC largely held the view that unions of like-minded churches were desirable. But in practice they were not interested in union with anybody who was even a little bit unlike them. The PCA had little interest in ecumenism and was somewhat suspicious of it, though they occasionally gave some attention to union proposals, and they did succeed in merging with the Reformed Presbyterian Church, Evangelical Synod, in 1982. But they did little to encourage the OPC to join them, and some respected members like Francis Schaeffer spoke eloquently against such a union.

So the two denominations rejected union in the 1980s and continue to reject it to the day of this writing. That left the outward-facing OPC churches in a difficult position. The original New Life Church in Philadelphia eventually transferred from OPC to PCA, and other like-minded churches followed suit. By around 1989, Dick came to feel that this was the best course for New Life/Escondido. It was not difficult for him to persuade the session and membership that this was the right course, though there were some who disagreed, including Bob Strimple, who began attending ECRC after New Life made the change. In presbytery, Dick explained that there was a difference in "vision" between the two positions. The dominant view of the OPC was that we should strive above all to achieve historical authenticity—to be a church like those of the original Calvinistic Reformers. Dick's view was that our goal should be to carry out the Great Commission by making disciples of contemporary people. Some felt that these visions were compatible. But after all the battling that position didn't seem credible.

Many in presbytery sympathized with our decision, but others talked of "betrayal" and spread on presbytery's minutes a number of insults directed to the churches and ministers who made this move. But they were unable to keep us from leaving. I joined the group that left the OPC, for I agreed with Dick's argument, and I wanted to be in the same denomination as New Life, the denomination of which my family would be members. So that year I became a PCA "Teaching Elder." That was the PCA lingo, and of course I had to learn it.

During that time I did a lot of thinking about denominations. Eventually I came to reject the very concept of a denomination as unbiblical. In the NT, nothing like a denomination plays any role in church government. And in 1 Cor 1, Paul speaks out against the kinds of divisions in the church that later have led to denominationalism. Therefore, there is in the Christian life no place for denominational pride. We should, rather, seek to reverse the forces that have created more than 40,000 Christian denominations in the world, and the forces that continue to drive them further apart from one another. I developed this argument in the book *Evangelical Reunion*.[2]

New Life

The numerical growth of New Life Church continued until 1992. That year, our attendance was usually in the 400s, and Dick challenged us to invite family and friends to raise our Easter attendance above 500.[3] The week after Easter, with a twinkle in his eye, Dick announced that our attendance had failed to reach a 500 number ... rather, God be praised, it was over 600!

But alas, that was the high point, and our attendance then plateaued at lower numbers. Part of the problem was a recession, which led a number of our members to move away. Another part, I think, was that we missed an opportunity. Zan Stanton, one of our deacons, had cultivated a group of young people from a poor area and brought some to church, indicating that he could have brought many more. But the kids sometimes misbehaved, making it difficult for other kids to learn. Zan appealed to the church to help him to evangelize this group, but he felt a rebuff and ended up going to another church. Resisting an evangelistic opportunity was uncharacteristic of New Life, and I think that was the beginning of harder times.

Dick also moved on. In the late 1980s, some had approached Dick about planting a PCA in New York City. He visited there and spent some time praying with friends and family about whether to accept the opportunity. Some of us pled with him to stay. Dennis Johnson tried to convince him that the Pacific Rim was at least as crucial to world evangelism as was New York. After some time, Dick determined to stay in Escondido. Tim Keller became the founder of Redeemer PCA of New York, and God blessed it with astonishing growth. In fact, the growth was hard to manage. So Tim called Dick to ask him a second time to move to New York. This time he would become "executive pastor" of the church, charged with training leaders and helping to organize its ministries. Again, Dick asked us to pray with him about this opportunity. But this time he judged that the Lord answered differently.

---

2. Grand Rapids: Baker Book House, 1991. Now available at http://www.framepoythress.org/wp-content/uploads/2012/08/FrameJohnEvangelicalReunion1991.pdf.

3. Dick was not one of those people who thinks that "numbers don't matter." I am not either. The New Testament frequently considers numbers important enough to report (as Acts 2:41 and 4:4).

So he left us in 1994, spent five years with Redeemer in New York, then returned to San Diego in 1999 to plant Harbor Presbyterian, a church that like Redeemer was multi-site and gospel-centered in every ministry. Mary and I attended some of the organizational meetings of Harbor and some of its early services, before we too left the area.

When Dick left us in 1994, he was concerned that the church had become ingrown, less evangelistic, less centered on grace. This was at least part of the reason for our declining membership.

After Dick left, Dennis Johnson, who taught NT at WTS/C, became acting pastor of the church. We appreciated Dennis's preaching ministry and his winsome manner. Dick's successor as senior pastor was Dan Deaton. Dan was a former PCA pastor who had spent some years as a Navy chaplain, attending New Life regularly. He preached several sermons after Dick left, which we very warmly received. Many started asking, "Why not Dan?" With very little controversy, Dan became our next senior pastor.

Dan hoped that we would support a building program for a new main auditorium and other facilities. But pledges fell far below goals, and the project was abandoned. Meanwhile conflicts developed between Dan and various individuals and groups in the church, particularly some of the deacons. Around 1999, Dan was accused of moral failure, and he left the pastorate. Again Dennis Johnson stepped in as interim pastor. The ensuing pastoral search, after I had left the area, led to Ted Hamilton, for some years a lawyer and recently a graduate of WTS/C. I am told that under Ted's ministry at New Life the church has flourished.

Family

As the '80s passed into the '90s, both Debbie and Doreen were married. Debbie married George Rubio, a pastoral intern at the local Emmanuel Faith Community Church. Eventually, they moved to Hesperia, CA in the high desert where George was first the assistant pastor, then senior pastor, at the Sonrise Evangelical Free Church. They had five children: Rebecca, Amanda, Adam, Olivia, and Kristina. Debbie, who graduated from San Diego State College, worked as a high school teacher in the public schools, specializing in bilingual education.

Doreen married Dennis Kester and moved with him to the vicinity of Eugene, OR, where his family lived, and where he became a fire fighter. Doreen graduated from the University of Oregon with a fine arts major. They have one daughter, Malena.

For David (Skip) the '90s were the decade of finishing high school (Santa Fe Christian) and attending Palomar Community College and San Diego State University. He left college without a degree, but he did well without it. He became a photographer's assistant and later was able to set up his own business as a photographer. He has photographed many weddings and has done much of the commercial photography for the Advocare Co. Often he has visited us in Orlando, FL while visiting the area for photo shoots.

For our little boys, Justin and Johnny, the '90s were for home schooling. Christian families in that time had basically three alternatives: public schools, Christian private schools, and home schools. Mary and the older kids had used the public schools before they moved to California. After the move, Debbie, Doreen, and Skip had gone to Santa Fe Christian School. Now home school presented a different opportunity and different challenges.

We perceived the public schools to be a spiritual danger to children, both because of their secular ideology and because of the moral condition of the peer culture. We respected Christian parents who used the public schools (either for economic reasons or as a means of Christian witness). But we believed that if our kids went to public schools we would have to spend much time un-teaching them things they learned in the classroom and opposing the example of their peers. Christian private schools like Santa Fe offered many advantages, but in our area they were expensive and distant.

As with our ministry to street people, the chief burden of home school fell on Mary. I was amazed at the amount of work she willingly undertook, both with the home school and with the street people we continued to minister to. She also taught in the New Life children's ministries. At first she developed a curriculum for a pre-school program called "Kids' Time." Later she taught in the Sunday School. She was not content merely to read through a prescribed curriculum. Rather, for every class she made careful and elaborate preparations of visual aids, hands-on crafts, and games.

I helped by supervising the kids' practicing on musical instruments. (Both boys took piano lessons; Johnny also played violin, and Justin cello.) For a time, we got up at 6 AM and would practice until 7. I also often drove them to their lessons, sat through the lesson, and drove them home. I also helped with the logistics for their athletic activities. The boys played a number of sports, especially soccer. They were both good athletes; I thanked God that I hadn't passed my non-athletic genes on to my sons. Mary and I watched most all of their games. Sports ignoramus that I am, I was surprised at how much I enjoyed watching my boys play.

We were all involved in a home school support group. Alas, like a Christian denomination, the organization went through a split between one faction that used teaching materials offered by the public schools and another group that thought Christians should have nothing to do with the public schools at all. We supported the first group—really supporting friends of ours who had a financial need for the public school assistance. Our group met occasionally during the year, for graduations, arts festivals, instrumental recitals, and so on.

We also had a group-within-a-group: three families (the Hoflands, the Tanakas, and us) that regularly got together to teach various units of instruction. One year the group studied native Americans, dressing up in Indian costumes, holding banquets of Indian food, etc. Another year, we studied "early settlers" in Pilgrim costumes and cowboy hats. Once we studied anatomy, and Janice Tanaka wrote a song about the epiglottis. The ladies' creativity flourished!

Janice's husband Warren was not a Christian believer when we first met him. His family was of Buddhist background, and he was a somewhat skeptical engineer. But he did not object to Janice raising their two children as Christians and home schooling them. But Warren was curious about the Christian faith, and he watched closely the developments in the lives of his children and their home schooling friends. At times, he went to church with Janice. But he resisted making a commitment to Christ. Toward the end of our time in Escondido, however, on Christmas Eve, God got Warren's attention. He and Mary drove separate cars with the kids to an outing in the mountains. It had snowed and the roads were slippery. Warren's car, with our son Johnny, overturned on the road. Mary stopped to call for help. They got everybody home safely, but Warren thought that he should attend the Christmas Eve service at New Life. Dan Deaton's sermon was "An Upside-Down Christmas," about how God almighty came in humility, all the paradoxes of the incarnation. That sermon took on special meaning for Warren and the kids who had literally spent part of the day upside down. On the way home, Warren and Janice noticed a shooting star and commented that it had been a day of strange things.[4]

After that day, Warren asked for some help in understanding the Christian faith. Jay Sesto, a deacon at New Life, brought together some course materials, and I was invited to be part of a Sunday morning class

---

4. On the way back from the accident, they had noticed a big "Jesus Saves" sign. Warren and Janice agreed that it had been a day of strange things. Certainly God was at work.

with the Sestos and Warren. Warren had particular problems accepting the resurrection of Jesus, and I was able to help him with that.[5]

Later I baptized Warren, with his daughter Elizabeth, in the Sestos' pool. They asked for baptism by immersion, and I complied, though some might have said that my compliance was not truly Reformed. I had assisted at the baptisms of my sons, but to the best of my recollection the Tanakas were the only others I have baptized. This was one of our happiest experiences in Escondido.

Seminary

In 1988, Bob Strimple announced his retirement from the presidency and his return to the classroom as a fulltime professor of systematic theology. Replacing him as president was Bob Den Dulk, who had come to California as our director of development. This was the first time Westminster had a president from the business side of the seminary rather than from the academic side. But the presidency is, of course, very much a fund-raising office. It was in this case also an honor for Bob Den Dulk's outstanding service to the seminary over many years.

At the turn of the decade, there were several faculty changes. Meredith M. Kline, the son of Meredith G., left us, by mutual agreement, to return to New England. He did not care for the area, evidenced by his poem "Southern California Ugly." From the administrators' point of view, Meredith was not making fast enough progress toward his doctorate. (Yikes! I thought. If they had applied that rule to me I would have been gone fifteen years earlier. Besides, Meredith had stronger excuses than I had, related to academic bureaucracy.) I missed him, a gentle, gracious, insightful presence.

Replacing him was Mark Futato, a student at WTSP in the late 1970s, with a doctorate from Catholic University and pastoral experience (OPC) in Maryland. The Futatos had sons roughly the age of ours, and we got to know them well through New Life. In 1996, Iain Duguid, a Cambridge Ph.D., church planter, and guitarist joined Mark in the OT department.

Allen Mawhinney, who served us well as academic dean and professor of New Testament, left us to help plant a new seminary in Orlando, a second

---

5. Nothing particularly presuppositional about my approach. I used the traditional evidences of the resurrection, just as Josh MacDowell or John Warwick Montgomery would have done. If Warren had given epistemological resistance, like Hume's arguments about the impossibility of establishing a miracle, I would have dealt with those arguments presuppositionally. But there's no need to discuss epistemology if there is no epistemological problem.

campus of Reformed Theological Seminary of Jackson, MS. I would join him, and RTS/Orlando, in 2000.

Replacing Al in the NT department was Peter Jones. Peter, whose wife Rebecca is a daughter of Edmund and Jean Clowney, had served as a PCA missionary, mainly as a teacher in the French Reformed Seminary at Aix en Provence. He had a Th.M. from Harvard and a Ph.D. from Princeton Seminary. His youngest son became one of our boys' best friends.

H. David Schuringa joined us in practical theology, with an M.Div. from WTSP, a Th.M. from Calvin Seminary, and a Ph.D. from the Theological University of Kampen in the Netherlands.

Around this time, Jay Adams left the seminary to plant a church in South Carolina, assisted by his son-in-law Bill Slattery. Replacing him as head of the D.Min. program in preaching was Joseph A. ("Joey") Pipa, who had a Ph.D. from WTSP and twenty years of pastoral experience. He serves today as president of Greenville Presbyterian Theological Seminary, Taylors, SC.

After five years in the presidency, Bob Den Dulk decided to return to his family's almond-growing business in northern California. His successor as president was Bob Godfrey. While Den Dulk was primarily a fundraiser and administrator, Godfrey had a distinct theological agenda. Similar to J. Gresham Machen years before, Bob had been an activist in the Christian Reformed Church for orthodox theology, centered on the Reformed confessions. The CRC was in some turmoil at the time over the issue of women in church office. Godfrey maintained a vigorous presence in the denomination, arguing the traditional church position, that the offices should be open only to men. When the CRC opened all of its offices to women, Bob and a number of others left the denomination to found the United Reformed Churches of North America.[6] The ECRC and other conservative CRC churches also left to join the new denomination. In Bob's inaugural address, he stated the purpose of the seminary as promoting the teaching of the Reformed Creeds and Confessions, and resisting opposition to these teachings. It seemed to some of us to be a very "in-house" vision of the work of the seminary: a program for purifying the Reformed churches, rather than for reaching out to the non-Christian world.

Bob's vision of the seminary's work drew on Machen's passion for sound doctrine, and properly so. But at the beginning and throughout his presidency he did not seem to me to appreciate sufficiently the outward-facing dimension of the gospel—our witness to the world. Or that Westminster

---

6. I applauded Bob's leaving the CRC, but I thought, do we really need another denomination? Another wound in the body of Christ?

historically is not merely a defender of Reformed tradition, but was also a strong force for what I have called theological creativity within the bounds of orthodoxy.[7] Bob's view of theology was historically oriented: based on our study of the Reformed confessions and the Reformed theologians of the sixteenth and seventeenth centuries. He did not appreciate my own concept of theology, following that of John Murray: the direct application of Scripture to current questions.[8] Under Bob's leadership, the seminary took on more and more the qualities of the "truly Reformed," of whom I have spoken in earlier chapters. In this era, the operative description of WTSC was "confessionalist."

My Troubles

The Godfrey presidency accelerated forces at WTSC that would eventually make it necessary for me to leave. But those forces were developing years earlier.

In the mid-1970s, some of the friends of Cornelius Van Til became somewhat critical of my work in apologetics. Van Til himself liked my article "Van Til the Theologian" (1976), and I believe it was he who arranged to have it published as a booklet. But shortly afterward Van Til began to have second thoughts, influenced, I think, by some of the younger men who surrounded him. One of these was Jim Halsey, a student who undertook to write an article opposing my approach. I had no objection to anyone writing critiques of my efforts, but I noted something odd about Halsey's project. Although he was a student of mine, he never spoke to me personally about his difficulties with my thinking. I learned of his project indirectly. At one point, Jim's pastor actually came and posed questions to me that evidently came from Jim. The pastor and I were friends, and I answered the questions as best I could. But I wondered how much loss of communication there was in the movement between Halsey, his pastor, me, his pastor, and back to Halsey.

Sometime later, I walked into a faculty meeting and noticed that Bob Knudsen, then managing editor of the *Westminster Theological Journal*, was proofreading an article that mentioned my name in several places. When

---

7. Bob is the first president who did not earn a degree at Westminster (his M.Div. was from Gordon-Conwell). For all my complaints about the ingrownness of Reformed faculties, I think this was a case in which an administrator was hindered by his lack of experience as a Westminster student.

8. Of course, this difference was a difference in degree. I do see value in historical theology, and Bob sees value in exegetical theology.

I tried to get a better look, Bob did his best to block my view. Eventually, the *Journal* came out, with Halsey's article in it. I have often taken a fairly positive view of negative responses to my work, but Halsey's I thought was inexcusably ignorant and inept in its argumentation. Nevertheless, I started hearing of people who were taking Halsey's critique of me with some seriousness. I responded to Halsey in my class lectures, and when I put together my *DKG* I criticized Halsey's article therein very thoroughly, refuting it (in my estimation, of course) about as fully as any article has ever been refuted.

Before I left for California, someone suggested that Halsey be hired as my replacement in Philadelphia. That move forced me to confront Halsey directly in a faculty interview and to challenge his argument. I was pleased that he was not offered the position.[9]

I thought that was the end of it all. But in 1985, in California, Meredith G. Kline asked to speak to me in my office. The conversation turned to apologetics, and Meredith indicated that he had been persuaded by Halsey's argument that I had not been true to Van Til. That disappointed me, for Meredith was one of the men I admired most as a Christian scholar, and I had thought we had a good relationship. But this incident confirmed an impression I had formed about him. Meredith was brilliant in his own field—I would never have dreamed of arguing with him on a point of Hebrew exegesis—but Meredith seemed to think that his pre-eminence as an Old Testament scholar made him an expert in many other fields as well, not least apologetics. I thought, however, that his reasoning was far less cogent in apologetics than it was in OT studies. I offered him the unpublished manuscript of *DKG* in which I had confronted Halsey's arguments with, I thought, some care. To my surprise, however, Kline refused the offer. So although he was willing to take Halsey's arguments at face value, he was not willing to give any attention to my replies to those arguments.

We parted as brothers and as colleagues, but I believe we each regarded the other with less admiration than before the meeting. As a student I had looked up to Meredith as a major example of "creativity within the bounds of orthodoxy." In his courses, he had been very critical of "traditional views," trying to correct the traditions by a closer reading of Scripture. In that stance he had attracted critics, but I thought he had dealt with those criticisms graciously and cogently. But his criticisms of me did not seem to make any allowance for differences over apologetics. In fact, I did and still do differ with Van Til over some matters, which I discussed at some length in

---

9. My replacement was David W. Clowney, the son of Edmund Clowney, who remained at WTSP until 1988, when he left in disagreement with the seminary's view of women in office.

the book *Cornelius Van Til: An Analysis of his Thought*.[10] But I thought that given Westminster's embrace of creativity, most notably in the work of Kline himself, the school could look at minor differences as points of academic discussion, rather than as challenges to Reformed orthodoxy.

After our meeting, I hoped again that would be the end of it. But Meredith wrote a letter to President Strimple complaining about my alleged unfaithfulness to the Van Tillian tradition.[11] Strimple did not seem to be much impressed. Kline only spent one semester a year on the WTSC campus; the rest of the year he spent in Massachusetts. When Strimple got the letter, Kline was gone. So Strimple told me that he intended to treat the matter with "benign neglect."[12]

So the discussion stopped for a few years. But I began to hear suspicions from some students about a more serious matter, the orthodoxy of my own work. I came to believe that Kline had influenced these suspicions. Kline's problems with my work were not limited to my apologetic approach. I came to see more and more that Kline also saw me as too close to Greg Bahnsen and to Norman Shepherd, to whom he had developed strong antipathy in the late 1970s. I had never been a follower of either man, but I thought the conventional criticisms of them (including Kline's) were overblown.[13] But Kline evidently expected his colleagues to follow him very closely, both in convictions and in attitude. Although Kline had once been a model of creativity within the bounds of orthodoxy, he had come to routinely oppose such creativity in others, at least when they differed with his ideas.

Around 1990, there was something of a student revolt against my teaching. Several began "bad mouthing" me outside of class, attacking my intellectual competence, my theological position, and my character.

While Kline had objected that I was not Van Tillian enough, these students seemed to think that I was *too* Van Tillian. They objected that I did not give equal time to non-presuppositional approaches.[14] If they had listened

---

10. Phillipsburg, NJ: P&R, 1995.

11. I look back on this complaint with some irony. Doubtless Meredith was pleased to see me leave WTSC in 2000. But my successor in apologetics, Michael Horton, had spent many years as a well-known critic of Van Til. And although after 2000 he found some things to commend in Van Til's work, WTSC has never since been known as a center of Van Tillian presuppositionalism. I wonder if Kline ever took Horton aside to complain that his allegiance to Van Til was not Simon-pure.

12. This was Daniel Patrick Moynihan's phrase for the way the government should respond to demands for more welfare programs.

13. On Bahnsen/theonomy, see the treatment in my *DCL*. On Shepherd, see the discussion of justification in my *ST*, and my reflections in chapter 6 of the present volume.

14. This criticism of me evidently got to the ears of an accreditation team, which

to me more carefully, they would have known that my purpose in the course was not to explore all the different views of apologetics, as a college course in comparative apologetics might try to do, but to equip students with what I considered the most biblical strategy for engaging non-Christian thought.

But there was one fairly public incident. During a lecture I gave in the Modern Mind course, a student went off the subject and began to criticize me on a highly personal level. My positions and arguments, he said, were not sufficient to deal with the objections to presuppositionalism, and my teaching methods were not helpful in preparing the students to be good apologists. Student after student arose to agree with these criticisms. I tried to hear all of this with grace, to accept it for what it was worth, and I offered little or no self-defense. But I was devastated.[15] Apparently there was a group of around ten students who shared these negative evaluations of my work. One of those was Michael Horton.

While these students were with us, the student evaluations of my courses turned negative, more negative than ever before or since. Dennis Johnson, then academic dean, was greatly disturbed by this, and he told me that President Den Dulk was disturbed as well. I'm pleased to say, however, that after this group of students graduated, the evaluations rose again to the high favorability rating they had enjoyed before. In fact, I believe that I was known as a fairly superior teacher. John Sowell, our student recruiter and director of admissions, frequently asked me to speak at prospective student conferences. He announced to the faculty that when students described what had drawn them to WTSC, they most often mentioned (1) the counseling program and (2) John Frame's teaching.

But I needed to rethink some things in my own life and thought. Sensing some confusion about my apologetic position, among people who should have known better, I reviewed all of Van Til's writings and produced two books in the middle of the decade. *Apologetics to the Glory of God*[16] came out in 1994 and would be my regular apologetics text.[17] The other book was a study of Van Til himself, *Cornelius Van Til: An Analysis of His Thought*, published in 1995, the hundredth anniversary of his birth.[18]

---

contributed to some of their negative criticisms of the seminary.

15. I grant that this occurred during a decline in mental sharpness. I was developing symptoms of sleep apnea and was far from my best, especially during the afternoon when the Modern Mind course was held.

16. Phillipsburg, NJ: P&R, 1994.

17. 2014 was the twentieth anniversary of *AGG*. We celebrated by bringing out a new edition of the book (2014), with notes and additional articles by my good friend Joseph Torres.

18. This book deals not only with Van Til as an apologist, but with his overall

I was happy that Sowell found me to be popular among prospective students. But after students came to WTSC, their affection for me did not always continue. I began to notice that students often came to WTSC in part to get my teaching, and they greatly enjoyed their first-year experience in my Christian Mind course. But in the second and third years they soured on me somewhat.

Part of the problem was that in the 1990s the seminary community grew factionalized. A number of professors accumulated groups of adoring students who agreed with everything they said. I was one of the few professors who had no such group, in part because I discouraged the formation of such groups.

Joseph Pipa's entourage was one example. He joined the faculty in 1990 as the head of our D.Min. program in preaching, replacing Jay Adams. On arrival, he announced that he was planting a church. I questioned whether Escondido needed another Reformed church, in addition to the ECRC and New Life. But Dick Kaufmann, as was his custom, looked on the bright side: Escondido really needed about eighty churches, to take advantage of all the evangelistic opportunities and to reach the population/church ratio of the early 1900s. I agreed, of course, that if the new church were truly evangelistic, then it would more than justify its existence. But Joey's vision was different from Dick's.

When Joey began the Bible study that led to the formation of Trinity PCA, almost immediately people began to question me, asking "Why do you reject the regulative principle of worship?" Where, I wondered, did that come from? In my own mind, I did not *reject* the regulative principle (namely that everything in worship must have biblical warrant), but I did reject some traditional applications of it.[19] Lay people generally don't come up with issues like this on their own. Most likely, it seemed to me, Joey had implicitly or explicitly been criticizing my approach to worship and that of New Life. When Trinity began services, they were designed to be "historically Reformed," "reverent," "simple," musically minimalist and traditional. A number of people from New Life who preferred a more historical approach to worship and church life left New Life and joined Trinity. In my opinion, that movement left New Life weaker.

---

theology, including topics like common grace and divine incomprehensibility. I honestly think I have solved the "Clark Controversy," but not many partisans on either side seem to agree. If you are trying to choose between this book and *Van Til's Apologetics* (Phillipsburg: P&R, 1998), published about the same time by the late Greg Bahnsen, remember that Bahnsen's book deals more narrowly with apologetic matters, while mine is more broadly theological. And Bahnsen is less critical of Van Til than I am.

19. For my account of the regulative principle, see *DCL*, 450–86.

Sometime in 1997, Peter Jones, sensing that there were some divisions within the faculty, proposed a faculty discussion of "hermeneutics." I went to the meeting prepared to speak about theology as application, perspectivalism, and the like. But Joey and others more or less hijacked the meeting to discuss the regulative principle. I hadn't been prepared for that, but a number of speeches were made evidently directed against me. It seemed to me that this meeting could become (typical of Westminster) the beginning of a larger theological controversy, like the Shepherd issue. At that point, I announced to the group that if my theological position were to become seriously controversial I would not stay at the seminary, hashing it out for seven or eight years as Norman had done. Rather, I would immediately send out my résumé and seek a new position.

At that point, I would almost have welcomed a call from another seminary. But Bob Strimple and Bob Godfrey took me out to lunch and told me quite clearly that they wanted me to stay, and they did not see anything in my theology that should lead me to separate from Westminster. At that point I assured them that I had no plans to leave and would not leave because of Joey's accusations.

But there were other factions as well. Jim Dennison, the librarian, taught courses in Bible and preaching. Often his sermons in chapel were magnificent examples of careful research, thoughtful illustrations, and Christ-centered focus. His view of Christ-centeredness was similar to that of Clowney and Bergsma: the preacher is to focus on how every text bears witness to Christ. I loved Jim's preaching and was glad that the students had access to his example, though I doubted that most busy pastors would be able to do the intensive research Jim expended on his sermons. But as I often do, I found more to praise in what Jim was for than in what he was against. He hated preaching that was centered on morals, culture, or on the "how-tos" of the Christian life.[20] That sort of preaching he discounted as "moralism."[21]

Jim gathered around him a good number of students, many of them Korean or Korean-American, who accepted everything Jim said as gospel and who rejected anything that contradicted Jim's approach or de-emphasized Jim's distinctives.

Meredith Kline also gathered a faction. These were students who, like me in 1961–64, were dazzled by Kline's exegetical footwork and deeply impressed by the creativity and thoughtfulness of his proposals. But unlike 1961–64, Kline had developed also a sharp polemical tone against those

---

20. By contrast, Jay Adams encouraged students to preach on the "how tos."
21. For my evaluation of this controversy, see my *DCL*, 29–32, 271–97.

he took to be his opponents, and he came to equate his views dogmatically with Reformed orthodoxy. Whether he named them or not, therefore, it was plain that anyone who opposed his distinctive ideas was an enemy, not only of Kline, but of the Reformed faith itself. Many students climbed on board the Kline bandwagon and were prepared to do battle with anyone whom they thought was inadequately Klinian.

Another faction developed toward the end of the 1990s. In 1997, R. Scott Clark joined us as academic dean and professor of historical theology. I thought that Scott had been a good friend of mine during his student years in the 1980s. He often visited my office then, and we'd talk in a friendly way about biblical and theological matters. He then became a pastor in the very conservative Reformed Church in the United States.[22] When some people in that denomination attacked my orthodoxy and that of the seminary, Scott defended me. But then Scott went to England and obtained a D.Phil. from Oxford University, writing a dissertation on Caspar Olievianus. He has said that his studies in Reformed historical theology convinced him that the distinctives of my teaching were non-Reformed and therefore seriously wrong. Scott's history-of-doctrine focus was essentially the type of confessionalist theology Bob Godfrey wanted the seminary to exemplify.[23] Scott led a sizable faction of students to agree with his position. Thus, another faction was born.

I was, alas, not part of any of these factions. I discouraged students from starting any faction in my name. But for the most part the students needed no discouragement on that account. My teaching was the target of the other factions. All of them claimed to speak for "truly Reformed" orthodoxy, and whatever else they believed, they were convinced that I was not in that category. And, as I have described truly Reformed orthodoxy elsewhere in the book, they were right. I was not "truly" Reformed and did not want to be.

To be honest, I should also say that I was not as persuasive to the students as were the party leaders. I tried to avoid contradicting any of my colleagues, because I was trying to maintain the collegiality that I had

---

22. This denomination is a remnant of an old German Reformed denomination. When that denomination merged with other bodies, the RCUS stayed out.

23. In his book, *Recovering the Reformed Confession* (Phillipsburg, NJ: P&R, 2008), Clark sets forth his distinctive position. In his view, theology should be primarily a study of the Confessions and of the classic Reformed theologians of the sixteenth and seventeenth centuries. For him, theology is a species of church history. For my reply, see my review of this book in my *TET*. For the similar viewpoint expressed by Richard A. Muller in *The Study of Theology* (Grand Rapids: Zondervan, 1991) see my review article "Muller on Theology," *WTJ* 56.1 (1994), 438–442 (http://www.frame-poythress.org/muller-on-theology/).

boasted of in the 1980s. And when I did set forth my own positions, the factionalized students listened to me as they might listen to Arius, Pelagius, or Arminius. They began with general disagreement, and they sought to identify particular points they could argue against. Not the best atmosphere for teaching God's word.

There were a few students who defended me. Among those my readers might know are Greg Welty, my teaching assistant for four years, who after seminary earned his doctorate in philosophy with Richard Swinburne at Oxford. He now teaches philosophy at Southeastern Baptist Seminary. Steve Hays, another good friend and teaching assistant, helped to develop Triablogue, probably the most thoughtful, interesting blog in evangelicalism. Phil Marshall was also my teaching assistant and, having completed a Ph.D. at the Southern Baptist Seminary, is now a professor of Old Testament at Houston Baptist University. Mike Kruger, after finishing his doctorate at the University of Edinburgh became professor of New Testament, and then president of RTS in Charlotte. These men were the best thinkers at WTSC, and significantly they were not wedded to any of the factions.

But many others were faction-bound. Often a student would be very thankful to me for my teaching after the first-year Christian Mind course. But in his second year (after courses with my colleagues) he would come to me with "concerns." I could satisfy some of those concerns, but not all of them.

The factionalism actually resolved itself somewhat toward the end of the decade. Joey Pipa left the seminary in 1997 when WTSC discontinued the D.Min. program in preaching. He became president of Greenville Presbyterian Theological Seminary in Greenville, SC. Jim Dennison later left the seminary to plant the new Northwest Theological Seminary in Lynnwood, WA. So two factions largely dissipated.

The D.Min. program was replaced by an academic degree program in historical theology. I am not opposed to historical theology, but I expected the program to become a hotbed of the Godfrey-Clark focus I complained of earlier. That happened, and so the history faction grew stronger and in effect joined forces with the Kline faction. The key to the merger between these two factions was a man who joined the faculty in 1998, Michael Horton.

Horton was recommended to us as "the most famous graduate of Westminster in California," and indeed he was. Even before he studied with us, he was known as an author, speaker, and leader of movements. He founded *Modern Reformation Magazine* and the radio discussion program *White Horse Inn*. After his seminary graduation, he wrote a number of books and eventually earned a doctorate at Wycliffe Hall, Oxford (through Coventry University) in England. Theologically he was a close disciple of Kline and

Godfrey, and he attracted many students to Westminster who were his close followers. After the war of the factions, it was this Kline-Godfrey-Clark-Horton faction that won out.

And there were a number of us that lost out in the new configuration. Even before 1999, it had become evident that there was no room at the seminary for teachers who were not considered adequately confessionalist. In the late 1980s, Dick Kaufmann had resigned from his course in evangelism after a visit from Bob Godfrey, who criticized him for assigning readings to students from the "church growth" school. I thought even then that if the seminary had no room for Dick, it probably had no room for me either.

In the mid-1990s, David Schuringa was asked to leave, for reasons I never entirely understood. Part of it was this: David had gotten involved in ministry to prisoners, and he had planted an independent church called Wellspring, intending to provide for released prisoners a welcoming congregation. But some at WTSC had objected to the idea of an independent church.[24] David later served for some years as president of Crossroads Bible Institute, which ministers to prisoners and their families through Bible study.

In 1998, Mark Futato left us in the aftermath of a family crisis. The Futatos had developed illnesses because of Dyazinon poisoning: a highly toxic insecticide had leaked from the garage to the home through the air ducts. No traditional doctors were able to help. But there was a naturopathic physician who gave them some relief. She was an evangelical Christian, but she advocated some types of treatment that were not sanctioned by traditional medicine. At Mark's recommendation, a friend went to one of her seminars, but he reacted very negatively to her teaching, and declared her to be "new age." Then he accused Mark of theological error, because he had recommended her.[25] This incident threatened to become another Westminster "case," like the Clark Case and the Shepherd Case. Hearings were held at New Life, at the seminary, in the presbytery. Papers were written. Mark was given the improbable job of writing an analysis and evaluation of his doctor's theology. And so it went on.[26] God rescued the Futatos, however, by the intervention of Reformed Theological Seminary, where we both happily

---

24. For my view of independent churches and such, see my *ER* (http://www.evangelicalreunion.org/).

25. Mark recommended her, not as a theologian, of course, but as one who might have some useful ideas about health and healing.

26. There's an old saying that "if all you have is a hammer, everything looks like a nail." To WTSC and the Reformed churches, everything looked like a theological controversy.

serve today. RTS offered a contract to Mark to teach Hebrew and Old Testament, and that was the end of that.

In 1999, however, it was my turn.

There was a student named Josh, a close follower of Horton and Clark. After he took my first-year course, he gathered signatures for a petition. Once when he was in my office on another matter, I asked him about the petition. He seemed aghast that I would actually ask him about that, and he searched for words. "Oh," he said, "that had *nothing* to do with *you*. We were only asking the seminary to replace Christian Mind with a traditional prolegomena course . . . without triperspectivalism." I was not entirely successful in concealing my laughter. Josh wanted the seminary to replace my course with another course, taught, presumably, by someone other than me, who would not share my basic approach, . . . and that had nothing to do with me!? Nothing!?

In August 1999, Bob Godfrey showed me a letter from Josh to the faculty. He had received it in May, but for some reason had not shown it to me for three months. Josh made all sorts of accusations against my academic competence, theological orthodoxy, and Christian character, all of them false, confusing, or half-true. He also managed to get another student to write a similar letter, a student who had my course three years before Josh, but who somehow remembered me as saying the exact same heretical things. It was all baloney, and I wrote a letter to Bob, refuting these letters very thoroughly. Neither Josh nor the other student had talked to me before sending out these letters, and for that reason Bob Godfrey proposed the letters be kept, but not discussed in faculty. At that point, Josh determined to write a similar letter to the board, a course Bob evidently talked him out of.

But early in the fall, Scott Clark, whom many of us thought was far too inexperienced to be an academic dean, summarized to the faculty some exit interviews of seniors that he had taken in the spring. The most significant finding was that John Frame and Peter Jones were "unconfessional." Peter was furious, and protested eloquently that he had expended huge efforts in the defense of the Reformed faith. Since nobody took Peter's side, I chimed in, making a similar defense of Peter and of myself, and wondering aloud whether it wasn't time to make good on my 1997 pledge to leave WTSC if my theological position was challenged.

I then composed a letter, trying to explain to my colleagues more fully what my theological position was, why it had been challenged, and why I found myself uncomfortable in the new confessionalist version of WTSC. The letter went way too far. I said many things that I later regretted and for which I later apologized. The letter contained negative reflections on some colleagues and some students by name. I should have known better, and I offer no excuse here.

But the letter had burned all bridges between me and WTSC. Godfrey told me in a letter that my apology was "too short."[27] From then on, nothing I said or did would help. I was a pariah on the WTSC campus, though a very few continued to speak cordially to me. Peter Jones continued to treat me as a friend. Bob Strimple took me to lunch to suggest that I should try to stay at the school, but he emphasized that he would not try to twist my arm, and he did not.[28] Ed Clowney called to say that it would be better for me to leave; he himself left in March of 2000 to join the staff of a Texas church. He said that even if I escaped the ongoing controversy I would likely be charged by Scott Clark with heresy over the doctrine of the Trinity.[29] Later, George Scipione asked his colleagues to speak to me in my office and urge me to stay. But none came by. None even offered to counsel and pray with me.

Godfrey set up a couple meetings to promote "reconciliation," but those could not have been less conducive to that goal. They mostly consisted of attacks on me, accusing me of every ill that had befallen the school: I had divided the community by attending New Life rather than ECRC, I had slowed donations by "teaching a non-Reformed view of worship", and so on. When I thought it appropriate, I would ask forgiveness. But forgiveness rarely came. Bob's purpose at these meetings was to reiterate that WTSC was a confessionalist school, and that my teaching was out of accord with confessionalism.

In my own mind, I did not disagree with the Reformed confessions, except in minor ways.[30] Indeed, nobody pointed out any specific area where I had violated my vow to uphold the confessions. No specific charges against my orthodoxy were ever registered. The opposition to me, rather, concerned the personal offenses for which I had confessed sin, and also my lack of adherence to Reformed traditions in worship, church life, and teach-

---

27. I wondered about the tax collector, who repented of his sins by saying "God, be merciful to me, a sinner" (Luke 18:13). I tried to imagine God replying to him, "sorry, but your repentance was too short."

28. Not one person, including Godfrey, actually urged me to stay. The public statement by the seminary released on my departure claimed that I had been asked to stay and refused. That was hugely misleading. As I mentioned earlier, I had been asked to stay in 1997 during my skirmish with Joey Pipa, and I had indeed stayed for two years after that. But 1999 was a different controversy, and nobody urged me to stay that year.

29. Believe it or not, Clark's complaint about my doctrine of the Trinity was that I defended Van Til's position. For that defense, see my *DG*, 703–4. At one time, Van Til was the very criterion of orthodoxy at Westminster. This was the beginning of a slide in Van Til's status. Today one rarely hears anything about Van Til from WTSC.

30. See "My Exceptions to the Westminster Standards" in my *SSW* 2.

ing emphasis.³¹ One colleague brought up my vote in support of Shepherd's orthodoxy twenty years before. But no one had any idea of the specific issue that I voted on at that time.³²

Nobody, friend or opponent, made any effort to understand my position or to build a bridge between colleagues in these matters.³³ Not one board member called to ask why I was leaving WTSC. They all evidently bought the administration line without question.

The bottom line was the same as at Blue Bell Church in 1979: they did not respect my Reformed commitment. Now some of them thought perhaps that I did not care about the Reformed faith, that I did not care whether colleagues considered me to be Reformed or not. But I did care, very much, and still do. I could never teach at a school that did not respect the Reformed character of my work.

I think that any honest and well-informed reader of my books will acknowledge their Reformed character. But I do not endorse idiosyncratic versions of Reformed theology validated only by parochial traditions. That is to say, I am Reformed, but not "truly" Reformed. And that is why I left Westminster.³⁴

Making the Break

The decision to leave WTSC is one of the hardest I have ever made. It marked the end of the missionary adventure I had begun in 1980. I had experienced many good times over the twenty years since, at Westminster and at New Life, and there would be no more. Still, moving away seemed by November 1999 to be a necessary step. There was no alternative, and it had to be done without flinching. That removed much of the difficulty from me individually. But the change would certainly be more difficult for my family.

Mary had read the terrible letter I wrote to my colleagues. She would have wisely advised me not to write it and, having written it, not to send it.

---

31. That is, in my teaching I emphasized the Bible more than the confessions and historical theologians.

32. Review chapter 6.

33. After I left, a friend sent me an article written by a psychologist about "mobbing." Mobbing often occurs in an office, in which everybody singles out one person and blames him for all the difficulties that have taken place, without any regard for facts or evidence. It was nice to have a word that I could apply to what happened to me at WTSC.

34. The above account sets forth accurately the factors leading to my departure, as I remember them. But it is not exhaustive. There were other matters, especially personal matters, that led to my decision and those of my colleagues.

But once I reached the point of no return, she accepted our situation with grace and gladly undertook the enormous extra workload that fell to her. She took charge of cleaning, repairing, and selling our house in Escondido. She also brought to a graceful end the ministries we were involved in. And she continued to home school our two boys. She went with me to Orlando on two occasions to meet with people in our new venue and to help me buy a new house, as I shall narrate in the next chapter.

My dear wife had moved six times before. She was positive about only one of these, our move to California in 1984. She was always sad that she could not live closer to her family. Now we would be scattering the family even more. We would move away from California, leaving Debbie, Doreen, and Skip on the West Coast. That brought agony to Mary in 1999 and has been a great sadness to her ever since. She had hoped to be a good grandmother, to have a close continuing relationship with her grandkids. Since the move, she has visited them many times, but that has not been nearly enough.

Our move also brought an end to our ministry to homeless people. And our homeschool support group would never meet again.

The boys would lose many of their home school friends, and friends from the North San Diego Soccer Leagues. Toward the end, Toby Jones (Peter and Rebecca's son), one of their best friends, visited with us, and I drove him back home for the last time. He wept deeply, and I wept with him. Something good was coming to an end, and for no really sufficient reason.

The boys would have to stop their lessons in piano and strings, with their wonderful music teachers. After the move, they would not find any comparable teachers, and the boys would abandon classical music.

We would not worship again together at New Life. And I would lead worship only very rarely afterward.

My truly Reformed colleagues thought that by expelling me they were ridding their community of a near-heretic, and that would be a good thing. The report was that after I left there was much more unity on the WTSC campus. Of course, there is always more peace, after a fashion, when all the dissenters leave. So perhaps my leaving was a good thing for the seminary, as it was for me. But I don't believe it was good for Mary, or Justin, or Johnny, or for our friends at church, or our homeschooling friends, or for our homeless friends. My break with WTSC ended a number of good things. That fact deserves to be recorded and noted, not just the theological issues. Our life in Escondido was, as David Wells said of eighteenth-century Wenham, MA, a "delicious Paradise lost."

I have no bitterness, however, toward WTSC or toward the faculty there. WTSC was not obligated to preserve for the Frames a paradise in

Escondido. I pray only the best for their ministry. They have done much for the kingdom, and will continue to do so. WTSC stands for Christ and the gospel, and in that I rejoice. I am sad that the school missed a major opportunity. Southern California is still a very secular area, much in need of evangelism. It needs also an outward-facing, missionally focused seminary. Unfortunately, WTSC embraced a type of Reformed theology that is focused in on defending one Reformed tradition and community rather than the work of making disciples in the unbelieving world. Of course, the "truly Reformed" community has as much right to have a seminary as anyone else, to supply their churches with pastors. And certainly their work is much better than nothing. So despite our differences, I support them in prayer, and I look forward to seeing what God will do with this ministry to which I gave twenty years of my life.

Still, I maintain the right to comment theologically on the issues that stood between us. As a teacher of theology, I consider that to be part of my job. Such comments can be found in this volume, and in a number of my other books.[35]

---

35. Particularly *DCL*, *ST*, and *TET*.

9

Winsomely Reformed at RTS

FROM TIME TO TIME over my years in California I had received invitations to move elsewhere. In 1988, Bob Knudsen called to ask if I would be interested to return to WTSP after Dave Clowney's departure. I said no, I was quite happy at WTSC, and at the time that was entirely true. Also in 1999, when my position at WTSC was imploding, I was able to tell my colleagues that I was already in conversation with another seminary about a position there.

Trinity Evangelical Divinity School

That seminary was Trinity Evangelical Divinity School in Deerfield, IL. Several men on that faculty were former students of mine: Wayne Grudem, Kevin Vanhoozer, Willem VanGemeren; and others knew my work well (Don Carson, John Woodbridge). Trinity had expressed interest in me before that time, and there was much about the school that appealed to me. My sister Martie and her family lived in nearby Northbrook. Trinity's scholarship was first-rate. I also thought (as the WTSC people kept telling me) that I might be happier in a school that was more broadly evangelical than Westminster—a school that did not seek to be "truly Reformed." Trinity was a seminary of the Evangelical Free Church of America. Many of the faculty were Reformed (such as those named above), though some were not. But I thought I could easily be comfortable there.

The only theological rule at Trinity was the short doctrinal statement of the Evangelical Free Church. Most of the statements in it were easy for me to agree with. But I had some difficulty subscribing to one statement that affirmed the premillennial return of Jesus. At Westminster, most of the teaching in eschatology had been amillennial, though John Murray had veered toward postmillennialism toward the end of his life. I was myself somewhat inclined to postmillennialism, but I had never taught eschatology at the seminary level, and I had never thought that any of the millennial positions was so clearly taught in Scripture as to be a valid test of orthodoxy.

When I talked to one of my friends at Trinity, he told me that the premillennial statement should not be a problem: the school did not take it seriously. But later Wayne Grudem talked to me about it, and he assured me that the statement was indeed taken seriously. I would either have to confess premillennialism, or I would have to go through some process that would allow me to take exception to it. Wayne actually spent maybe a half hour on the phone trying to convince me to be a premillennialist. Actually his arguments were pretty good. He pointed out to me some Bible passages in which it seemed as though God was personally ruling on the earth, but his enemies had not yet been finally judged. Could these refer to the millennium period?

But issues like this typically take me a long time to muddle through. I concluded that I could not and should not consider a doctrinal change in the midst of a job search.[1] I told that to Wayne, and we ended the call cordially.

Trinity, however, was not ready to leave me alone. Someone there set up a plan whereby I would become a kind of visiting professor, as John Gerstner had done years before. I received in the mail a large amount of paper, representing all the hoops I would have to go through in order to achieve that status. For even if I reconciled myself to becoming a visiting professor, I would still have to persuade many administrators and representatives of the faculty and church that I was fit to teach theology at Trinity. And, for all of that, in none of those sheets of paper did this program mention the possibility that I could actually take exception to the church's premillennial position.

In the course of this discussion, I received a five-page letter from Kenneth Kantzer, the retired academic dean, who had put Trinity on the map of academically advanced seminaries. Kantzer urged me to accept the invitation to join the faculty of the seminary. He said that when he became dean years before the seminary had promised him that the premillennial statement would never be used to inhibit him from choosing the best faculty available.

I considered it a privilege to receive this letter and affirmation. I greatly respected Kantzer, one of the giants in American Evangelicalism. My book

1. I recalled a Presbyterian student of mine of some years past, who with the speed of lightning became a Baptist when a job offer came his way. I was resolved not to do that.

Perspectives on the Word of God[2] consists of lectures that I gave at Trinity around 1989 in honor of Dr. Kantzer. But I thought that evidently there had been a problem of communication between him and the current administrators of Trinity who in the stack of papers I received certainly made my teaching at Trinity contingent on my full acceptance of the EFCA statement.

So I thanked Trinity for their interest in me and turned in other directions. During this period I also received some tentative feelers from Covenant Seminary in St. Louis, affiliated with the PCA, and from the ministries in Moscow, ID, associated with Christ Church there, where Douglas Wilson is pastor. But the final destination of my search turned out to be Reformed Theological Seminary.

Reformed Theological Seminary

My memories of RTS go back to its founding in the 1960s. In my senior year as a student at WTSP, Morton H. Smith taught practical theology as an adjunct professor. I took his course in Public Worship, and it was from him that I first learned about the Reformed regulative principle of worship. His argument was not very persuasive to me, and it took some mental anguish before I thought I could embrace this doctrine. Some think my formulation is not true to the regulative principle; I think it is. But to say so requires a bit of "creativity within the bounds of orthodoxy." Morton Smith doubtless rejects the reformulation of that principle found in my books.[3] Still I thought he was a good teacher on the whole, and our relationship was cordial. In the mid-1960s, when I was at Yale, I received notice that Morton and others were starting a Reformed seminary to serve the southern states, as Westminster had served the north. Though I was only a poor graduate student, I sent them a little money, and thereby I got on to a mailing list from which I have never been dropped.[4] From then on, I was fairly well informed about developments at RTS. It became my second seminary.

RTS began in Jackson, MS, in 1966, in the wake of much prayer for the spiritual condition of the churches of Southern Presbyterianism. In 1989, it established a daughter campus in Orlando, FL. It now has nine campuses, the rest located in Charlotte, NC, Washington, DC, Atlanta, GA, Memphis, TN, Dallas and Houston, TX, and, New York City. Richard Pratt was one of

---

2. Phillipsburg, NJ: P&R, 1990.
3. See especially *DCL*, 464–86.
4. At seminaries, professors are dispensable, but contributors are not. President Reagan once said that the closest thing to immortality on earth is a "temporary" government program. I nominate seminary donor mailing lists for second place.

the teachers that moved from Jackson to Orlando. He had been a student of mine at WTSP. We had corresponded several times, and I recommended his introductory apologetics book *Every Thought Captive*.[5] In the late 1980s, I received a packet of letters from students at RTS/Jackson. Richard had assigned to them parts of my *DKG*, and he evidently urged them to write me thank-you notes for the book. I was encouraged and delighted to get them.

In following years, I heard some reports connecting me with RTS/Orlando. (1) Evidently some student recruiter there was telling prospective students that RTS was planning to offer me a position.[6] At the time I heard that rumor with much curiosity and, I confess, some hope. I was not eager to leave WTSC until 1999, but I was becoming increasingly uncomfortable there through the 1990s, and I might well have accepted a position at RTS if it had been offered to me.

(2) Luder Whitlock, president of RTS, whom I had known as a fellow student at WTSP, had a conversation with Bob Godfrey in which he presented to Bob the rumor that WTSC was trying to get rid of me. Bob insisted then (maybe around 1995) that there was no truth to that rumor. But Bob did call me into his office to discuss it. I told Bob that I did not feel that way,[7] and I had not told anybody else that I did. What I had said to some people was that I thought that WTSC had made a sharp right turn toward traditionalism and confessionalism, and I was having a hard time handling it. Bob told me not to worry. He was happy to have a variety of views represented at the seminary, including mine.[8]

I mentioned earlier that Allen Mawhinney, academic dean at WTSC from 1980–89, left for a similar position at the founding of RTS/Orlando. Sometime in 1997, the Mawhinneys visited Escondido, and my wife and I had lunch with them. I shared with Allen some of my problems (then mainly problems with Joey Pipa's faction). Allen said that there were no positions open at RTS. But, he said, if I ever decided to leave WTSC I should contact him. Some days later, he called me from Orlando, asking if he had "dropped the ball" on a potential opportunity for RTS to get me. By then, Bob Strimple and Bob Godfrey had taken me to lunch, assuring me that they wanted me to stay despite Joey's challenges. So I told Allen, as I had told the two Bobs, that I intended to stay in Escondido for the foreseeable future, but if I ever changed my mind I would certainly call Allen.

---

5. Phillipsburg, NJ: P&R, 1979.

6. Since my move, I asked about this to friends at RTS, and they have all confessed ignorance about it.

7. Though, of course, I did feel that way in 1999.

8. In 1999 his viewpoint would not be so tolerant.

Then came 1999. Although I had been talking to Trinity, I thought it would be wise for me to see what might transpire with RTS. So I called Allen and told him that I was no longer able to stay at WTSC. We talked a bit about the circumstances. He asked if I had any of the RTS campuses in mind, in particular. (At the time, there were Jackson, Orlando, and Charlotte.) I replied that I thought the Orlando campus was the liveliest of the three, but if there is no opening there I would be happy to think about going elsewhere in the RTS system. Shortly afterward I had phone and email communications with Richard Pratt and Luder Whitlock. Richard gave me a much-needed opportunity to hash out the whole ugly situation with a good friend.

Luder presented his vision for RTS. He said that RTS was unapologetically Reformed, but had good relationships with all evangelicals. They had good relationships with the local Episcopal diocese and students from there, and they also, amazingly, had good relations with Anglicans who were fleeing the Episcopal Church to form new parts of the Anglican Communion. There were a number of Baptists in the student body,[9] and Independents. A number of RTS students and professors were involved with the 8,000-member megachurch, Northland. Some of them were also involved in the ministry of First Presbyterian Church, Orlando, a conservative congregation within the liberal PCUSA denomination. The headquarters of Campus Crusade, Wycliffe Bible Translators, and Pioneers Mission were in the area, and RTS had good relationships with them too. I saw this as a kind of ecumenism I had never experienced at either Westminster,[10] a strong affinity with my *Evangelical Reunion*.

Two of the older professors, Roger Nicole and Charles MacKenzie, favored women's ordination, a position that would never have been tolerated at either Westminster. I disagreed with their view, but both men were very distinguished and effective defenders of the Reformed faith, and I was glad that their view of women's ordination did not prevent their teaching at RTS. RTS took these issues seriously, but they resolved them with an ecumenical spirit far beyond that at WTSP and WTSC.

Common at RTS was the slogan, "We're Reformed, but not angry." In the PCA, people were inclined to classify people as TR, "truly Reformed" (i.e., demanding duplication of some historical movement) and BR, "barely Reformed" (i.e., Reformed in name only). RTS designated itself WR,

---

9. Roger Nicole, who taught systematics, had been a Baptist for many years.

10. I recalled that once at WTSC the faculty rejected a candidate for a staff position, on the ground that she was a member of a conservative PCUSA church.

"winsomely Reformed." That was how I wanted to be known. And it was a substantive contrast from self-descriptions typically heard at WTSC.

Luder also told me of the entrepreneurial spirit of RTS. In addition to the campuses at Jackson, Orlando, and Charlotte, RTS had extension centers in Atlanta and Washington, DC, and they hoped to develop a large association of seminaries throughout the southeast.[11]

Luder's vision touched my heart, and from that time I deeply hoped that God would allow me to join the faculty of RTS.

The Transition

By mid-November of 1999, Bob Godfrey's "reconciliation" meetings were over, and I felt free to proceed forward with RTS. Peter Jones urged me to wait, to undergo a "process" before resigning from WTSC. What kind of process? A heresy trial? I wasn't about to do that. Besides, the faculty rules at WTSC required anyone resigning their position to give the seminary five-months' notice. Since the new academic year began in July, I would have had to resign by January if I were to accept other employment in July. So there was no time for a "process," and frankly I had had my fill of Westminster "processes."

The first step was for Mary and me to visit RTS in Orlando. The only time that satisfied everybody was Thanksgiving week. We stayed in the Holiday Inn Select at University and Alafaya in Oviedo, near the University of Central Florida. On Sunday, our friend Allen Mawhinney came to take us to church. We went to an early service at St. Paul's PCA, which had good preaching (by Mike Malone), traditional music, and a liturgy that was rather formal for a Presbyterian church. Afterward, Allen took us to the church he regularly attended, Willow Creek PCA,[12] nearer the seminary. It was very different, with contemporary music and a sermon by Pete Alwinson aimed at reaching out to unchurched career people. We saw the Futatos also at Willow Creek. Then we had lunch with the Mawhinneys. Afterward, they gave us the keys to a large old Buick that had evidently been donated to the seminary, and we drove back to our hotel.

---

11. This kind of expansion was also uncharacteristic of WTSC. After the initial planting of a western campus of Westminster, WTSC passed on a number of opportunities to teach courses in other areas, such as in the Los Angeles area.

12. I was told the name of the church had nothing to do with Willow Creek Church in Illinois. There actually was a creek by that name in Winter Springs, where the PCA was located.

Confirming my sense that RTS should be our next step was the familiarity of the faculty. At that time the RTS/Orlando faculty included *seven* of my former students: Mawhinney (NT), Futato (OT), Richard Pratt (OT), Reggie Kidd (NT), Chuck Hill (NT), Frank James (church history), and John Muether (librarian). In addition, there was Luder, whom I have known since we were one year apart as Westminster students. There was also Steve Childers (practical theology) who told me when we met that he has been developing all his courses in a tri-perspectival way. There was Steve Brown (preaching), a former member of the WTSP board and a wonderful preacher of God's grace. Steve and I had corresponded about a friend of his who was held up unfairly as he sought to enter our presbytery in Southern California. I took the side of Steve's friend, and he thanked me. And on other RTS campuses there were Jim Hurley (counseling, Jackson), Mike Kruger (NT, Charlotte), John Sowell (head of the Atlanta extension), and Andy Peterson (head of the RTS distance learning operation). Allen Curry, whom I had known in Pittsburgh and Philadelphia, was academic dean of the Jackson campus. Hard to imagine that there would be so many people from my past. Certainly God arranged the reunion. For me, coming to RTS was like coming home.

There were others to whom I had not been introduced, but even among them there were "small world" echoes of my past life. Rick Gamble taught systematics. Rick and I had corresponded when he was at Calvin Seminary; he gave me a warning about somebody in Grand Rapids who was misrepresenting my views. When I met him in Orlando, he told Mary and me that he had grown up in the Pittsburgh area, not far from the church founded by Mary's dad. He greeted us warmly and prayed with us.

Scott Coupland taught counseling at RTS, but in a past life he had worked as a cowboy out West. One ranch he worked at was owned by a professing Christian, who invited children and teenagers to stay there for some days and weeks to get a feel of ranching life. Among those kids were ours: Debbie and Skip. I don't know if our kids ever met Scott, but we thought of that as another of many God-orchestrated coincidences.[13]

Charles Sherrard MacKenzie and I had never met formally, but I remembered him as a guest preacher at Beverly Heights sometime in 1965–66. "Sherry" was a distinguished philosopher who had been president of Grove City College and was humanly responsible for largely returning the school to evangelical orthodoxy. He had been a hero among conservative

---

13. Scott's senior colleague at the time was Gary Rupp, who was not the subject of any of these "God-orchestrated coincidences." But Gary left RTS after another year and was replaced by Jim Coffield. Jim taught one year at The Master's Academy Christian high school, and our son Justin was in his class.

Presbyterians in western Pennsylvania. In 2000 he was semi-retired, an advisor to Luder as well as a teacher, and one of the most beloved figures on campus.

Still, it was not a foregone conclusion that I would join the RTS faculty. When I arrived, John Muether the librarian (formerly one of my teaching assistants at WTSP) told me that Bob Godfrey and Mike Horton were among his best friends, and that his theological position was very close to theirs. But, he said, if I came to RTS he would seek to be a colleague to me "in the fullest sense." Bringing me that news must have been difficult for John, and I respected him for speaking so honestly to me.[14] As I expected, he spoke against me as the faculty prepared to vote on my candidacy. But since that time John has been exactly what he pledged to be, a colleague in truth. I have deeply valued him as the seminary librarian. He also asked me to help him with a book he was writing about Van Til, and I was happy to do so. Although I have not always agreed with him, I have appreciated the intelligence and Reformed conviction he has always brought to our faculty discussions.

There was one other problem that inhibited my joining RTS. Ronald Nash at the time taught the courses in apologetics, ethics, and history of philosophy. He was actually one of the most famous of the RTS faculty, having written a great many books and articles, though he was not a popular professor at RTS. There were evidently conflicts at the time between him, Richard Pratt, and others. Ron had edited the Festschrift for Gordon H. Clark, and he saw Richard and me as disciples of Van Til, who was famous as an opponent of Clark. When Ron heard that I might be coming, he registered objections, and Luder arranged for a meeting in the Faculty Lounge between Ron, Sherry, and myself. I dreaded that meeting, but as with so many things in my relation to RTS, the Lord seemed to go before.

I thought that Ron would first question my relation to Van Til, at which time I was prepared to talk about my differences with Van Til and my attempt to resolve the Clark Controversy.[15] But God made it much easier. For some reason, Ron chose to ask me, not about Van Til, but about Dooyeweerd, with whom he thought Van Til had been close. Ron worried that Dooyeweerd had been critical of logic, and he thought that was theologically disastrous. I was able to tell Ron that in 1962 I had written a paper on Dooyeweerd for Van Til's class. In preparation for that paper, I scoured the WTSP library and found a book *Dooyeweerd and the Amsterdam Philosophy*

---

14. If that had happened with my opponents at WTSC I might not have come to RTS.

15. See my *CVT*, 97–114.

by a young scholar named—Ronald Nash. It may have been Nash's first published book. Years later now, I was able to tell Ron that my paper on Dooyeweerd (like my later published work on Dooyeweerd) was very critical, and that at many points I was helped by the young Ron Nash. I could also tell Ron in good conscience that I did indeed believe in logic and would not tell students to violate the law of noncontradiction. I am told that when the faculty voted on my coming, Ron voted in favor of my appointment.

That meeting with the whole faculty took place in the Conference Room, and I answered questions. They asked me a number of questions on theology, biblical criticism, etc. When the subject of practical theology came up, one question I recall concerned women in the student body. Did I believe that women should be ordained as pastors? I answered no. Well, then, how would I deal with women who came to RTS believing that God had called them to be pastors? (That was not a hypothetical question; there were such women in the student body.) I answered that I would present my case against women's ordination when it came up in the regular curriculum. But I would not put pressure on any woman to agree with my position. That was my usual attitude toward those who disagreed with me. Further, if a woman student considered my argument in a serious way and determined nevertheless that she was going to proceed toward ordination, I wanted to equip her to be the very best woman pastor that she could be. That seemed to please the assembled group.

Then I was asked to step into the Faculty Lounge while the vote took place. The wait was longer than I expected. But after some time I heard the result: the vote in my favor was *nearly* unanimous.

While we were in Orlando, we looked at some potential housing and tried to get the lay of the land—locations of churches, Christian schools, and the like. In the evenings, we were invited to dinner by several families, to get acquainted with faculty couples and staff. I don't know what happened, but we were about forty-five minutes late for each of these. Somehow we were never able perfectly to follow directions, and we drifted far off the mark. God had wonderfully orchestrated the big events, but in going to evening dinners he reminded us that even Orlando was part of the fallen world. Since we moved here, we have learned that the area is not a difficult place to drive in, and of course internet directions, not to mention GPS devices, have come a long way since then. But in 1999, our bad sense of direction stood out like a sore thumb. Still, we began some good friendships during those evenings. The last night we visited Luder and Mary Lou Whitlock, with Rich and Gena Pratt and we had a good time of prayer together.

The most impressive meeting of the week was the chapel service on Tuesday morning. Faculty candidates were expected to speak once in chapel and also to present one class lecture to students. For my class lecture, they brought me into Rick Gamble's Sanctification course, and I presented some of my standard material on the sanctifying power of the word of God. It went OK I think. Gamble commended it, though I felt the students weren't paying close attention. But the chapel service was wonderful. I used a message on Gal 3 I had presented earlier at the WTSC chapel. On that earlier occasion I had received suspicious looks from people who evidently wondered how a near-heretic could possibly believe what the passage taught on justification. But at RTS it was entirely different. I had emailed the written message to Reggie Kidd, the RTS dean of the chapel. Reggie was also on the ministerial staff of mega-church Northland, and he arranged to have Tim Tracey, the church music director, playing the piano, with three lady singers from their worship team: Teresa Lee (now McCaskill), Eleanor Tracey (Tim's wife), and Michelle Lindahl (now Alexander).[16] I was deeply moved, especially, by an arrangement of the hymn "Arise, My Soul, Arise" by Eleanor Tracey. I had always liked the hymn, but the Louis Edison tune usually found in hymnals seemed to me to contradict the text. Edison's tune crawls along with patterns of three repeated notes, while the text cries out for jumping and dancing. Eleanor's arrangement added a chorus, in which the word "Arise" jumped a full fifth, and the rest of the text was set was set to a memorable melody.[17] That song, in that arrangement, has been my favorite hymn ever since, and I hope if possible that it will be sung at my funeral.

Response to that service was wonderful. No theological suspicions, just praise to God. That seemed to underscore to me the difference between RTS and WTSC.

Wednesday we returned to Escondido. To Westminster friends who asked my impression of RTS, I raved: RTS was wonderful in all sorts of ways. Particularly it impressed me as a seminary run by adults. I could not conceive the possibility that what happened to me at WTSC could have happened at RTS. Going from WTSC to RTS was like dying and going to heaven. I would say that many times, even after we actually moved to Orlando.

The RTS faculty approval of my appointment was important, but it was not decisive. Board action was also required. For that I needed to go to the original RTS campus in Jackson, MS, to meet with the executive committee. This meeting was sometimes called the "new professor's pilgrimage to

---

16. My memory is a little foggy here. It is possible that the third singer was Sharon Diachesyn rather than Michelle.

17. Nowadays, churches often use a version from Indelible Grace; but that seems almost too bouncy for me—too much, in any case, to fittingly describe Jesus as the "bleeding sacrifice" with his "bleeding wounds." The Tracey arrangement is lively when it should be lively and quiet when it should be quiet.

Jackson." The committee gave me a somewhat skeletal theological examination, and then they gave me the lecture that every new RTS appointee, especially those who had come from Westminster, had to hear: RTS is a board-run institution, not a faculty-run institution.

Now both WTS and RTS had been formed in response to the liberalization of other seminaries in their respective areas, but they had responded to this situation in different ways. WTS had believed that a faculty-run institution could best prevent the imposition of liberalism by an authoritarian board. So at WTSP and WTSC there were long faculty meetings and long debates as the faculty sought to make decisions about everything under the sun. RTS, however, reasoned that liberalism was the result of domination by theologians, and that a board of lay people and ruling elders would be better able to keep the school straight. So they sought to limit the power of the faculty and magnify that of the board. That board, represented by its executive committee (which took an extraordinary role in the day-to-day operations of the school), wanted to tell each incoming professor that his power was limited. For example, RTS did not give tenure to faculty members (though it did pay them better than WTSC did). When a faculty member's views came under suspicion at Westminster (as in the Shepherd case), there was a seemingly endless cycle of due process, with discussions, papers, counter-papers, trials, and appeals. But when that happened at RTS (and it has happened), the executive committee had the power to fire the employee without ceremony. And at RTS, faculty meetings were short. They were largely informational, though there were a few cases (like the addition of faculty to their own campuses) where the professors needed to debate and vote.

As a seminary student at WTSP, I often looked longingly at the closed doors of the room where the faculty typically met all day Saturday (according to rumor—without lunch), and wished that I could take a role in the debate, thinking I could set them straight about a few things. But when I joined the faculty in 1968 and entered the dark faculty room, I found that I had almost nothing to say. My senior colleagues, as it turned out, had far more wisdom than I on the important matters. And the often-long discussions of unimportant matters bored me no end: I didn't want to say anything then for fear of prolonging the meeting. Again, as with many other matters, I thought the RTS system was superior, much as it was sometimes denigrated as a "top-down" approach. Occasionally I would chafe at a board decision I disagreed with, but for the most part I was happy for them to make the institutional decisions and to let me have more time to teach and write.

In January 2000, Mary and I made another trip to Orlando, this time with Justin and Johnny, then fourteen and twelve. We wanted primarily to look at housing and schools. Again, the RTS people were welcoming. We stayed at a seminary-owned condominium in the Plantation Cove complex, with a lake in the back yard, and we drove another seminary-owned car. We looked over several churches we had missed on the first visit. We visited Northland for the first time, and we were overwhelmed by the quality of its music and preaching. We also attended for the first time Covenant Presbyterian Church, which would be our home church through our time in Orlando. I shall have much more to say about it later.

The first house we visited with our realtor was a two-story on Kingsbridge Dr., within walking distance of the seminary. It had four bedrooms, a bonus room, a den, four bathrooms, and a pool, everything in good shape. We visited many other houses, in Oviedo, Winter Springs, and Chuluota, but we kept saying about each house, "this isn't as good as the Kingsbridge house."

We looked at several Christian schools. There was a K-8 Christian school connected with Covenant Presbyterian of which there were good reports. But Justin was too old for it, and Johnny would have only a year or two there before he would have to transfer to somewhere else. We visited The Geneva School, which presented itself as a "classical" school. Johnny had a great time there. He went to recess with one class and his athletic talent made him instantly popular. Justin was not as enthusiastic. Then we visited The Master's Academy, a broadly evangelical, largely Baptist school, that was planning to move to Oviedo the following year. They put more of an emphasis on sports, which appealed to Justin. As we might have predicted, then, Johnny and Justin voted opposite ways.

Mary went by herself to visit the Orangewood Christian School, connected with the Orangewood Presbyterian Church. It was the school from which the Geneva School had broken away. It had the most mature sports program of the three schools. But Justin and Johnny didn't want to visit a third school; their minds were made up.

In the end we bought the Kingsbridge house and enrolled Justin at The Master's Academy and Johnny at The Geneva School. In time, we had second thoughts about all these decisions. The distance of the Geneva School from Oviedo brought us all sorts of transportation headaches. But for the most part we stuck by our choices.

Back in Escondido, New Life threw us a lavish farewell party. There was good food and songs and prayer. Glen Campbell, Justin's cello teacher, came and played with him and me a Vivaldi piece (I seem to remember) for two cellos and piano.

WTSC also honored us, at a trustees' dinner at the end of the academic year. At first I refused to attend, thinking (rightly) that the tribute was intended mainly as a face-saving measure for the seminary. But Bob Strimple convinced me that healing words would be spoken. I had second thoughts about that decision. Our reconciliation meetings in the fall had not done much toward reconciliation; why should I assume that a trustees' dinner would be any different?

Bob Strimple, Dennis Johnson, and Bob Godfrey did say some gracious words about Mary and myself. But it was a highly artificial situation in that none of them mentioned the sources of our division. And after dinner, our short conversations with other diners were dances on eggs—earnest endeavors to avoid giving offense.

Then at the end of May, the Bekins Company packed our belongings into their truck, and a day or two later we left our delicious paradise lost, in two cars, a 1991 Previa and a 1991 Camry. Mary drove one, I the other, and there was one boy in each. Occasionally we exchanged boys.

Our first stop was Hesperia, CA, to see Debbie, George, and their kids. Then to the Grand Canyon. In all our years in southern California, we had never visited there, and we were determined to expose our boys to the awesome experience of that great work of God. Then the Petrified Forest and the Painted Desert. For the most part after that, we just drove. We stayed overnight in El Paso and the Florida panhandle. For much of the trip, we listened to a CD by DC Talk. For the four-hour trip from the panhandle to Orlando, Justin and I listened to CDs of Josh Harris's lectures, "I Kissed Dating Good-bye."

The Futatos graciously hosted us for several days, while we prepared the Kingsbridge house for occupancy. Our older son Skip also joined us and played the role of a handyman. He went with Mary to buy closet racks and shelving, and they installed them very well. (I was excluded from that job for reasons of quality control.) Mike Tuttle, the seminary maintenance man, piled some of my books into his truck to be unloaded in my seminary office. That office was slightly larger than the one I inhabited at WTSC and had a great view of the parking lot. Most of the rest of my thousands of books went in the garage of our home. On the advice of many, we did not put them with the cars and garden tools. Rather, we had the third stall of the garage air-conditioned and put the books in there, to keep them in fairly decent shape.

For the next few days, my main job was shelving books in my seminary office and in the garage, plus a few upstairs in my den and in the bonus room. My family agreed on one thing: we would not allow Dad to cover the downstairs living area with shelves of theological books, as he had done in Escondido.

Covenant Presbyterian Church

One high priority for us was finding a church. We visited a great many of them in the area. Northland was by far the most impressive. Since Joel Hunter became their pastor around 1985, they had grown from 250 members to around 8,000. Attendance was even more than that, at their seven weekend services. And they discovered that in the area there were about 15,000 who said that if they would go anywhere they would go to Northland.

Northland was founded by a group of Christians who sought more creativity in worship. When we attended, that creativity was astonishing: professional-level singers and instrumentalists, graphics, lights, audio. Almost every week there was a "Wow!" moment. And yet those who were part of the worship ministry were godly people. They didn't promote themselves, but sought to use their astonishing ability and creativity in the service of God. Joel's sermons, too, were extraordinary. He is a great storyteller, but his goal is always to present a biblical passage that God would use to draw people to himself. Often he would give an invitation to people to receive Christ. He also sought to draw believers toward spiritual maturity.

The theology of Northland was more Reformed than anything else, though Joel's background was in the United Methodist Church. The music ministry was intensely Christ-centered. The church taught its theology directly from the Bible, rather than through the lens of a historical tradition, and I like that very much. The church has a doctrinal statement, but does not subscribe to a historical confession. It offers both covenant baptism of infants and believers' baptism.

The church has led its people into many social service projects and is well known in the community for its aid to the needy and its service in disaster situations, both near and far. They have partner-relations with a number of churches throughout the world and send teams of members to many countries to help in many ways.

People often ask the secret of Northland's growth. When I ask what the church was like in 1985, before its major growth, people tell me "pretty much the same as now, only smaller." Joel says that they never followed a "strategy for church growth." Rather, they "just tried to help everyone who came through the door."

At WTSC there would have been grave suspicion of anyone involved in such a ministry. But Northland had, and has, many significant ties to RTS. The Northland Counseling Center was originally a cooperative effort with RTS and it used RTS office space. Joel for some years taught a course in church leadership at RTS. Reggie Kidd, who teaches NT and worship at RTS, had his ordination credentials at Northland and frequently led worship there. Later the Futatos became members at Northland. Several staff members of RTS were and are members of Northland. Several of their worship team members have been students at RTS.

Early in our stay in Orlando, we went to Northland on a Sunday night. Afterward, I went past the stage to the door. I heard a voice asking "John Frame?" It was Teresa, one of the worship singers. She was one of the three who had sung at the chapel service where I preached in November of 1999. She also knew me because Reggie had used my *Worship in Spirit and Truth* as a worship team Bible study, and because Teresa herself was enrolled at RTS and would have me as a teacher. She brought me up on the stage, where I met other singers and instrumentalists, who all greeted me warmly.

Joel Hunter also met me at the door, recognized me, and said, "we'll have to partner together." We did; I accepted several teaching opportunities at the church.

When Johnny started at the Geneva School, Mary attended a parents' meeting and found herself praying in a small group with Eleanor Tracey, whom I mentioned earlier as a Northland singer, arranger of "Arise, My Soul," and wife of Tim the music director. The Traceys' two children were students at Geneva. A year or two later, the Geneva School would use some rooms at Northland for their middle-school students. Johnny and the Traceys' son Michael became good friends through Geneva. Michael took Johnny exploring, through all the nooks and crannies of the Northland building.

Nobody would have thought to call Northland a "truly Reformed" church, and many things about it would have incurred the ire of the truly Reformed: its size, its creativity in worship, its contemporaneity, its lack of denominational or traditional identity. But as I compared Northland with the Bible, I could not find one thing wrong with it. Northland had problems over the years, but they were very good at solving them. To at least the occasional visitor, Northland seemed to be a place where all was going well. There was no doubt in my mind that Northland was a work of God.

So our family could have slipped into Northland very easily. And in many ways, we considered Northland to be our second church. We often attended Northland on Sunday night, when the Presbyterians had no services. But I must now say something about our first church.

Randy Oliver was an email buddy of mine, from the mid-1990s. Raised in New York, African-American, he took classes at Westminster/Philadelphia and led worship at Emmanuel Chapel in South Philadelphia where Mary's brother Wilson was pastor. Randy somehow started reading my books and articles and he wrote for clarification. In time, he left Westminster for RTS/Orlando, primarily for financial reasons. He kept writing to me from Orlando and we became good friends. Randy confirmed the rumors I was hearing that RTS might offer me a position there. But I waited and waited, and it didn't happen until I went begging for a job in 1999.

Randy led worship in a PCA inner-city church that eventually folded. Then he went to Covenant PCA, where he was appointed worship leader and became a ruling elder. When Mary and I visited RTS in November 1999, Randy tried to get me to preach at Covenant (henceforth CPC), but Allen Mawhinney advised that it would not be a good idea to add that to my schedule. Randy did attend my teaching audition in Gamble's class, and we got to talk briefly in that context.

I had my first extended conversation with Randy during our January visit. He lived in a Plantation Cove condo, near where we stayed, and we talked at length. We attended a CPC worship service on that trip, went to a Wednesday family dinner, and talked with some folks about the CPC-affiliated Christian school.

When we arrived in Orlando in June, Randy came to visit us in our new home, and again we talked and talked. I was interested in getting him to be my teaching assistant, among other things. But a day or two after that conversation Adele Futato called us fairly early in the morning, with the devastating news that Randy had passed away. That was a terrible shock. Randy was only thirty-nine, and he had given every appearance of good health. I thought that I had heard Adele wrongly. There was an older man named Leroy Oliver in the WTS/Philadelphia community, whom we knew. So I had to check on Adele: are you sure you are referring to *Randy* Oliver? Yes, she was.[18]

It was that sad event that did more than anything else to connect us with CPC. We went to Randy's memorial service, where Luder Whitlock spoke. Randy, Luder said, was a student who "made a difference." And although we visited some other churches through the summer, we kept coming back to CPC. We went through the mourning process with the church.

The church's web site describes concisely its early history:

> In 1969 Covenant Presbyterian Church (CPC) started as Immanuel Evangelical Presbyterian Church, located in the Goldenrod community in Winter Park as a plant of the Reformed Presbyterian Church, Evangelical Synod (RPCES). The growth of the church coincided with the founding in 1972 of Covenant Christian School as a ministry of the church.

---

18. When I heard of Randy's passing, I also thought of Lem Tucker, an African-American student of ours at WTSP in the 1970s, who had worked with John Perkins in Mississippi. Lem too had died suddenly and mysteriously, at far too young an age. I would later compare these, with some bewilderment, to the case of Anton McCollum, an RTS/O graduate, also African-American, who died at thirty-two.

The church's association with the Presbyterian Church in America (PCA) came in 1982 when the RPCES merged with the PCA. The church was then renamed Howell Branch Fellowship shortly thereafter. The church attained its current name in the late 1990s.[19]

Despite its thirty-year existence, CPC was not a large church. When we first visited it was somewhere around 150 people. In the past the church had ups and downs. One split led to the formation of Orangewood Church, which grew rapidly and was mother church, around 1990, to Willow Creek and St. Paul's. But CPC didn't share in this growth. A number of people joined the church, but it also lost members to the above churches and to Northland. CPC became known as a missions-oriented church because of its yearly missions conference and the attendance there of a number of international students from RTS. So a large part of the CPC budget, too much in the view of some, went to missions, mostly to those who had attended the church during their student years.

We first attended in January 2000, during the transition between Pastor Jack Arnold and Pastor Jim Fitzgerald. Jack had encouraged the church's missions emphasis, and in 1997 had founded Equipping Pastors International, which supported him on teaching missions to pastors in Africa and elsewhere. In the mid-1990s, Jim was Jack's assistant. He went with Jack on some missions trips and had pastoral responsibilities in the church. On our first Sunday in the church, during our visit in January 2000, Jim was ordained to the gospel ministry and installed as senior pastor of the church, in place of Jack, who had formally retired. Jack and his wife Carol continued to attend CPC when he was in the country.

That first Sunday, Jack introduced himself and invited us to the Chinese restaurant 3-5-7 after church. Jack had played basketball under the great coach John Wooden at UCLA, and he gave to each of our boys cards with Wooden's autograph. He talked up the church and the Christian school and left a good impression with us, which of course would be deepened in June when we learned of Randy's death.

Jack preached for CPC a number of times in the next few years. On 10 January 2005, he died while preaching about heaven. We were there and had a remarkable experience. He finished the main part of his sermon, and then began to reflect informally: he said he did not want to stay on this earth one moment beyond the completion of the work God had given him here. Then his last words, "and when I get to heaven . . . ." He stopped and looked upward. I imagined later that as he looked up he saw angels coming

---

19. http://www.cpconline.net/History.

for him. Then he collapsed. A lady nurse in the congregation ran to him, and someone called 911. But he had evidently died right then. A number of news outlets, including Paul Harvey, picked up the story of the preacher who died with heaven on his lips.

There was much for us to like at CPC. Roy Lowrie, headmaster of The Master's Academy, attended the church, and he taught one of the best adult Sunday School classes we had ever attended. The youth program was fine when we arrived: Jim Fitzgerald himself led the young people's meetings as he had under Jack. But Jim soon left that ministry and gave it over to RTS students. Some of them did better than others, so the youth work had ups and downs.

Jim was a good friend to us, and we admired him as a man of prayer, with a heart for reaching the lost. But under his pastorate the church had a number of ups and downs. Later Jim evaluated his own ministry triperspectivally: he had done better as a prophet (preacher) than as a king (leader of the whole ministry) and a priest (nurturer to the flock).[20] Jim's sermons sometimes reached heights of eloquence and motivated our love for Jesus. But at their worst they scolded us, without giving us enough grace, or telling us the "how tos." As in his self-evaluation, he was not the best "executive." Someone needed to give the whole ministry a comprehensive analysis, evaluation, and future plan. Jim was not gifted to do that. But nobody else among the church's leadership was equipped to do that either.

Mike Beates, the RTS dean of students, was the church's associate pastor. A Hebrew scholar, Mike often got us deep into the Scriptures. His presentation of infant baptism helped Mary to see the rationale of that practice better than any other teacher had done up until that time. The Beateses' eldest daughter, Jessica, was very seriously disabled from birth, unable to talk, walk, or perform any tasks for herself. Mike and his wife Mary took her to church regularly, and they taught us much about welcoming and helping the disabled. When Jessica responded emotionally to the singing, she often brought tears to us "differently abled" people.

The Beateses had also adopted African-American chidren, whom they raised alongside Jessica and their other biological children. Others in the church also had bi-racial families, and several African-American families were part of the church—most unusual in the PCA.

The Women's ministry was very impressive, according to my dear wife. She mentioned that many of the women were very mature believers, very knowledgeable in the Scriptures.

20. See his book *Triplex: The Three Faces of Leadership*, available as ebook for Kindle. (http://www.amazon.com/Triplex-The-Three-Faces-Leadership-ebook/dp/B004CYEXCG).

The maturity of the congregation was both a blessing and a challenge. Many of the people had ministries elsewhere: Campus Crusade, Wycliffe Translators, Ligonier Ministries, Third Millennium, The Master's Academy, RTS. But the church itself had never mobilized these substantial gifts to reach its neighborhood for Christ (as Dick had done at New Life). As of this writing this is still a problem at CPC.

The worship team led the songs with a contagious enthusiasm. Jack once asked my interest in becoming worship leader. I said no, for a number of reasons (1) From 2000–2005, at least, I intended to do a lot of traveling and would not be regularly available. (2) The Florida churches seemed to have an entirely different repertoire of contemporary songs from the ones I knew. (3) I had little experience, and no successful experience, at leading worship teams. (4) I thought the CPC team was pretty good as it was, and better than it would have been with me as leader, at least at that time. It wasn't perfect, and I might have mastered the skills it would have taken to bring the team to a higher level. But 2000 was not the time for that. All of that reasoning still makes sense to me. But I'm sad that my move to Orlando meant the end of my life as a worship leader, even a worship accompanist. I have at different times been asked to supply prelude music, offertories, and music during the Lord's Supper, but it hasn't been the same. For several years, the worship team pianist was David Ridenhour, who had studied choral conducting, and David gave me the opportunity to accompany the choir for Christmas and other special programs. But I did not then have the time to practice very much, and I was somewhat ashamed of my performances. When David left, the choir programs ended, and with them a large chapter of my life with God.

So we joined CPC. Technically, I never became a member, because I became a teaching elder of Central Florida Presbytery, by transfer from South Coast in California. It is an odd part of Presbyterianism (one that I would like to see changed) that ministers are not members of local churches. My local church was presbytery. Often that is a laughable fiction. But Central Florida Presbytery took it seriously and tried to make it real. In fact, CFP turned out to be the best presbytery I had ever been part of. In each meeting, the entire morning was given to teaching, prayer, and worship. The business meeting did not begin until after lunch. Often I was greatly moved and helped in my spiritual growth.

But I also attended the church membership class led by Jim at CPC, with Mary, Justin, and Johnny. We were pleasantly surprised that Jim used, as his text, the OPC booklet *Confessing Christ*, written by Mary's Dad, Calvin K. Cummings, Sr. The class was a blessing, and CPC became our church.

I had no formal role in the church. I had some invitations to teach, but I turned them down because of my desire to travel for RTS. Jim and I had lunch several times a year. We talked about all sorts of things, including many of the issues facing the church. I think Jim was expecting more wisdom from me than I was able to deliver.

Around 2002, a storm did some damage to the façade of the church building, and there was discussion of how much, if anything, we should spend on a church face lift. A number of people, including Jim, had thought that the condition of the building was one reason for our lack of growth over the years. Jim came eventually to the position that a change of location would be good for the church. The church had done many different things to attract the community, but none availed. That part of Winter Park was a highly Roman Catholic area.

What moved us to make the change was the possibility of a move to Oviedo, specifically to the new RTS Chapel. It seemed inevitable that there would be a PCA church in Oviedo, to support, and be supported by, the PCA students and faculty at RTS. The idea that we could be the "seminary church" ignited our enthusiasm. The idea of a move also enthused those of us who envisaged change. Mary and I thought that this was an opportunity for CPC to become another New Life, with a truly outward-facing stance. Jim and many others in the church talked about the move as a "church transplant"—i.e., reforming the church as if it were being planted afresh.

Chuck and Karen Griffith were an older couple who had worked for some years in ministries at Willow Creek, while Chuck finished his seminary program. We respected Willow Creek as a good example of church growth, and the Griffiths seemed to have lots of ideas that could be put into effect. Mary shared with Jim many materials from Dick Kaufmann's ministry, and we suggested a number of the practices that had worked well at New Life, such as (1) scheduling church before Sunday School so as to increase Sunday School attendance and making possible a sermon response class for adults, (2) holding "church chats" at homes occasionally for Sunday lunch, inviting visitors and some church leaders to answer questions, (3) rethinking children's ministries for age-appropriate communication, with better understanding of children's attention spans, visual learning, movement, crafts, etc.

The church experimented with these and other ideas, but in the end the old patterns prevailed. We couldn't worship at 9:30, we were told, because other churches in the area all worshiped at 10:30 or 11:00. Other ways of connecting with visitors, they said, were as useful as church chats. Sunday School volunteers couldn't be expected to put much creativity into children's ministry.[21] In time, the Griffiths came to feel that the church was intent to keep the status quo. Chuck resigned and returned to Willow Creek.

This was the unfortunate pattern of the church in those years. Occasionally there would be a new member, or a new idea, that would promise a new beginning. But there was always pressure to return to the tried and true. If the new ideas weren't brilliant successes from the beginning, and they never were, the church would quickly abandon them. So from time to time there were conflicts over this practice or that, or more broadly over "philosophy of ministry."

In the course of one of those conflicts, around 2008, Pastor Jim resigned as pastor. The events left a bad taste in many mouths. Mary had been urging me for some years to visit other churches with her, concerned that she was not being fed. And, in the ups and downs of the youth ministry, most of Justin's and Johnny's friends had left the church. So we visited many other churches as a family: PCAs, Calvary Chapels, Assemblies of God, Independent Baptist Churches, and so on. We visited Northland again, and also Summit Church, another dynamic megachurch, founded by Joel Hunter's son Isaac with others from Northland.

We liked Isaac Hunter's preaching best of all of them. The boys later went to Summit on a part-time basis. Justin became a member there, or "partner" as they say. The music is very loud, electric guitar dominated, with lyrics that are a little quirky. When I worship there, I put a lot of thought into the words, and after a while I am typically moved by them. Summit is clearly a church for younger people than I, but I was delighted by the quality of its ministry.

But Summit endured a terrible tragedy. Isaac left the ministry because of moral failure, and after a year he took his own life with a gun. With Justin and Carol (Justin's wife, see below) we attended his memorial service. It was jam packed with Northland and Summit people. Given the extent to which God had touched us through Isaac's ministry, the service was a celebration of Isaac's life, without any hesitation or condemnation. I too celebrated Isaac. I had often listened to his recorded sermons on Sunday afternoon, with much profit. I don't know what demons he eventually yielded to, but I have no doubt that God really saved him and that God's work in him was not in vain.

There were two churches to which we seriously considered transferring our membership. One was Lake Baldwin Church, a PCA which stressed Jack Miller's "Sonship" doctrine, strongly grace-oriented, a little disparaging

---

21. However, Mary taught Primary Sunday School for several years, and both children and parents loved it.

about law and obedience. We were there for several months and greatly enjoyed the ministry there, especially the preaching of Mike Tilley and Dave Abney. But at one point the church offered a membership class, and we felt we needed to make a decision about our role there. In the end, we decided that Lake Baldwin Church was too far from our home for us to have real fellowship with its people.

The other church we visited at length was University PCA, which had grown large under Mark Bates' ministry and was then under the pastoral leadership of Mike Osbourne. Mike was also a strongly grace-oriented preacher, and we benefited greatly from his sermons. But as we conferred as a family, we concluded that University, like Lake Baldwin, was too far for us to be active members.

So the question was, where could we find a Reformed church close enough to our home for us to enjoy fellowship with the people? And the only answer was, back to CPC! So after maybe six months of church hopping, we came full circle. The people welcomed us back, without any discernible resentment. The godliness of the people had always been the greatest strength of CPC, and to me it felt very good to be back.

After resigning the pastorate, Jim became more deeply involved with Equipping Pastors International. This was the organization Jack Arnold had founded to bring biblical teaching to African pastors and churches. After Jack's death, others had continued the ministry, especially Jack's widow Carol, who was in much demand for her teaching on marriage. Jim focused his attention on northern Africa—particularly Egypt and Tunisia. This was a highly volatile area, but Jim was quite fearless and made a number of trips over there in support of church planting and the development of a seminary.

In the midst of all this, Jim was diagnosed with cancer—multiple myeloma. Many of us prayed for him and his wife Carole during this terrible ordeal. It now appears that he is cancer free, but he has had many problems with the aftermath of the drugs and chemo.

Meanwhile, the church looked for a new shepherd. For a year the church engaged a delightful retired pastor named Rod, as interim pastor. In addition, we heard one or two candidates for the permanent pastoral role. In 2010 we called Randy Greenwald, pastor of a PCA in Bradenton, near Sarasota, FL. I had met Randy once or twice, had preached in his church once when Allen Mawhinney wasn't able to make it.

Randy and his wife had three biological children and had adopted three African-Americans, two of whom, Jerusha and Colin, came with the Greenwalds to Oviedo. That made them a good match for the congregation, which had always welcomed mixed-race families. Shortly after they arrived, we faced another change in location. RTS was happy to allow churches to rent its premises temporarily, but it was not willing to be the permanent home of a congregation.

When we had sold the Winter Park property, we bought some desirable acerage on Route 419 in Oviedo, the road to the rural community of Chuluota. We hoped that we could eventually build on that property. Our idea was to sell part of the property to a developer, and with the money from that sale we would erect a building on the remaining acres. But the Real Estate market collapsed in 2008 and we had no way either to sell or to build.

It was not easy, then, to find an alternative location, but we were able to relocate to the cafeteria at Partin Elementary School, not too far from our own property on Route 419. Eventually, however, we sold that property to purchase an already-existing church facility on the other side of the same road. Our first service there was on 3 August 2014.

Randy's sermons are intelligent and soundly biblical. Since Randy came, God has brought a number of new people to us, particularly students from the University of Central Florida. Randy's coming, however, ignited a controversy concerning "confrontational evangelism." Several members of CPC have been involved in open-air preaching on the UCF campus, and another man has witnessed to girls seeking abortions at the Orlando Women's Center. Randy made it clear that he does not support such a direct approach. He believes that evangelism should be gentle, sensitive to each person, and based on the establishment of a friendship. He wants the church to be a "safe place" for people who have been hurt, especially by unwise Christians.

Several of the confrontational evangelists have left the church over this disagreement. My own belief is that friendship evangelism is ideal, but there are times (as when an unborn baby's life is at stake) when Christian witness needs to shift to an emergency mode.

I indicated that Jim evaluated himself as a better prophet than a priest or a king. Randy, I think is a better priest: a nurturing, gracious pastor who understands the hurts of each of us and is willing to take much time in ministering to those in need. But the various ministries in the church, from children to youth to community outreach, need much more thought, staffing, and planning.

Mary has become a volunteer teacher in the pre-school children's church. When she first visited this ministry, she was disappointed to find that some teachers merely came in each week and read to the kids out of the teachers' manual. Mary insisted that her own teaching would be developed as a serious ministry of the church. As with all her teaching, she expended a large effort in developing lessons that are age-appropriate and well-illustrated. Each Sunday she has arrived at Partin with a trunkload of teaching material which we have unloaded into the Art room at the school and which we have loaded back after church. Again, the children and their parents have greatly appreciated Mary's work, but we have heard some murmuring to the effect that other volunteers find this quality of teaching too difficult. Again we found that the status quo has a powerful constituency at CPC.

We have also hosted a weekly prayer meeting in our home, which usually numbers four to six people. We are convinced that CPC will never overcome its problems until it becomes saturated in prayer.

Family

After the move we did not consider ourselves competent to continue home schooling. We had lost our support groups, and with them the pressure to continue the practice. Further, we thought that it was time for Justin (fourteen) and Johnny (twelve) to get some experience in a standard classroom. So, as mentioned earlier, we enrolled Johnny in The Geneva School (TGS) and Justin in The Master's Academy (TMA).

TMA had just completed its building in Oviedo, so it was easy to drive to. We became good friends with the headmaster, Roy Lowrie, and his family, who attended CPC. I mentioned earlier Roy's excellent adult class.

We wanted Justin to continue his cello lessons, because he seemed to have some real talent for the instrument. He was playing pieces of greater difficulty than I played on the piano at his age. His teacher in San Diego, Glen Campbell, had recommended a teacher in Orlando, but she had very limited teaching hours. TMA's soccer program had attracted us, but the year we arrived they started a football team, and Justin wanted to be part of that, playing football in the fall and soccer in the winter. But any schedule for cello lessons conflicted with football practice. Well, it often happens that teenage boys reach a point where they must choose between classical music and athletics. In that choice, classical music rarely has a chance.[22] I continued my interest in classical music through high school, mainly because of my extreme athletic incompetence. At some point, Justin told us honestly that although he had spent hours practicing, going to lessons, and playing for recitals, he never really enjoyed classical music, but only played it to please his parents. At this point in his life he was happy to quit. Mary and I were sad to hear this, but we came to accept the inevitable.

Justin did play football, though he didn't have the body for it. He spent most of his time on the bench at first, but got more playing time in his last two years. He got more time, and more enjoyment, from soccer which was

---

22. Rock music, of course, is a different story. Eventually, Johnny gravitated to that, but Justin did not.

now offered as a winter sport. But TMA did not support the soccer program as they once had. The coaching was uneven, and the potentially best soccer players tended to play only on the football team.

Justin hoped that playing sports would be a way of making friends at TMA. His only permanent friend, however, was Darryl Ayers, who welcomed him early in his TMA experience. They have kept in close touch for many years and have shared in business ventures.

TMA was saturated with the Scriptures and the gospel. Everything, even in the athletic program, was to be done for Jesus. Much as Reformed people like to talk about having a "full-orbed world- and life-view," we thought that the Baptists at TMA were often better at integrating faith and learning than were the classical teachers at TGS.

Johnny chose to attend TGS in spite of their athletic program rather than because of it, but he managed to play in a number of sports and became a soccer star. A varsity player in the sixth grade, by high school he stood out so that the audience frequently expected big plays, yelling "Go, Johnny, Go!" He was really too small to achieve the heights of soccer fame, but I loved to watch his footwork as he took the ball away from much larger guys.

For two years, ninth and tenth grades, he left TGS to attend TMA, where he and Justin were able to play on the same sports teams. Johnny made a number of friends there, whom Justin inherited after Johnny returned to TGS.

TGS gave Johnny a genuine love of learning, which I had not seen in him up to this point in his life. By his high school years, he and I carried on theological and philosophical discussions that were beneficial to both of us.

But TGS did not seem to me (compared, e.g., to TMA) to have a very good understanding of the spiritual development of young people. They taught Bible to the younger students, in Kindergarten, the grades, and middle school. But in the high school they taught doctrine more abstractly and academically, in philosophy, apologetics, and systematic theology courses—almost a seminary curriculum. There was little application of Scripture to the specific issues of teenage life: drugs, sexuality, media, vocation, etc.

Chapel services at TGS were rather formal, preoccupied with historical liturgical practices. These were academic exercises—to teach students about the history of the church—rather than attempts to reach the hearts of the young people. In this environment, Johnny encountered temptations his parents did not expect him to find in a Christian school, and these inhibited both his learning and his growth in grace.

Partly to be near our son, partly to exercise her own teaching gifts, Mary became involved at TGS. First she volunteered to help the first grade teachers, who were under a difficult mandate. Florida required every school to teach the history of Florida to its students. Most public schools taught the Florida History unit in fourth grade, but for some reason TGS determined to teach it in the first grade. The first grade teachers were frustrated with this duty. Mary offered to put together a curriculum that would teach the Florida History unit to first graders in an age-appropriate way. She prepared lessons using visual aids hands-on projects, and field trips. The teachers were happy with her work and TGS used this curriculum for many years. Possibly they are still using it today. Also, together with Carole Mawhinney who had experience in theatrics, Mary put together a production of "Peter Rabbit" for the children to present to their parents and others.

So Mary became a familiar figure around TGS. One year, Mary applied to be interviewed for a teaching position there. She expected them to interview her for a third-grade position, but as it turned out she interviewed for kindergarten instead. Kindergarten was perhaps a better match for her gifts. She worked under the formidable master teacher Carol Reeves and has often spoken since of the invaluable lessons she learned from Carol. There were three sections of kindergarten, taught by Carol, Robin Candeto,[23] and Mary. After five years, TGS decided to drop one of the three sections and the administration chose Mary to be laid off. We were very sad and disappointed at this. Mary was greatly beloved by the children and by their parents, and her teaching was well-appreciated. But evidently the administration thought otherwise.

Since then, she has worked as a substitute teacher in public schools, mostly at the Stenstrom Elementary School, walking distance from our home. Over the years, she has gotten more and more calls to substitute, indicating her growing acceptance among the children, administrators, and teachers. She has been given two long-term assignments, helping with a class whose regular teacher has been ill. Mary also took a "nanny" job for a single mother of two girls. The mother is of Hindu background, but she and her children have shown much interest in religious questions. Mary desires to represent Christ in both of these situations, though it is difficult to know what kind of witness is appropriate at each time.

We had always assumed that the boys would go to college. In both Mary's family and mine, this step was taken for granted. Current (2017) discussion calls this assumption in question. Many are asking whether colleges are worth the cost, and in the last few years we have joined in asking that question. But we never questioned in 2004 whether Justin should go to college, or in 2007 whether Johnny should go.

23. On February 8, 2011, Mrs. Candeto was diagnosed with Creutzfeldt-Jakob disease (CJD), a rapidly progressive fatal brain disease and died tragically on May 31. For her testimony, see https://www.youtube.com/watch?v=HbGcrkqoE1U.

Mary and I hoped that the boys would get the advantages of Christian colleges, but we gave them a choice: either a secular college near home, or a Christian college elsewhere. Justin, with Mom, visited a number of Christian colleges: Covenant, Bryan, Colorado Christian, Grove City, and Geneva. Geneva is located in Beaver Falls, PA, near Pittsburgh. It's a fairly small school, run by the Reformed Presbyterian Church of North America, the exclusive psalm-singing "Covenanters." Several members of the Cummings family had gone there, and Mary knew a number of people on the faculty and administration. To Justin, Geneva seemed like the most friendly of the schools, with the least amount of academic pretentiousness. So in 2004 I drove him up there, joking with him about going back to his ancestral homeland.[24] I stayed with him long enough to get him set up in his dorm room and to get the results of his running test for the soccer team (he passed easily).

I was glad that Justin was able to take basic Bible and worldview courses at Geneva, but after a year he wanted to come home. He had a great many complaints against the school, which I could not enumerate here. The main problem seems to have been that Geneva was organized as a commuter school for Pittsburgh residents, and they did not make very good provision for people who lived a distance away. So the dorms closed up entirely during vacation periods, and the like.

So I went up to drive Justin home. I will long remember the two trips: to Geneva in the fall, home in the spring. On the way up we listened to Odyssey tapes—a home-school staple. On the way back, we listened to gentle rock songs by Ben Folds, an interesting measure of Justin's growing up.

We had arranged that he and Johnny could go to Mexico in the summer of 2005, to visit a CPC missionary and then to join another group for an immersion experience in Spanish. But Justin had a bad experience there as well. He had lost his passport on the plane and the Mexican authorities kept him away from the group he traveled with, locked in a holding cell overnight.[25] The next day, they sent him on a plane to Miami and then to Orlando, while Johnny and the rest of the group went on to their destination.

---

24. Mary and Johnny stayed home and experienced the worst hurricane we've had in Florida, "Charlie." They stayed for a time squeezed together in our innermost powder room. We had a lot of tree damage and some damage to our roof and pool screen. A tornado may have passed close. Neighbors helped a lot.

25. I remembered this when recent stories appeared of Americans being arbitrarily held in prisons by Mexican police. Mexican law enforcement seems to have little respect for people who get into bureaucratic problems with border enforcement; but many Mexicans expect the American government to give free rein to those who enter the country illegally. I will never go to Mexico if I can help it. Only the gospel can overturn that corrupt system.

That was a perplexing turn in God's providence. But we decided to use the time to enroll Justin in the University of Central Florida for the fall term. Justin had been easily admitted for the Fall of 2004—with a hefty scholarship—so we thought there would be no problem in enrolling him for 2005. We were wrong. There were piles of forms, many trips to offices, fees for this and that. The scholarship money they had offered him before was no longer available. But he did get in, and he spent the next three years in a business major, then another year and a half in a stressful MBA program. If God hadn't interrupted Justin's Mexican trip, we wouldn't have had time to deal with UCF. God was right again.

Because of problems mentioned earlier, Johnny graduated from TGS in 2007 without academic distinction. But he was admitted to Covenant College. His first year was fairly challenging and he told us that he didn't want to continue there. Returning home, he took some courses at Valencia Community College, but lost interest in them. Then he did some of his own research and found a Roman Catholic school in Hawaii, Chaminade University, which accepted most all applicants, was not far from the beach, and had some courses he was interested in. We knew that most likely the Hawaiian surfing was the biggest attraction, but we thought it would be best to honor Johnny's academic initiative. So he spent a year there. He says he only got to surf there maybe twice, and he did not want to continue there beyond one year. So he decided to try to return to Covenant, and the college did receive him back.

As with Justin's year at Geneva, I was pleased that Johnny got some good basic Bible and worldview courses at Covenant. He also got a good taste of philosophy from Bill Davis. Bill was my student at WTSC in the early 1980s (see chapter 7), and our three older kids took math courses with him at Santa Fe Christian School. Now our youngest also came to know Bill as a teacher, advisor, and friend. I had thought Johnny was headed for a philosophy major, but philosophy writing assignments were not his cup of tea, and he turned to sociology. Sociology was a good field for him, I think. Among other things, it gave him the opportunity to work with a church in Chattenooga that was giving after-school help to inner-city children. He seemed to enjoy that experience more than anything else at Covenant, except playing two years of varsity soccer.

And his band. After he dropped piano and violin lessons in Orlando, he took up rock guitar, and in college he was able to join a band of classmates called Raenbow Station. They recorded some selections on the internet and played for a number of venues in Chattenooga and beyond.

I visited Covenant to give the Reformation lectures in 2011, on the authority of Scripture. These were based on my 2010 book *The Doctrine of the Word of God.* It was good to see Bill Davis again and to get acquainted with other Covenant faculty. They were interested in my work, because they were largely against the "two kingdoms" theology of WTSC and stood for a largely transformationalist view of Christ and Culture.[26] One man I met was Brian Fikkert, co-author with Steve Corbett of *When Helping Hurts.*[27] Brian was the son of Henry Fikkert, my pastor at Blue Bell Church in 1961–62. We figured out that Brian wasn't born until after Henry and Doris had left the church, but it was neat to have that connection. After the lectures, I stayed on a bit. Johnny and I had lunch in Chattenooga, and we visited the huge aquarium they had downtown. I stayed another night to watch him play soccer.

Our family in 2008

Johnny did graduate from Covenant in 2013 after some struggle to finish his Senior Integration Paper in sociology on time. His paper was the kind of paper I would have written, examining the epistemological foundations of the very discipline of sociology. I read it at several points in its preparation, and it was excellent in many ways. Quite presuppositional. But faculty readers at Covenant seemed to think that it was not a proper kind of research for a real sociologist. In time they came around to give it a passing grade, but it was touch and go.

When Justin graduated, he visited Debbie, his older sister, in Hesperia, CA for a time. Debbie had been through divorce from George, and the five children needed friendship and care. Skip had married Sharon, who also had divorced her first husband. Skip and Sharon had a son, Gavin, and they also raised the four boys by Sharon's previous marriage. So, as with Mary and me, the shadow of divorce hung over these two families, with its attendant difficulties.

26. Michael Horton, however, was asked to give the Reformation lectures in 2012.
27. Chicago: Moody Press, 2012.

Justin also traveled in Africa, Malawi, with our California friend Marilyn McDonald, who ran a ministry to women in San Diego County. After they returned, Justin was invited to spend some time in Uganda, by Dave Eby. Dave pastored a PCA church not too far from New Life for some years, and then was called to help start a theological school in Zana near Kampala, Uganda. He worked with Emma Kiwanuka, a graduate of WTSC, pastor of a Presbyterian Church in Zana. Dave asked if Justin would be willing to come for a year to administer some of the business affairs of the new Westminster College and Seminary. Justin agreed to go.

The arrangement did not turn out well. Justin did not feel that his knowledge and gifts in business were being used, and he thought they were expecting too much of him in their social gatherings. Justin, alas, inherited my introverted personality, and he tended to be quiet in social settings rather than to liven them up. So he resigned his position with the Westminster School. But he did not leave Africa immediately. He tried, rather, to set up businesses that would enable him to make a living there. He set up, for example, a computer café; but that failed when the owner of the building refused to keep the electricity on through the day.

But as it turned out, Justin had another reason for wanting to remain in Africa. We began to hear in his calls and emails about a beautiful lady: the kindest, the sweetest, the most wonderful. Language like this was somewhat out of character for Justin. So we were introduced to Aidah, who later wanted to be known to us as Carol. We gave Justin all our usual warnings about marriage, and the additional difficulties of cross-cultural communication, but these did not discourage him at all. On 23 December 2010 Justin and Carol were married. Johnny, Mary, Skip, and the Kesters were there; I was not. I believed I needed reliable electricity to work my CPAP machine,[28] and I had no assurance that such was available in the Zana area.

The family brought back some memorable tales. Mary and Johnny had flown to London, which was in the grip of a major winter storm. They had to spend several days there, with a lot of heavy luggage, before they could get service to Entebbe. Mary's cell phone didn't work, nor did her credit card, which she had been relying on. But God sent two reassurances that he was on the throne. One was that as it turned out Johnny was very adept at traveling. He did have a reliable credit card. He suggested that instead of trying to find a place to stay at the airport, they should take the "underground" (subway) and visit some of the sights. So they went to London Bridge and the familiar London buildings. The second indication of God's providence

---

28. Continuous positive airway pressure (CPAP) therapy is a common treatment for obstructive sleep apnea.

was that Skip showed up. Skip had come on a completely different plane, but somehow God brought him together with Mom and Johnny. They combined resources and had a good time.

They arrived in Uganda late in the preparations, but the day before the wedding. They met Carol, many of her family, many of the church people.

After the wedding, Mary, Johnny, Skip, and the Kesters went on a Safari, saw a number of African beasts and vistas.

Justin and Carol spent another year in Uganda trying to make a living together, but the process was discouraging. They came to the US briefly with Carol carrying a tourist visa. At that time they visited family in Philadelphia, Orlando, California, and Oregon. Later, they made the decision to move permanently to the US. Getting a residence visa for Carol was very difficult and time consuming. I consider it a huge injustice that the US government puts so many barriers before US citizens who want to bring their spouses to live in the US. But after months of waiting, Carol's residence visa arrived, and the couple came to live with us in Orlando. They have started a number of business ventures, and we are waiting to see which, if any, turns out to be profitable.

In 2013, Johnny also joined us, but a few months later he went to live with some friends closer to his workplace. He became a general manager in a Chipotle restaurant. I kid him that that is the logical destination for sociology majors. But I admire his intention to work his way up the ladder. He has never worked so hard in his life, and he has never before kept so closely to a rule book.

Teaching

When I was planning my move to RTS, I talked with Al Mawhinney about my likely teaching schedule. Even in 2000, I thought of myself more as a writer than a teacher, and I would have been very pleased if someone had offered me a "research professorship" like Trinity had given to Don Carson and Kevin Vanhoozer. But that was not to be,

Teaching at RTS

and beggars cannot be choosers. So what Al offered me was a fourteen-credit-hour schedule, the minimum teaching load for one with a full-time salary.

Luder had said that in setting up the faculty for the Orlando seminary he had not added professors simply to fill "openings" in pre-established slots. Rather, he chose good people who were available and arranged the curriculum around their specialties and interests. In the 1990s, he hired people who were already known as mature scholars: Elmer Smick and Rich Pratt in OT, Roger Nicole in systematics, R. C. Sproul in systematics and apologetics, Ronald Nash and Charles MacKenzie in philosophy. Chuck Hill (NT) though young, was internationally known as a patristics scholar, as were Frank James and Rick Gamble for their Reformation scholarship.

So there was, strictly speaking, no "opening" for me. I would have to take courses away from men already on the staff. So I was asked to replace Nash in the ethics course, and Gamble in the first systematics course (Doctrines of Scripture and God). I took on three weeks of Rich Pratt's theological introduction course—actually a convenience to him, since he was our most traveled colleague and he needed to be absent from the course for three weeks. I also was asked to teach History of Epistemology. That course had been taught by Charles MacKenzie as part of the M.A. in Christian Thought program that he oversaw. That left room for me to teach some electives. In my early years at RTS, I taught Modern Views of God, Modern Views of Scripture, and the Thought of Cornelius Van Til.

In 2002, Steve Childers asked me to teach an intro to theology course for the D.Min. program, which he supervised. I was not naturally attracted to the D.Min. program, but Steve gave me a special enticement: I was to co-teach the course with my dear friend and former pastor Dick Kaufmann. I never felt completely competent in the course, but it was good to see Dick again. We taught together also in 2004. In 2006, Doug Swagerty was my partner, and in 2008 and 2010 Scotty Smith of Nashville, TN, whom I respect very much. But after eight years, I thought I had done enough.

That teaching load was certainly enough to keep me busy, but I also received invitations to teach summer courses and courses at other RTS campuses. The summer courses were grueling. For a three-credit course, we would meet from 8:30 to 5:00, with an hour off for lunch, for a week. Normal RTS courses were "block scheduled"—three hours per week, all together in a block. That was physically taxing for me, but the summer course schedules were almost too much.

When I taught at other RTS campuses, they would either ask me to teach for several weekends during the term (maybe 7:30 to 10:00 Friday night and 8:30–3:00 on Saturday) or to teach one long block during fall break, spring vacation, or summer. I taught at all the campuses that were connected to RTS at the time: several times in Washington, Charlotte, and Atlanta, once in Jackson. I also taught several times in an innovative program organized by Spanish River PCA in Boca Raton—a church where I worshiped back when I visited my parents in the 1970s.

Despite the physical challenges, teaching at RTS was for the most part more enjoyable than it had been at WTSC. I was, for one thing, very proud to be part of the Orlando faculty. My first year, I decided to audit Rich Pratt's Intro to Theology course. I had been asked to teach three weeks of it toward the end of the course, and so I wanted to get the hang of what Rich was trying to do. It was held on Monday evening, and when I arrived the parking lot was nearly full. None of the classrooms were large enough to hold the students, so they met in the Fellowship Hall. The course was intended for first-year students, but a number of older students and alumni came to audit, thinking that it would help them to hear the material a second time.

Rich was a spellbinder, one of the best pedagogues I have ever known. He was a master of PowerPoint graphics, state of the art in 2000, and he seemed to carry on a personal conversation with each of the maybe 120 students in the room. His lectures in the course aimed to expound a "deference construct," by which Christians could come to assurance about biblical doctrines. To gain assurance, they should give deference, first to Scripture, then to tradition and church teachers, then to the work of the Holy Spirit working in the heart—normative, situational, and existential in effect. Rich had four or more teaching assistants. He divided the students into teams named after unclean animals—pigs, snails, etc., and had them carry on internet dialogues about the lectures with their team members. Rich gave me some credit for all this: the large team of TAs was similar to what I was doing at WTSP in the late 1970s. And of course the triperspectival scheme owed much to my work. But I had never been as good a teacher as Rich was in that course. The students loved him. He seemed to me to be the heart and soul of the seminary.

In the middle of the 2000 decade, Rich left us to spend more time at Third Millennium Ministries, the work he had formed to bring multi-media recordings of theological courses to Third World pastors and churches. I felt sad about his departure, though I was excited about ThirdMill. When Rich was with us, he seemed to constitute something distinctive about the whole seminary, a direction we were all trying to follow. I still miss him here, but God has brought other able people, many of whom understand well the direction in which Rich led us. Scott Redd was one of our best students in the early 2000s. Eventually he finished his doctorate in OT at Catholic University and returned here in effect to replace Richard. Scott also took on the work of dean of students and he brought a great spirit to the campus. After a few years, the board recognized his gifts for leadership and made him president of the RTS/Washington campus.

Other faculty members brought other strengths to the teaching at RTS Orlando. As I mentioned, James, Gamble, and Hill were well known in the professional academic community, well beyond the evangelical boundaries. Gamble later left us, replaced by Scott Swain, a well-respected young theologian who is now our president. Reggie Kidd had a profound understanding of the dynamics of human culture in communication, reflected in his work in New Testament exegesis and worship. Reggie was one professor who became a great friend of many students. Like Mike Glodo, who returned to RTS after a period as the stated clerk of the Evangelical Presbyterian Church, Reggie had a keen eye for youth culture and "hung out" with many students.[29] Bill Eckenwiler taught Christian education, with a passion for the church and knowledge of biblical principles. Mark Futato's love for the Hebrew text, and his great gift for making it live in his sermons, was unique.

Allen Mawhinney was known as the best Greek teacher on the planet. When he moved from Escondido to RTS/O, Allen hoped to become more of a scholar and less of an administrator. But Luder prevailed in getting him, not only to become academic dean, but also to regard that as a calling from God. Al was certainly one of the best academic deans I have ever worked with. Sadly, he left us after several years, under bad circumstances. He divorced his wife Carole, under circumstances that brought criticism upon himself, and he felt he had become "radioactive" at RTS.[30] When he left, Mark Futato became dean, and a few years later he was succeeded by Scott Swain. Both men did excellent work in that office.

"Sherry" MacKenzie was admired for bringing the gospel to Grove City College and, at RTS, for his grandfatherly graciousness to everybody. Steve Childers urged the students to get serious about missions and evangelism, and many came to share his vision "for the nations." He spoke all over the world on church planting and evangelism, and often he brought RTS students with him. The counseling teachers, Rupp, Coupland, and later Coffield, brought both biblical values and academic rigor to their discipline. Steve Brown was one of the most interesting preachers around. He was a

---

29. RTS has always sought to deal with the lives of students, not just their academic development. So it has been important that there be some professors around who are at ease in getting to know students. Reggie and Mike were among the best of us in that regard.

30. I never learned the details of the story. Al did not confide in me, because my wife was a good friend of Carole, and Al wisely wanted to preserve that relationship. Hearing Al's side of the story, he thought, could prejudice that relationship.

great theological humorist, and the chief irony in his sermons was the irony of grace, which hits us with God's love when we least expect it.

We had a special blessing in the senior members of the faculty: Roger Nicole, Simon Kistemaker, Charles MacKenzie. They brought a wealth of knowledge in their fields and a huge amount of experience in teaching. Simon ("Sam") Kistemaker and his wife Jean lived up the street from us in Kingsbridge, and when we moved in they welcomed us with Dutch goodies. Sam had taught my dear wife at Dordt College back in the 1960s. We had several meals with them and they were godly role models to us.

Roger visited my office soon after I arrived. He was preparing a plan to bring charges against the open theists who were members of the Evangelical Theological Society (of which Roger had been a founder in the 1940s). I had published my *No Other God: A Response to Open Theism*,[31] and Roger graciously praised it. He asked me to read and comment on some things he had written in the context of the controversy, and we worked together on the project.

MacKenzie often talked with me about philosophy. He had written two volumes on Pascal. I think he was disappointed that I did not get involved in the American Philosophical Association, in which he participated. But I just didn't have time to add another activity to my schedule. And although I didn't tell him this, I was coming to think that the professional academic world was not a friend to Reformed thought, let alone the training of Reformed pastors.

Luder Whitlock retired as president of RTS in 2001. That was a surprise and shock to me, because he had been president for twenty-three years, and I had been attracted to RTS by his vision for the seminary. The reasons for his resignation were never very clear to me, evidently some differences of opinion between him and some of the board members in Jackson. Luder told us about some of these differences, but later the board sent a representative to tell us the board's plans for the seminary's future, and I could not distinguish Luder's view from that of the board's representative. I have missed Luder, though he and Mary Lou have had Mary and me to their home on several occasions since his resignation. The Orlando campus had a special meaning to him, as he was a native Floridian, and he put his great innovative energies into making this a special place.

As it turned out, the early 2000s were a time of retrenchment, not innovation. Post 9–11,[32] the country, and the RTS system, faced financial

---

31. Phillipsburg, NJ: P&R, 2001.

32. On 9–11, I drove my car to a photographer's studio in Winter Springs to have a picture taken for RTS publicity. I heard on my car radio a report that a plane had struck a building in New York, but I thought that this was a situation with a small plane

reverses. Some contracts were not renewed, including those of Christian education teacher Bill Eckenwiler, my friend Mike Beates who was dean of students, and Ron Nash. About the same time, Gary Rupp, director of our counseling program, left and was replaced by Jim Coffield.

After Luder's departure, the seminary reorganized somewhat. Ric Cannada, whose father Robert long chaired the executive committee of the board, succeeded Luder as the overall head of RTS, now called "chancellor and CEO," rather than "president." Under the new arrangement, each campus of RTS would have its own president, and Frank James was chosen for that job at RTS/O. Later, Ric retired in favor of Mike Milton, but Mike had to resign in the face of a debilitating illness. The chancellor today is Ligon Duncan, longtime pastor of First Presbyterian Church in Jackson, who has often taught systematics at RTS. The president of RTS/O since 2010 has been Don Sweeting, who doctored in church history at Trinity Evangelical Divinity School and had pastored several churches, recently the large Cherry Creek Evangelical Presbyterian Church in Greenwood Village, CO (near Denver). Don has been effective as a pastor to us as well as an executive and fundraiser.

Nash's departure left some of our courses unattended. I was asked to teach the Apologetics course, and Sherry MacKenzie taught History of Philosophy. A few years later, Sherry cut back on his teaching responsibilities, and I was asked to teach History of Philosophy as well. So I had four courses in the required curriculum for M.Div. students.

I turned sixty-five in 2004, and I began then to get income from my Westminster retirement program and Social Security. So I decided to cut back on a schedule that was becoming too difficult for me to handle. I told the RTS administrators that I would prefer to curtail my travel to teach at other campuses, though I did make a few such trips for what were described as special occasions. I also turned down opportunities to teach summer courses. I also quit accepting invitations to speak at various conferences. From 2000–2005 I spoke at many conference settings, on worship and other matters. My friend Jeff Ventrella invited me for several years to speak to

---

that had wandered away from its assigned air space. I got the picture taken, then drove back to Oviedo for a haircut. The barber had his radio on, from which I learned what a tragic day this was for the country. I remember being very pleased that President Bush understood that we were at war with Al Qaeda and other militant Islamic groups. In a week or two, an Imam named Musri came to RTS to urge peace between their religion and ours. He said that Islam and Christianity agreed about 95 percent about Jesus of Nazareth. (Yes, I thought, we probably are as close to Muslims as we are to liberal Protestants. But sometimes it's the 5 percent that is most important.) A week or two later, Steve Childers eloquently replied to Musri and indicated the vastness of the gulf separating Islam from the gospel.

Christian law students at the Blackstone Fellowship conference in Phoenix. But I never felt that I was a good conference speaker. I never felt that my prepared material quite matched what the conferees expected and needed. At Blackstone, they took speaker evaluations, and mine were not encouraging. So since the mid-2000s I have been pretty much a homebody.[33]

After 2005, too, I accepted fewer preaching invitations. By my own estimation, reinforced by that of my wife, I am not a good preacher, and I think I can accomplish more for the kingdom by other means. Some ordained ministers think there is something wrong about regularly turning down preaching opportunities. In our Presbyterian circles, one often hears about the "centrality of preaching": if one doesn't preach, what is the point of his being ordained? But as usual I think that some more distinctions need to be made. Usually when people talk about the centrality of preaching, they are referring to the sermon preached in a church on Sunday morning. But in the Bible, the preaching that is "central" is the preaching in the synagogues and marketplaces: *evangelistic* preaching, done where the unbelievers are. The New Testament says almost nothing[34] about formal sermons in post-resurrection Christian worship. One may argue that something like a formal sermon is a *useful* way of teaching God's people; but one may not, I think, claim that such sermons are "central" to Christian worship, or that they must be central in the calling of every minister.

Although I turned down many opportunities from 2005 on, I did, however, agree to join the RTS online teaching program, at the urging of Andy Peterson, an old friend from San Diego. They wanted to use recorded lectures of mine in the distance-ed versions of the courses Apologetics, History of Philosophy, and Ethics. (In ST1, they wisely chose to use a complete systematics sequence by Doug Kelly of RTS/Charlotte.) For these three courses, they asked me to help them develop lecture outlines, study guides, exam questions and answers, etc. In 2008–9 I began to be the "professor of record" for the online versions of these three courses. Each day I would

---

33. Perhaps I am a homebody by nature. I have always been "socially awkward," or as some put it "introverted." I am not fond of that language because it suggests that I am a victim of something genetic, whereas I think it is more likely that some of my social phobia is rooted in my own sinful attitudes. But I have tried many times, by prayer and discipline, to be more useful in social contexts and have never changed much. As I grow older, indeed, I have become arguably worse. Many times I hate even going to class, though after I force myself to go, I usually do fairly well as a teacher. I will go far to avoid having to go to a party, and I hate any occasion with a dress code, especially an occasion requiring academic regalia. In Philadelphia and Escondido, I volunteered to play the organ for ceremonial occasions on the condition that I not have to wear regalia. But RTS has not bought into this arrangement.

34. There is the reference to a "lesson" (*didache*) in 1 Cor 14:26.

receive assignments and questions from students in the distance learning programs. Each course had a midterm and final, which included multiple choice questions (to be graded automatically) and essay questions (which I was to evaluate). Then each student submitted a term paper, which I was to read and evaluate.

It was not a difficult assignment, and I did receive extra pay. But as the numbers of online students increased, the job turned out to be very time consuming. And the job of evaluating essay exams and term papers was one that had become increasingly distasteful over the years. In my early years as a teacher, I developed the reputation of reading student essays very thoroughly. Reflecting the influence of Miss Elliott from high school days, and my work as editor of the student literary magazine, I learned how to closely proofread everything, checking for detailed mistakes of grammar, style, paragraph structure, transitions, etc. And I also read papers very carefully for theological content, especially for bad arguments, which abounded in the papers of seminarians. But giving such attention to student writing became an unpleasant experience for me.

Further, I have always hated the business of grading, especially when the system requires the professor to evaluate the student's work in hundredths of perfection (100, 99, 98, etc). There is always a degree of arbitrariness and subjectivity, and there are always unpleasant arguments with students who think they should have received a 92 instead of a 91. Grading has some value, I think, in courses that are essentially quantitative like mathematics and science. But I've lost any confidence in it for theological thinking. The renewed emphasis on grading (or "assessment," as accreditors like to say) is based on a false analogy between theology and the quantitative sciences.[35] We are in the business of preparing people for church ministries, and I don't believe that writing research papers plays any meaningful role in most such ministries.

In my Orlando campus courses, I gave more and more of these responsibilities to teaching assistants. At first I hesitated to delegate this task. I remembered how much I had resented it at Yale when my wonderful paper on Athanasius was graded dismissively by a teaching assistant. And I got the impression that many seminarians, too, resented it when their diligent efforts were read, not by the professor, but by a peer. But in time, as I aged, that impression disappeared, and I asked TAs to grade papers. But no such delegation was possible for the online courses. I was expected to read the essays and papers myself. Someone, indeed, gave me the impression that

---

35. See my *ACT*.

the accreditors required that, that the essays and papers must be read by the "professor of record."

I continued to work in the distance education courses from 2008 to 2013, but at the end of that period, I declined to continue. I was reluctant to leave this work, because apart from the paper-grading it was a pleasant enough task. I enjoyed interacting with student questions.[36] I offered at one point to continue my informal interactions with students, but to drop the grading of papers and essays. But that offer was rejected by those concerned most about accreditation.

When I was spending a lot of time on distance courses, I was able to count some of those hours toward my teaching load. But when I dropped the distance courses, my teaching load dropped to eleven credit hours a year. Scott Swain, our academic dean, suggested that I elevate those hours to fourteen again by teaching electives. As I mentioned, I had taught electives earlier, but they were not well attended, and I found them increasingly irrelevant to the mission of the seminary, to prepare students for ministry. Bringing those electives up to date would require an enormous effort on my part, and I did not think that effort was worth it, either to the seminary, or to my own ministry.

I am now a heart patient, though I have not had symptoms.[37] I do get very tired at the end of the day, especially on days when I have to teach three-hour blocks of classes. That tiredness may be related to the statin drugs I have been taking. I can still teach, but if I teach I want it to count for something, not to be a kind of busy work in order to rise to a certain workload.

Scott was willing to allow me to teach eleven hours in 2014–15 on a full-time salary. But after that I cut back both in teaching and also in salary and was no longer on the full-time list. At that point, I guess, I met one definition of retirement.

---

36. For many years I have answered questions emailed to me, even from strangers. If the question requires research, or a long response, or a series of responses, I have learned to decline the task. But if I can respond meaningfully to a question in five or ten minutes, I sense an obligation to God to do that. A few years ago, we tried to assemble a list of these theological questions and answers, and we discovered that the number of these on my computer totaled around 18,000.

37. I have not had a heart attack, or even chest pains. But the doctors' machines—the electrocardiograms, the stress monitors, and the sonograms have led to "procedures" in which a surgeon inserts stents into the arteries leading to my heart. I have a general skepticism about this. Both Mary and I have had suspicions about "traditional western medicine." But for the time being I am following the wisdom of a traditional cardiologist.

The students at RTS have been wonderful. I say that, not because I am expected to, but because I have taught in other schools where students were often difficult. At both WTSP and WTSC there were many good students who to this day are friends of mine. But there are also students like Josh (chapter 8), who try to present themselves as more knowledgeable and smart than their peers and their professors, and who do what they can to undermine the teaching of their supposed enemies. There were a very few RTS students like that during my early years here. But most RTS students have learned somehow to be respectful of their instructors. Part of it may be Southern culture and etiquette. But I would prefer to think that RTS's intention to be "winsomely Reformed" rather than "truly Reformed" has a lot to do with it. We seem not to get students who have a chip on their shoulder, who think that there is something terribly wrong with the evangelical or Reformed church and that they have the duty to fix it. Would-be factionalists understand that there is nothing for them at RTS. Rich Pratt made that a major theme in his first-year Introduction to Theology. Many of us also read Roger Nicole's paper "Dealing with Differences,"[38] and have taken its biblical advice to heart. It is hard for me to imagine that RTS/O could ever experience the kind of factionalism I experienced at WTSC.

One of the most frequent topics of faculty discussions is how we can spiritually nurture our students. We proclaim in our literature that we try to do this. The seminary's motto is "A Mind for Truth and a Heart for God."[39] One of the major difficulties in this has been that we do not have a residential campus. The lack of dorms makes it difficult for us to create a community. But the seminary has put together a lot of social and spiritual events and conferences. There is a chapel service once a week. In my early years Reggie Kidd was dean of the chapel, and the worship was very contemporary, somewhat like Northland. In years since, others have planned the services, and there has been some turning toward traditional liturgy: scripted prayers, responses, with a lot of kneeling and standing. Ceremony is not my cup of tea, though the more traditional type of worship has given me some opportunities to play the organ. (I don't see any biblical basis for saying that worship should incorporate practices of past generations. In Scripture, worship was always in the cultural language of those who participated in it.) Still, I try to sympathize with those who find that such practices move them toward God. Many feel this way, and a high liturgy need not be a discouragement to church growth, witness St. Paul's and St. Andrew's churches in

38. http://www.ligonier.org/learn/articles/dealing-differences/.

39. The Orlando campus, under Don Sweeting's leadership, has added "a life for ministry." That makes the slogan triperspectival, and also adds a necessary practical element.

our area. Significantly, Reggie Kidd has recently been ordained in the Episcopal Church, USA, and has delighted in the liturgy as a true expression of his heart for God. He has become Dean of St. Luke's Cathedral in Orlando. Perhaps one day God will lead me too to feel at home in that kind of tradition, but it hasn't happened yet.

Writing

RTS faulty

My move to Orlando inaugurated the most fruitful time of my life in writing and publishing. When I arrived in 2000, P&R was editing my *DG*, the second volume (after *DKG*) in my Lordship series. Someone told me that if I stayed in Escondido, Scott Clark would bring charges against me for the doctrine of the Trinity presented in the book (i.e. for my defense of Van Til). Somehow, Ron Nash was also worried about that. But I wondered, how did Ron come to know about that from 3,000 miles away? Gossip seems to travel fast and far in the Reformed community. At any rate, no charges were ever brought. *DG* turned out to be my most honored book.

I had written it, more than my other books, with traditional academic criteria in mind. I quoted a lot of historical figures and contemporary theologians, "interacted" with a lot of thinkers, as they say. P&R submitted it for the Gold Medal in one of the categories distinguished by the Evangelical Publishers Association, and it won! I thought that *DCL* (2008) was equally worthy, but P&R did not submit that for consideration.

DG wasn't actually released until 2002. I had written P&R to tell them that I would be willing to take some of the *DG* material, add to it some analysis of the writings of open theism, and have them publish it as a critique of open theism. They liked the idea. They postponed the release of *DG* so that they could release the open theism book, *No Other God*, earlier. So it was a 2001 release.

Shorter writings followed. The seminary asked me to write a booklet about life at seminary, resulting in "Studying Theology as a Servant of Jesus." That one was a bit negative on the dangers of seminary life, so a few years later I balanced it with "Learning at Jesus' Feet," a kind of case for seminary training. Since my "Proposal for a New Seminary" (1972)[40] I had been known as an advocate for nontraditional ministerial preparation. But I still thought there was something special about the traditional three years of seminary.

Al Mawhinney introduced me to Mark Sigmon, head of the Institute for Theological Studies in Grand Rapids. The ITS put theological lectures on tape and sold them to seminaries around the country and around the world. At this point, Mark wanted a "survey" course in systematic theology. I liked the idea, because I thought it would minister to people in diverse locations, and because it would help me to become knowledgeable in the areas of systematics I had never taught at the seminary level. It was not necessary, but I thought I should write my lectures out word-for-word, so as not to have a lot of starting and stopping. I recorded these lectures in a couple of trips to Grand Rapids. That went very smoothly, and they told me that I was free to use those written lectures in any printed format I liked.

I told P&R about this and made two suggestions: (1) that we publish the lectures more or less as they were as an "introduction" to systematic theology, and (2) that I expand the lectures on Christology, pneumatology, and eschatology to make up another "Doctrine of" book in the Lordship series. They favored the first suggestion, so in 2006 *Salvation Belongs to the Lord* was published. This was one of the books with which I was most satisfied. It was used in a lot of church Sunday Schools and adult Bible studies, and I have heard from a lot of individuals who say they have profited from it.

I also recorded some lectures on ethical decision-making for Third Millennium Ministries (Richard Pratt, president). These lectures were written by my friend Ra McLaughlin, based on the lectures I gave in my Ethics course. Ra is brilliant in his writing and in his ability to illustrate. He wrote the script to correlate with graphics. I read the script from a teleprompter—the first and only time in my life that I have done that. They released *Making Biblical Decisions* about the same time as my *DCL*.

---

40. http://www.frame-poythress.org/proposal-for-a-new-seminary/.

DCL itself came out in 2008 and has been my main ethics text ever since. We released it at the meeting of the Evangelical Theological Society. In one session, I responded to rather gentle critiques of the book by Doug Moo and Russ Moore.[41] The most challenging question came from a member of the audience who asked why I had not referred to Stanley Hauerwas, Oliver O'Donovan, and other significant Christian ethicists. I made some specific comments about those gentlemen, but eventually I came to the central truth: I do not see Christian ethics primarily as a conversation between myself and other academic ethicists. Rather, I see it as a conversation between myself and the Bible. I'm willing to learn, and I do learn, from reading the writings of others. But I do not think that candidates for ministry are best served by hearing debates between ethicists; rather, they need to come to grips with what the Bible teaches.

In 2009, P&R published a Festschrift in my honor, edited by my good friend John Hughes. It was Hughes' idea to make the volume a series of responses to my work, rather than a traditional "essays presented to" volume in which the essays could have been about anything. I agreed to this proposal somewhat reluctantly, knowing the book would be characterized as an ego trip (since the 1970s, I have always had readers who took my work in the worst possible way), and knowing that such a volume would require additional work from me: John made several suggestions of essays I should write. But I thought the volume would serve a good purpose—further explaining ideas I had sought to set forth elsewhere, and I had long since given up on trying to persuade those who regarded me as an enemy.

2010 was the year of *DWG*, which of all my books is the one I personally like best. The published version is much shorter than what I originally intended. I had envisaged something more like *DG*, with lots of quotes, references, analyses of historical and contemporary views. I had thousands of pages of research sitting around, accumulated since my days at Yale. But I considered my advancing age, and the number of years it had taken to get *DG* together, and decided on a simpler plan. I would set forth the gist of my argument for biblical authority, the argument I had used for many years in my seminary course on the subject. There would be some debate with alternative positions, but that would mostly be in the "Appendices" section, and it would consist of short papers and reviews that I had published or posted elsewhere. As it turned out, I like it better than *DG* and *DCL*. It presents a clear, concise argument, avoids rabbit trails for the most part, and contains everything that in my opinion a seminary student needs to know. Others liked it too. My editor John Hughes is very bold in seeking endorsements

---

41. My responses to those papers can be found in my *SSW* 1, 256–74.

from famous people, and he got some very favorable comments from people like Don Carson and John Piper. To my astonishment, James I. Packer was willing to write the Foreword, where he recommended it as a complete treatment of the doctrine of revelation and Scripture.

After I left Escondido, the "Escondido theologians" produced a number of articles and books. Some of these took critical digs at my work. By the late 2000s I felt that their position (confessionalism and "two kingdoms") was making considerable headway in the evangelical and Reformed movements. Even popular magazines like *Christianity Today* were taking the Escondido line for granted. I read a number of their books and wrote reviews of them. I intended those reviews at first for the web page I shared with Vern Poythress (www.frame-poythress.org), but as they accumulated I thought I might try to publish them.

I have always had an affection for book reviews as a genre. In the 1970s, most of my ideas were first stated in book reviews. I thought of them as an ideal vehicle for exchanging views. In a review, a writer is forced to interact with what the author specifically says, rather than with abstract stereotypes and generalizations about schools of thought. To do this well, of course, the reviewer must write at some length, making his case cogently from the author's text. Eventually, however, the *WTJ* greatly restricted the word-length allowed for reviews. The new policy encouraged reviewers to use a style more common in trade periodicals: tell generally what is in the book, commend or criticize briefly. The criticism, when it existed, would often be a short comment about the author's "emphasis." To me, that new policy took all the fun out of writing reviews, and I shifted to other genres. But I always enjoyed writing reviews when I could do them my way, and I really got caught up in the project of writing reviews about the Escondido literature.

I sent the manuscript of *The Escondido Theology* to John Hughes, and he suggested I send it to Marvin Padgett, who was evaluating manuscripts for P&R. Time passed, and I came to the view that the book was not a P&R title. P&R, for one thing, had published Scott Clark's *Recovering the Reformed Confession* (2008), a book that I criticize very harshly in *TET*. Of course, that did not exclude their publishing a critique of that and other such books. But my critique was so sharp that I thought they may have felt under pressure to choose sides. That would not have been good for P&R. P&R has to serve the whole Reformed community, regardless of where they stand on these controversies.

So I sent *TET* to various friends of mine for advice. One of them sent it on to Ken Talbot, president of Whitefield Theological Seminary in Lakeland, FL. Ken really liked the book and very quickly offered to publish it. I rejoiced in Ken's enthusiasm, and I accepted his offer. I then wrote Marvin and John withdrawing the book from P&R's consideration.[42] Whitefield released the book in 2011. It has not been widely circulated.[43] It is mainly available on the Whitfield website, along with a video discussion of the book between me and Ken.[44]

When *TET* was released, the cyberworld exploded with fervent attacks on my writing and my person. I had hoped that the book would lead to some thoughtful discussion about these important issues, but that was not to be.

A different issue led me to write *The Academic Captivity of Theology*, also published by Whitefield, this one in 2012. I mentioned earlier in this book the tension in my life between abilities and interests. The former have been largely academic and the latter mainly pastoral. Since I began teaching in 1968, I have tried to integrate these by developing academic concepts that supported church ministry. But I have never been entirely free of the tension between academics and pastoral concerns.

In 1972 *Christianity Today* offered a prize for an essay on something like the future of theological education. I entered the contest but did not win. The winner was an essay (by a man now widely known) arguing that the great need of modern seminaries was higher academic standards. This was a well-known theme of the postwar neo-evangelical movement and of *Christianity Today* as a creature of that movement. So its choice of a winning essay was no surprise to me. My own essay, however, took a very different turn, perhaps in some eyes an opposite one. I called it "Proposal

---

42. These events were falsified in Mike Horton's response to the book. He said that the book had been rejected by several publishers before it was accepted by Whitefield. That statement is false. Although I had made some approaches to P&R, Whitefield was the only publisher to formally consider the book. Horton also reproved me for having the work published by a "theonomic" publisher. But in fact I don't know what Talbot's position is on theonomy as such. The question of theonomy never came up in our correspondence, and it plays no role in the book.

43. Ken told me that someone at WTSC had been calling Ken's distributors, urging them not to carry the book. So much for free discussion.

44. http://whitefieldmedia.com/product-category/books/.

for a New Seminary."[45] The essay tried to pin down in general terms what the Scriptures themselves required for church leaders, and what traits of character, skills, and knowledge[46] were requisite for church offices.

In 1 Tim 3:1–7, Paul tells us that most of the qualifications for overseers are traits of character: "above reproach, the husband of one wife, sober-minded, self-controlled," etc. He must, in addition, have one particular skill: he must be "apt to teach." And of course if he is to teach, he must have some knowledge—knowledge of the gospel content of Christian teaching. But there is no suggestion in this passage or any other part of the New Testament that an overseer must have formal education of any kind. Paul himself had something like formal rabbinical training "at the feet of Gamaliel," and he made good use of it. But other apostles had no training of this sort. Certainly such training was not expected of non-apostolic church leaders.

Yet in the history of the church, academic learning has played a larger and larger role in the training of church leaders. The church fathers often took pride in their knowledge of Greek philosophy and incorporated that into their theological teaching. Greek thought came to dominate medieval theology. In the modern period, university education was considered an advantage to pastors, even though that university education was dominated by secularist unbelief.

My "Proposal" argued a return to something like an apprenticeship model in preparing church leaders and a turn away from the academic model. *Christianity Today* did not accept that proposal, and many others rejected it as well. I couldn't find anyone to publish the paper until 1978 when Jay Adams accepted it for his *Journal of Pastoral Practice*.[47] Jay's support emboldened me.

Still, I continued to teach in academic institutions, with only minor modifications of the academic model. And over the years I have seen theological education (at WTSP, WTSC, RTS, and other schools) become more and more academic in character. The chief evidence of this trend, to my mind, is the tightening bondage of seminaries to accreditation agencies.

In the 1950s and '60s the Association of Theological Schools, the chief organization that accredits seminaries, was known as a liberal organization, to the extent that many evangelical seminaries avoided any involvement with them. But from the 1970s on, many Roman Catholic and evangelical schools sought accreditation with ATS and called to others "come on in,

---

45. http://www.frame-poythress.org/proposal-for-a-new-seminary/.

46. For multi-perspective buffs, note the pattern. Character is existential, skills situational, knowledge normative.

47. 2.1 (1978).

the water's fine." The water was fine, because liberal seminaries were declining and evangelical seminaries flourishing; so the ATS became more and more dominated by evangelicals. There were fewer demands that evangelical seminaries conform to liberal ideas of the place of women, for example.

At first, ATS developed a set of "standards" providing criteria for financial and academic acceptability. But more recently they have asked the seminaries to come up with their own standards and prove that their teaching program achieves those standards. Those standards can be purely academic (e.g., competence in Hebrew grammar) or more personal (e.g., having a winsome attitude). But each must be *provable*. There must be a means of *assessment*, constantly in practice, to prove (to accreditors, of course) that the goals have been reached.

Asking a seminary to formulate its own standards may seem to give it more freedom than accredited seminaries had back in the old days. But the emphasis on "proving" and "assessing" tells a different story. How can you assess whether a student has a winsome attitude, so as to prove that conclusion to an academic accrediting agency? I don't think that is possible. I think that seminaries ought to encourage, if not inculcate, all the character traits Paul lists in 1 Tim 3:1-7. But in my judgment not one of those can be precisely measured.

At RTS, accreditors required us to institute a "Quality Enhancement Project" (QEP). As with most contemporary accreditation projects, the seminary was to choose its own QEP. But then it had to choose respectable academic ways to "assess" its success. We chose to increase our teaching in the area of Islam. I thought that was fine. Given 9-11 and recent persecutions of Christians in the Muslim world, it seemed important to include some solid teaching about the Muslim religion in our curriculum. I had some ideas on how my apologetics course could be modified to include more material on Islam. But nobody asked me.

Rather, what happened was that we received an edict from the QEP committee that in the forthcoming academic year about thirty-five class hours that had been devoted to other subjects would be devoted to Islam. (That seemed to me to be a bit much.) Further, two of my required courses, Apologetics and Systematics 1, would henceforth each be required to include two lecture hours on Islam. Still further, I would be required to assess the students so as to *prove* that they had gained knowledge of Islam. To *prove* this, it was necessary to require each student in each course to write a paper on Islam. Those papers constituted "artifacts" that can be presented to the accreditors as evidence that the quality of our instruction in this area had improved.

When I developed the ST1 course, I set it up so that students would not have to write a term paper. It seemed to me that there was value in giving the students more time to study the Scriptures and the assigned readings without having to do research and writing. In general, I believe that seminarians write too many research papers. The work of the pastorate rarely includes writing research papers, so it seemed to me odd that in a school intended to prepare students for the pastorate and other ministries that so much emphasis should be given to the development of skills in academic paper-writing. But the QEP required me to assign papers in that course, and it dictated to me what the subject of this paper had to be.

Accreditors are academic people, and they use only academic tools (papers, exams) to achieve the goals of seminary teaching. So every problem has an academic solution: more testing, more research assignments. I am reminded of the old saying that "if all you have is a hammer, everything looks like a nail." I've been persuaded that though the new style of accreditation appears to give freedom to seminaries, it really imposes authoritarian requirements that leave less freedom to seminaries to pursue non-academic solutions.

That was the issue that led me to write my next book, *The Academic Captivity of Theology*.[48] I hope that in the future the essays in that book may provoke more discussion than they have to date.

My 2013 *Systematic Theology*[49] is in one sense a summation of all my work in systematic theology. John Hughes encouraged me to write it by saying that of course I could abridge my four Lordship books, then enlarge *SBL*, and I could write a systematic theology based on that. The book that emerged is somewhat like that, in that a lot of text has been literally cut and pasted from the other books. But I have thought through every page afresh. Much has been deleted, new sections have been added. I am particularly happy with chapters 4–6, a biblical-theological section that summarizes under three perspectives the main narrative of Scripture. In the Doctrine of God section, I dropped much of the scholastic discussion about essence, attributes, necessity, contingency, and focused more directly on the biblical text. Chapters 29–32 provide a much clearer, more concise treatment of the argument I used in *DKG*.

Chapters 37–51 (on Christ, the Spirit, and eschatology) are expansions of *SBL*, with significant expansions. I do agree, however, with the criticisms that these chapters do not provide as rich a treatment of their subjects as

---

48. Lakeland, FL: Whitefield Publishers, 2012. Some of these essays, along with the related "Pratt's Boot Camp" can also be found in my *SSW* 2.

49. Phillipsburg, NJ: P&R.

chapters 1–36 provide on the subjects they explore. Yet those critics should have taken more seriously my observation that the *whole book* is Christ-centered. I show that each divine attribute, for example, is an attribute of Christ. So although my Christology chapters are relatively shorter than those in most systematic theologies, the treatment of Christology in the book itself is as extensive as any.

I confess, however, that the conciseness of my treatments in this section, particularly chapters 40–44, reflects in part my feeling that traditional theology has been somewhat guilty of overemphasis here. Recent discussions, especially of justification and sanctification, have been very scholastic, unnecessarily complicated. Important as these concepts are in Scripture, I think the crucial issues can be stated better with less complication.

History of Western Philosophy and Theology is an expansion of my lectures for our course in History of Philosophy and Christian Thought. Again, Frame and Poythress have coincided in their publishing programs. *HWPT* should be read together with Poythress, *Redeeming Philosophy*.[50] My book is historical in its orientation; Poythress' book is systematic, working through the problems of philosophy, especially in metaphysics.

Selected Shorter Writings is exactly what the title suggests. If the first volumes sell well, I expect that there will be others. As of now (2017), P&R has published volumes 1–3, but I suspect that the series is over for at least a time.

My last publication may well be a collaboration between me and my colleague Steve Childers. It is a variation on the lectures on systematic theology that led to my book *Salvation Belongs to the Lord* in 2006.[51] Steve's organization, Pathway Learning, seeks through recent technology to put seminary-level courses in the hands of students around the world. The course in *Applied Theology* will take my lectures and present them through animation and translation into other languages. It will include

Steve Childers and me

50. Wheaton, IL: Crossway, 2014.
51. Phillipsburg, NJ: P&R.

audio interludes in which I answer questions from Steve on the various topics.

And then there is this volume. Since 1985 I have written a journal. Mary was pregnant with Justin then, and I feared that, having a child at forty-seven, I might die before my child would ever know me. I've also heard that journaling can be a valuable spiritual exercise. My journal is not full of spiritual wisdom, like those of many great saints. It is just a way for me to remember how God has dealt with me.

So for most of the intervening years, I have written about one entry a day. The present volume is not that journal, nor a series of excerpts from it. I have, rather, here rethought the course of my life, as one often does at my age. The journal, no doubt, has quickened my memory at points. But the present volume is a reflection at seventy-seven, looking back on God's dealings with me. I hope you don't think it is an egoist exercise, for I have learned a lot about myself from writing it, including many things for which I have needed to repent. And I have learned much about the providence of my great God. I hope that one day he will give you the opportunity to rethink your life. Meanwhile, I hope there are some things in this book that will help you to rejoice in God's grace.

Slouching toward Retirement

I have always seen a period of retirement as desirable, not out of a desire to play shuffleboard, but because I saw it as a time when I could observe my own priorities. In my case, those are writing and publishing, not teaching, and certainly not participating in formal academic exercises like grading and appeasing accreditors. On the other hand, I have always tried to provide for my family. In recent years, my teaching responsibilities have not been too onerous, so I have gladly stayed on to teach, even at seventy-seven, my present age.

My health has been something of a question mark, as I mentioned earlier. I saw a doctor about a shingles problem in 2011. He did nothing for my shingles, but put me through a battery of tests and declared that I needed to see a cardiologist. That seemed strange to me, because I was feeling fine. No chest pains, no shortness of breath, no heart attacks or strokes. But my cholesterol and blood pressure were high, as was my weight, and there were evidently some irregularities in my electro-cardiogram. When I saw the cardiologist, he required me twice to have catheterization procedures that installed stents in the arteries leading to my heart. After those procedures I felt exactly the same as before.

I have felt very tired at times. To some extent, I have been tired all my life, and therefore unfit for athletics and such. Before 2000, teaching had never wearied me. But at RTS, most courses involve teaching in three-hour blocks. Since 2005 or so, those have left me exhausted after completing a block. So I have tried, as much as possible, to minimize teaching and to maximize writing and publishing.

So my teaching load came under discussion. In my early years at RTS I taught the minimum number of teaching hours, fourteen per semester, plus summer courses, courses at RTS campuses other than Orlando, and distance-ed courses. After I turned sixty-five in 2005, I dropped the summer courses and courses outside Orlando, in order to give myself more time to write. From everyone's responses, I figured that my writing contributed some value to the seminary's program and reputation; certainly it enabled me to have adequate textbooks for my courses.

In 2013 I resigned from my work in the distance-ed program. I did not observe carefully what that would do to my teaching load requirement, but, as mentioned earlier, in 2014 we discovered that it had declined to eleven hours. Scott Swain, the academic dean suggested that I could get back to fourteen hours by developing one or two electives. But that was not acceptable to me: (1) I wanted to do less teaching, rather than more. (2) It would mean that I would have to devote a large amount of time to preparing courses, which would retard my writing and publishing. (3) My elective courses have never been very popular or, in my own estimation, very good. Preparing electives would compromise my calling in order to fulfill formal requirements of a faculty rule book.

So I told Scott that I preferred to drop my "full time" status and to teach fewer courses rather than more. In 2014–15 I was allowed to formally violate the rule, and I taught four courses (eleven hours), all of them required courses in the M.Div. program. In 2015–16 I taught three courses, with a reduced salary and no benefits. That's OK; God is taking good care of us.

I first cut back on my teaching, not knowing whether or not I would be considered retired. I am no longer a full-time teacher. Nobody has made a fuss about that. But it seems to have been a workable arrangement: some teaching, an office, a lot of writing time, no shuffleboard.

But my present plan is for formal retirement as of June 2017. My reasons are: (1) My health. I now find it very difficult to teach a three-hour class session without physical exhaustion. (2) My retirement fund: apparently it is not possible to access that fund easily without formal retirement. (3) I want to have the freedom to join in whatever the family does. If they decide it would be best to move back to California, I would like to be able to join them without trouble. (4) Hints at RTS of a growing confessionalism of the sort that caused problems for me in California. (5) Linked to this development is a movement toward a greater academic emphasis, guided by concerns about accreditation. That is a development concerning which I have no enthusiasm.

Still, I have to say that my seventeen years at RTS have been my happiest ever, certainly my most productive years as a scholar and theological pastor.

Looking Ahead

Earlier, I mentioned Marilyn McDonald, our good friend from Escondido, who started the House of Sophia, a ministry of counseling to women. The ministry consisted of (1) distribution of food to the poor using a 501C3 status, and (2) starting a group home, in which people with mental and spiritual disorders could receive intensive counseling. Mary and the kids have helped out with this ministry, and Marilyn has become a good friend to all of us. At seventy-four, she began to seek out people who would carry on the work of the House of Sophia after her retirement from the work. As I mentioned earlier, she had traveled to Africa with Justin, and more recently she had met Justin and his Ugandan wife Carol. She would now like to work with Justin and Carol (with help from Mary and me) to provide for the next generation of the House of Sophia. At first, our planning had included a move back to California for all of us. But more recently Marilyn has moved in with us, and we hope she will be able to develop a House of Sophia ministry here in Central Florida. With Justin, Carol, and Johnny involved in other projects as well, our planning is very much up in the air, but we look forward to see what God will do.

Epilogue

As I read over this book, the following themes seem central to me. These are the chief lessons God has taught me through his providence in my life.

1. The lordship of the Triune God is the central fact of my life and of my theology. Given God's gracious work in my heart, this theme naturally arises to prominence in all my writings.
2. I never get over my amazement that Jesus, the Son of God, would die for such a wretch as me.

3. Our earliest church experiences are often the most formative. Indeed, many of us spend our lives looking for a church like the one in which we grew up.

4. There is an important role for academic study in the Christian life, but not conformity of our thoughts to those of the academic community. Rather, the Christian learns to study God's world so that he/she can be better conformed to God's word and empowered to *resist* the world.

5. God's lordship commands obedience to him, not only in worship and ethics, but in the life of the intellect as well.

6. The best thing about the Reformed tradition is that it directs us to Scripture. What is merely traditional is dispensable.

7. Total alignment with a historical tradition leads to spiritual shipwreck.

8. One tradition worth keeping, that we need to emphasize more, is that of "creativity within the bounds of orthodoxy."

9. It is indeed possible to be both Reformed and evangelical.

10. There are delightful blessings in God's kingdom, on earth as in heaven.

"Surely goodness and mercy shall follow me all the days of my life, and I shall dwell in the house of the LORD forever" (Ps. 23:6).

Name, Subject Index

9–11, 198, 198n32

Abney, Dave, 184
abortion, 58, 109–11
academic respectability, 94, 99, 209, 210–11
academic theology, 64–65, 71, 72, 76, 99, 209, 215, 216
accreditation, 137n18, 152–53n14, 202, 209, 210, 213, 215
acting out of character, 7n8, 131, 193
Adams, Jay, 92–94, 117–18, 133, 133n13, 134, 135, 135n15, 137, 149, 154, 155n20, 209
Africa Inland Mission, 48
alcohol, 37, 68, 69n33, 74
Alexander, Michelle Lindahl, 173
Allik, Tiina, 100
Allis, Oswald T., 51n3
Al Qaeda, 199n32
Alwinson, Pete, 169
American Philosophical Association, 198
Ames, William, 94
analytic philosophy, 94, 108
Andrew W. Mellon Junior High School, 19
Anglicanism, 29, 36, 168, 204
Anselm of Canterbury, xiv
apologetics, xvii–xviii, 90, 91, 150–51, 153–54, *see* Van Til

Apologetics to the Glory of God, 153, 153n17
Applied Theology, 212–13
Aquinas, Thomas, 75, 77
argument, 11
Aristotle, 43
Arminianism, 35
Arnold, Carol, 185
Arnold, Jack, 180–81, 185
artifacts, 210
assessment, 201, 210
Association of Theological Schools, 209–10
Athanasius, 75
athletics, 6, 66n28, 146, 187–88, 214
Atwell, Robert, 109–10
Augustine, xviiin2
Austing, John, 69
Ayers, Darryl, 188

Bach, J. S., 8
Bacon family, 77
Bahnsen, Greg, 100, 136, 136n16, 142, 152, 152n13, 154n18
Bailey, Jim, 45–46
Bainton, Roland, 74, 74n4
balance, 97
Baptist Student Fellowship, 35
baptism, 181
Barnett, Arthur, 47
Barnhouse, Donald Grey, 17, 34
Barth, Karl, 27n4, 27n5, 34, 79, 83, 95, 98n18

basic beliefs, 11
Bates, Mike, 185
Baugh, Stephen, 136
Beates, Mike, 181
Bedau, Hugo, 40n18
Beechview Presbyterian Church, 15–18
Bergsma, Derke, 137, 155
Berkhof, Louis, 95
Berkouwer, G. C., xviiin2
Beverly Heights Presbyterian Church, 3n4, 7–10, 17, 19, 24, 29, 34, 45, 47, 52, 69, 77–79, 85, 87, 109, 119n46, 170–71, 216
Bible memory, 4
Bible Presbyterian Church, 35
biblical theology, 57, 155
bibliography, 97n17
Blackmur, R. P., 44, 74n5
Blackstone Fellowship, 199–200
Blaise, Clark, 21–23, 23n7
Blue Bell Church, see Community Orthodox Presbyterian Church.
Boder, Bill, 9
Boettner, Loraine, 53–4n12
book reviews, 207
Bowman, A. A., 60n20
Bromberger, Sylvain, 39
Brown, Larry, 77
Brown, Steve, 170, 197–98
Brunner, Emil, 83
Bultmann, Rudolf, 38, 83, 93
Burnham, David, 21, 23, 27, 47–49
Burtner, Howard, 37
Bush, President George W., 198–99n32
Butler, Ronald J., 28, 40n18

Calhoun, Robert L., 73, 74, 76
California, 22, 102, 109, 117, 214–15
Calvin College, 68, 105
Calvinism, 35, 36, 37
Campbell, Glen, 175, 187
Campus Crusade for Christ, 85n17
Canadian Reformed Churches, 121

Candeto, Robin, 189, 189n23
Cannada, Ric, 199
Cannada, Robert, 199
Cantor, Norman, 39
Carnell, Edward J., 54
Carlsbad Caverns, 133
Carson, Don, 164, 194, 207
catechisms, 129n8
Center Square, see Community Orthodox Presbyterian Church.
Central Florida Presbytery, 182
centrality of preaching, 200
ceremony, 203
Chaminade University, 191
Cherbury, Lord Herbert of, 82, 83
Cherry Creek Evangelical Presbyterian Church, 199
Chiao, Raymond Yu, 44
Chikes, Tibor, 46, 52n7
Childers, Steve, 170, 195, 197, 199n32, 212
children's ministry, 146, 184n21, 186
Childs, Brevard, 76, 76n9
choirs, 7, 105
Christ Church, Moscow, Idaho, 166
Christian reconstruction, theonomy, 136, 142, 142n1, 208n42
Christian Reformed Church, 17, 68, 109, 116, 123, 149
Christian Science, 15
Christian, William, 73, 75
Christianity Today, 207, 208
Church
    as institution, 4–5
    growth, 158, 177
    history, 57
    planting, 141–142, 148, 154
    spirituality of, 110
Clark, Gordon H., 52n7, 82, 92–93, 107, 114, 121, 154n18, 158, 171
Clark, R. Scott, 156, 156n23, 157, 159, 160, 160n29, 204, 207
Clowney, David, 100, 151n9, 164
Clowney, Edmund P., 55, 57, 62n21, 64, 73n2, 74, 81, 91, 94, 98, 99, 101, 113, 117, 128,

128n7, 137, 139, 149, 155, 160
Clowney, Jean, 128, 149
Coastal Community Church, Oceanside, CA, 127, 141
Coffield, Jim, 170n13, 197
Coffin, William Sloane, 27
College Briefing Conference, 46, 47
collegiality, 139–40, 156
Columbia University, 73
common grace, 121
Community Orthodox Presbyterian Church (Center Square, Blue Bell), 69–71, 77, 103–6, 109, 118–22, 126, 192
Comprehensive exams, 80
computer, 139
concurrence, 29
confessions, 129n8, 149, 158, 160–61, 161n31
Confession of 1967, 79
confessionalism, 150, 159, 160–61, 167, 207, 215
Conn, Harvie, 90–91, 90n5, 105
contemporary Christian music, 92, 125, 127–28
Contemporary Worship Music, 128
controversies, 71, 107, 111
conversion, 9–13
Coppes, Leonard, 108
Corbett, Steve, 192
Cornelius Van Til: An Analysis of His Thought, 152, 153, 153–54n18
Côte St. Gabriel, 65
Cottrell, Jack, 67n29
counseling, 134, 215
Coupland, Scott, 170, 170n13, 197
Covenant College, 104n29, 136, 137, 191, 192
Covenant of Grace Orthodox Presbyterian Church, 125n1
Covenant Orthodox Presbyterian Church, Pittsburgh, 65, 109
Covenant Presbyterian Church, 175–187
Covenant Theological Seminary, 166
Covenanters, 3n4, 35, 190

Craig, Bryce, 138n22
Crawford, Percy, 67n29, 69n29
creativity, 56–57, 63, 86, 92, 93, 112, 112n40, 139, 150–52, 166, 177, 216
Cross, Elane, 133
Crossroads Bible Institute, 158
cults, 21
Cummings, Calvin Knox, Sr. 65–67, 113, 130–32, 182
Cummings, Calvin Knox, Jr., 67, 100n22
Cummings, David, 67, 100n22, 112–14
Cummings, Mary, 67, 130
Cummings, Wilson, 67, 100n22, 130, 178
Curry, Allen, 170

Dallas Theological Seminary, 50, 71
Davis, Bill, 137, 191
Davis, D. Clair, xii, 92–94
DC Talk, 176
Deaton, Dan, 145, 147
deference construct, 196
DeMaster, Ivan, 71, 104
Demeester, Tom, 109–10
Den Dulk, Bob, 123, 148, 149, 153
Dennison, Jim, 155, 157
Denominations, 141–44, 149n6
Dewey, John, 43
Dillard, Ray, 100
Diachesyn, Sharon, 173n16
dispensationalism, 17, 35, 37
dissertation, 82–84, 98
distance education, 200–202
Doctrine of God, 204
Doctrine of the Christian Life, 204, 206
Doctrine of the Knowledge of God, 138, 151
Doctrine of the Word of God, 128n7, 191–92, 205
Dombek, Dave, 120
Dombek, Ellen, 120
Dooyeweerd, Herman, 61, 86, 107–9, 131, 171–72

Dordt College, 130, 131, 198
Dowey, Edward, 53n12
Downer, Alan, 27
Downing, F. Gerald, 81, 83
Dreesen, Mel and Millie, 47
Duguid, Iain, 148
Duncan, Ligon, 199
Dupré, Marcel, 14, 15
Dutch Calvinism, 17, 59, 60, 61, 68, 71, 104, 107, 119–22, 123

Eastern College, 130
easy-believism, 115
Ebenstein, William, 27
Eby, David, 193
Eckenwiler, Bill, 197
ecumenism, 168
Eddy, William, 29–30
Edgar, William, 99
Edgewood Presbyterian Church, 3
Edison, Louis, 173
Edwards, Jonathan, 18
Eldersveld, Peter, 17, 68n30
election, 116
electives, 90, 100n22, 138, 195, 202, 214
Elliott, Virginia, 19, 20, 23, 201
Ellis, Carl, 103
Emmanuel Chapel, 178
Emmanuel Faith Community Church, 145
Epicurus, 96
Episcopal Church, U. S. A., 204
epistemology, 91, 148n5, 192
Equipping Pastors International, 185
Erasmus, Desiderius, 39
eschatology, 165
Escondido, CA, 123–63
Escondido Christian Reformed Church, 123, 124, 125, 126, 126n3, 143, 149, 154
Esposito, Joseph, 7, 8, 16, 38n13
Estevez, George, 16
ethics, 89, 95–96, 99
evangelical, 34, 68, 92, 115, 164, 209, 216

Evangelical Free Church, 145, 164, 166
Evangelical Presbyterian Church, 69
Evangelical Publishers Association, 204
Evangelical Reunion, 144, 168
Evangelical Theological Society, 198, 206
evangelism, 119n48, 125, 129, 141, 144, 149, 163, 181, 182, 186
"confrontational," 186
Evangelism Explosion, 130
Evans, Bob, 132
Evans, John, 46
evidence, 11
existence of God, 60
existentialism, 61

factions, 142, 154–56, 203
faculty meetings, 174
Faith Theological Seminary, 35, 51
Festschrift, 205
Fikkert, Brian, 192
Fikkert, Doris, 70, 192
Fikkert, Henry, 70–71, 104, 192
First Presbyterian Church, Jackson, MS, 199
Fitzgerald, Jim, 180, 181, 181n20, 183–85
Flew, Antony, 42, 42n27
Folk, Sheldon, 48
Frame, Carolyn Nalumansi, 193
Frame, Clark Crawford, 1, 2, 46, 53–55, 118
Frame, Clark Shannon, 3n3, 132
Frame, David, 3n3, 132
Frame, "Irish Jimmy," 1
Frame, Johnny, 134, 137, 145, 147, 162, 174–75, 182, 187, 187n22, 189, 191–94, 215
Frame, Justin, 134, 137, 145, 162, 170n13, 174–75, 182, 187, 189–90, 192–93, 213, 215
Frame, Mary Grace Cummings, 67, 130–35, 141, 146, 147, 161–62, 169, 174–78, 181, 182,

NAME, SUBJECT INDEX 221

186–89, 193–94, 197n30, 198, 202n37, 213, 215
Frame, Richard C, 25–26, 26n1, 46, 73
Frame, Violet McElphatrick, 2, 53–55, 80, 132, 133
framework hypothesis, 56
free will, 75
Frei, Hans, 76
French Reformed Seminary, 149
Frisbee, Bob, 14
Fuller, George, 63n25
Fuller Theological Seminary, 54, 64, 71, 136
Fullerton, Donald B., xii, xiii, 30–38, 30n9, 50, 52n7, 64, 71
fundamentalism, 30, 34, 34n11, 68, 69, 70, 71
Futato, Adele, 179
Futato, Mark, 102, 129, 148, 158–59, 158n25, 169, 170, 176, 178, 197

Gaffin, Richard, 94
Gamble, Rick, 170, 173, 195, 196
Gay, David, 29
Geneva College, 190
Gerstner, John H., 18, 18n4, 23, 35, 46, 52, 52n8, 53, 114, 165
Glasser, Arthur, 37n12
Glodo, Mike, 197, 197n29
Godfrey, W. Robert, 137, 139, 149, 150n7, 155–60, 160n28, 167, 167n8, 169, 171, 176
Gordon College, 130
Gordon Conwell Theological Seminary, 136
Gordon, Ernest, 27n4
Gordon, Kent, 65
Grace Theological Seminary, 50, 71
grading, 201, 213
Graham, Billy, 9, 54, 81
Grand Canyon, 176
Greenville Presbyterian Theological Seminary, 149, 157
Greenwald, Colin, 185
Greenwald, Jerusha, 185

Greenwald, Randy, 185–87
Griffith, Chuck, 183–84
Griffith, Karen, 183–84
Gropp, Doug, 102–3
Groves, Alan, 100
Grudem, Wayne, 100, 164–65
Guret, John, 84
Gustafson, James, 89

Halsey, Jim, 150–51
Hamilton, Ted, 145
Hamm, Mordecai, 81
Handel, George F., x, 79
Harbison, Edward, 39
Harbor Presbyterian Church 145
Harris, Frank, 84
Harris, Josh, 176
Hartt, Julian, 41, 73, 76, 78, 80n11
Harvard University, 73
Harvey, Paul, 181
Harvey, Van, 38
Hauerwas, Stanley, 205
Hays, Stephen, 157
health, 153n15, 202, 202n37, 213–14 see sleep apnea
Heidegger, M., 61, 96
Hempel, Carl, 28, 40
Henry, Carl F. H., 54, 82, 110n37
Hill, Chuck, 137, 170, 195, 196
historical approach to theology, 150, 150n8, 157
History of Western Philosophy and Theology, 138, 212
Hodge, Charles, 51, 95
Hoeksema, Herman, 121
Hofland, Fred and Alaine, 147
Holmer, Paul, 73, 81–84, 98
Holy Spirit, 11, 60
home schooling. 146, 147, 162
homeless ministry, 135, 146, 162
Horne, Fern, 25
Horton, Michael, 152n11, 153, 157–58, 171, 192n26, 208n42
House of Sophia, 215
Howard, David, 37n12
Howerzyl, James, 123–24, 126

Hughes, John, 100, 205, 207, 208, 211
Hume, David, 148n5
Hunter, Isaac, 184
Hunter, Joel, 177–78
Hurley, James, 99, 170
Hurricane Charlie, 190n24

improvising, 15–16
Institute for Christian Studies, 108, 109
Institute for Theological Studies, 205
Inter-Varsity Christian Fellowship, 31, 81, 85n17
introversion, 65, 71, 130, 130n10, 193, 200
Islam, 199n32, 210

Jackson, Martha Frame, 3n3, 132, 164
James, Frank III, 102, 170, 195, 196, 199
Jenkins, Joyce, 105, 120
Jenkins, Ron, 105–6
Jesus people, 125, 127
Jewett, Paul K., 54
Johnson, Dennis, 100, 136, 144, 145, 153, 176
Johnson, Robert C., 73–74, 74n3
Johnson, S. Lewis, 37n12
Jonas, Hans, 40
Jones, Peter, 149, 159, 160, 169
Jones, Rebecca, 149
Jones, Toby, 162
Jordan, Jim, 102
Josh, 159, 203
journal, 213
Journal of Pastoral Practice, 209
justification, 111–17, 111n39, 212

Kant, Immanuel, 83, 96
Kantzer, Ken, 165–66
Karlberg, Mark, 139
Kaufmann, Dick, 103, 124–30, 137, 142, 154, 158, 183, 195
Kaufmann, Elizabeth, 125

Kaufmann, Walter, 40–43, 76
Kardashian, Kim, x
Keller, Jim, 52, 76,
Keller, Tim, 144
Kelley, Bob, 8–9, 15, 18, 52, 53n10, 63
Kelly, Doug, 200
Kelso, James Leon, 18, 48, 52
Keiper, Ralph, 32
Kelsey, David, 80, 80n13, 95
Kester, Dennis, 145, 193–94
Kester, Doreen, 130, 132–34, 145, 162, 193–94
Kester, Malena, 145
Keswick, America's, 36–37
Key Klub, 45, 46, 47
Keyes, Richard, 99
Kidd, Reggie, 102, 170, 173, 177, 178, 197, 197n29, 203, 204
Kierkegaard, Søren, 12n11, 81, 81n14, 83
Kirk, Jerry, 45
Kistemaker, Jean, 198
Kistemaker, Simon, 198
Kiwanuka, Emma, 193
Kline, Meredith G., 55–56, 64, 92, 94, 95, 97, 98, 110n37, 136, 136n16, 139, 148, 151–52, 152n11, 155–56, 158
Kline, Meredith M., 136, 148
Knudsen, Robert D., 55, 61, 88, 90, 107, 108n36, 150, 164
Krabbendam, Henry, 104, 104n29
Kress, Arnold, 109
Kruger, Michael, 157, 170
Kuiper, R. B., 51n3
Kuschke, Arthur, 70–71, 113
Kuyper, Abraham, 35, 36,
Kuyper Club, 107

L'Abri, 49
Lake Baldwin Church, 184
Latourette, Kenneth Scott, 74, 74n4
Laverell, W. David, 104–5
law, 36
"Learning at Jesus' Feet," 205
Leithart, Peter, 102

Lessing, G. E., 83
Lewis, C. S., xv, xviiin2, 38, 41
Lewis, H. D., 75
liberalism, 23, 27, 34, 51, 60, 68, 74, 82, 89, 174, 199n32, 209
Lindbeck, George, 73, 75, 80
logical positivism, 28
Long, Bob, 21–22
Longman, Tremper, 102
lordship, 12, 96–97, 211, 215, 216
Louie, 20–21
Lowrie, Roy, 181, 187
Luther, Martin, 39
Lutheran Church, Missouri Synod, 75
Lynch, Cathy, 19

Macaulay, Ran, 49
Machen, J. Gresham, x, 34, 35, 51, 55, 58, 58n16, 66, 69, 89, 93, 98, 142, 149
Mahlow, William, 37n12
Making Biblical Decisions, 205
Malarkey, Bob, 104n27, 109–10
Malmberg, Arnold, 84
Malone, Mike, 169
Markham Elementary School, 5–6,
Marshall, Phil, 157
Martin, Al, 131, 131n11
Marx, Karl, 85
Mawhinney, Al, 136, 148–49, 167–70, 179, 194–95, 197, 197n30, 205
Mawhinney, Carole, 197, 197n30
MacKenzie, Charles Sherrard, 168, 170–71, 195, 197, 198, 199
McCaskill, Teresa Lee, 173, 178
McClain, Alva J., 50
McCollum, Anton, 179n18
McDonald, Harry, 54
McDonald, Marilyn, 193, 215
McDowell, Josh, 148n5
McElphatrick, G. Domer, 2
McLaughlin, Ra, 205
McLeister, William, 17, 77
McLeod, Don, 65
Meadowcroft, Alberta, 7, 14, 15

Meek, Esther, 102
Mehl, John, 46
Memmelaar, Joseph, 109
Merrill, Gerard, 126, 130
Metzger, Will, 69
Midget, 118
Mill, John Stuart, 96
Mille Isles, 65
millennium, 35
Miller, C. John, 92, 94, 104, 120, 124, 184
Milton, Mike, 199
Mininger, Larry, 133
Mira Mesa, 142
miracle, 148n5
missions, 64–65, 139–40, 180
mobbing, 161n33
Moltmann, Jürgen, 93
Montgomery, John W., 148n5
Montgomery, Robert P., 30
Moo, Doug, 205
Moore, Russ, 205
moralism, 57, 64, 155
Moreau, Bill, 77
Moreau, Jackie, 84
Morgan, Ed, 37
Mormonism, 22
Mote, Frederick, 39
Mt. Lebanon High School, 19, 23
Mt. Lebanon United Presbyterian Church, 45, 52–53
The Mounty, 19, 201
Movies, 87
Moynihan, Daniel Patrick, 152n12
Muether, John, 102, 170, 171
Murray, John, x, 55, 61–62, 62n21, 62n22, 62n23, 63–64, 88–90, 94, 98, 111, 150, 165
Musri, Imam Mohammed, 199n32
mystery, 11

Nash, Ron, 171–72, 195, 199, 204
Nasser, Gamal Abdel, 48
National Union of Christian Schools, 108
necessity, 115
neo-orthodoxy, 34

Net Nite, 130
New Haven Evangelical Free Church, The, 84–86
New Life Orthodox Presbyterian Church (Philadelphia), 92, 120–21, 124, 126, 129, 143
New Life Presbyterian Church (Escondido), 123–30, 133, 134, 141–45, 154, 162
New Wilmington Missionary Conference, 25, 88
Nicole, Roger, 168, 168n9, 195, 198, 203
Niebuhr, H. Richard, 74
Nietzsche, F. W., 85
No Other God, 198, 205
North, Gary, 112n40
Northland Church, 168, 173, 175, 177–78, 180, 184, 203
Northwest Theological Seminary, 157
Notaro, Thom, 138n22
Nyack Missionary College, 131

Obama, President Barack, 1n1
O'Brien, G. Dennis, 43–45, 86
Oceanside, Calif. 127
Ockenga, Harold J., 54
O'Donnell, Jerry, 130–31, 133
O'Donnell, David (Skip), 130, 132–34, 146, 162, 170, 176, 192, 193, 194
O'Donnell, Gavin, 192
O'Donnell, Sharon, 192
O'Donovan, Oliver, 205
Old Testament Theology, 128–29
Oliver, Leroy, 179
Oliver, Randy, 178–80
ontological argument, 44–45
open theism, 198
Orangewood Christian School, 175
Orangewood Presbyterian Church, 175, 180
Osbourne, Mike, 185
organ music, x, 8, 71, 77, 85–86, 105, 124, 203

Orthodox Presbyterian Church, 35, 36, 46, 52n7, 66, 69, 92, 104, 115n41, 123, 129n9, 141–44

P&R Publishers, 138, 138n22, 204, 205, 206, 208, 208n42, 212
Packer, James I., 42, 42n26, 207
Padgett, Marvin, 207–8
Painted Desert, 176
Palmer, Edwin H., 55, 62–63, 89
panentheism, 95
Pannenberg, Wolfhart, 89, 93
Parson, Geraldine McElphatrick, 80
Pascal, Blaise, 44, 198
pastorate, 64–65, 67, 71
Pathway Learning, 212
Payne, Michael, 103
Payton, James, 106, 119n48
pedagogy, 97–99, 102
Peniel Bible Conference, 107
Perkins, John, 179n18
personal revelation, 81
perspectivalism, ix, xviii, 44, 75, 91–92, 95–97, 101, 134n14, 155, 159, 181, 196, 209n46
Perspectives on the Word of God, 166
Peterson, Andrée Seu, ix–xv, 103
Peterson, Andy, 170, 200
Petrified Forest, 176
phenomenology, 61
Phonics and whole language, 5
physical education, 6, 28n8
pietism, 68, 92, 104
Pike, Kenneth, 101
Pipa, Joseph, 149, 154–55, 157, 160n28, 167
Piper, John, 207
Pitcher, George, 39
Pittsburgh, 1, 65–66, 78
Pittsburgh Theological Seminary, 9, 17, 52–53, 64, 73
Plantinga, Alvin, 11n10, 44n30
Plato, 96
postliberalism, 75
postmillennialism, 165
Powlison, David, 102

Poythress, Vern, xi, 101, 101n24,
    138, 139, 206, 212
Pratt, Gena, 172
Pratt, Richard, 57n15, 103, 139,
    166–68, 170, 172, 195, 196,
    203
"Pratt's Boot Camp," 211n48
prayer, 130, 181, 187
preaching, 155, 200
preceptorial system, 26, 102
premillennialism, 164–66
Presbyterian Church in America,
    105, 141–44, 180
Presbyterian Church in the United
    States, 3n4, 141
Presbyterian Church in the United
    States of America, 3n4,
    18n3, 35, 52, 66, 69, 79, 141
Presbyterian Church of America,
    69n37
presuppositions,
    presuppositionalism, 44–45,
    60, 82, 148n5, 153, 192
Princeton Evangelical Fellowship,
    30–38, 50, 56, 64, 69
Princeton Theological Seminary,
    27n5, 35, 50–51, 53, 107
Princeton University, 9, 25–50, 82,
    102, 106
Prichard, H. A., 96
process theology, 43, 52, 75–76,
    93, 95
"Proposal for a New Seminary," 205,
    208–209
propositional revelation, 81–84
Protestant Reformed Church, 121
Psalms, 119–20
psychology, 28
Pulliam, Paul, 46–47
Putnam, Hilary, 40

Quality Enhancement Project,
    210–11
Quine, Willard Van Orman, 40

Raenbow Station, 191

Ramona, 124
Rancho Bernardo, 142
Ramsey, Paul, 89
Reagan, Ronald, 109, 166n4
reconciliation, 160, 176
Redd, Scott, 196–197
Redeemer Presbyterian Church
    (New York), 144–45
Reed, Smith, Shaw and McClay, 46
Reeves, Carol, 189
reform school, 32
Reformed Church in the United
    States, 156, 156n22
Reformed Presbyterian Church,
    Evangelical Synod, 143, 180
reformational, 108
Reformed faith, 67–68, 216
Reformed Presbyterian Church of
    North America, 3n4
Reformed Theological Seminary,
    137, 139, 148–49, 158–59,
    164–216
Regulative Principle of Worship,
    70n38, 70–71, 154–55,
    154n19, 160, 166
relativism, 38
retirement, 202
Ridenhour, David, 182
Ripper, Ted, 15
Ritschl, Albrecht, 83
Roe v. Wade, 109
Rogers, Jack, 45
romance, 21, 106, 130–34
Rowat, Ron, 65
Rubio, Adam, 145
Rubio, Amanda, 145
Rubio, Debbie, 130, 132–35, 145,
    162, 170, 176, 192
Rubio, George, 145, 176, 192
Rubio, Kristina, 145
Rubio, Olivia, 145
Rubio, Rebecca, 145
Rupp, Gary, 170n13, 197
Russell, Murray, 48
Ryrie, Charles Caldwell, 37n12

Sabbath, 36

Salvation Belongs to the Lord, 205, 211, 212
sanctification, 212
Sanderson, John W., 55, 98
San Marcos, 123, 141–42
Santa Fe Christian School, 134, 137, 145, 191
Sartre, Jean-Paul, 96
satire, 19–20
Schaeffer, Francis, 37n12, 49, 99
Schleiermacher, F. D. E., 83
Schuringa, David, 102, 149, 158
Scipione, George, 134n13, 137, 160
Seidenspinner, Charles, 37n12
Selected Shorter Writings, 205n41, 211n48, 212
Sesto, Jay, 147–48
Shafarevich, Igor, xii
Shakespeare, William, xiv
Shepherd, Norman, xi, 63–64, 88–90, 105, 111–17, 136, 139, 152, 152n13, 155, 158, 161
Sider, Ron, 85
Sigmon, Mark, 205
Silva, Moisés, 100
Skilton, John, x, 55, 58n16
Slattery, Bill, 149
sleep apnea, 153n15, 193
small groups, 130, 130n10
Smick, Elmer, 195
Smith, Ben 1n1
Smith, Clifford, 52–53, 52n7
Smith, Morton H., 166
Smith, Scotty, 195
sociology, 192
Sonrise Evangelical Free Church (Hesperia, CA), 145
Sonship Discipleship Course, 92, 184
Sophists, 96
Southern culture, 203
Sowell, John, 153, 170
Spanish River Presbyterian Church, 196
Speaking the Truth in Love, 205
Special Program in the Humanities, 44–45
Spinoza, Baruch, 43, 82–84

spiritual formation, 203
spiritual gifts, 126
Sproul, R. C., 52n8, 195
St. Andrew's Chapel, 203–4
St. Luke's Cathedral, Orlando, 204
St. Paul's PCA, 169, 180, 203–4
Stanton, Zan, 144
Steele, Francis, 37n12
Stenstrom Elementary School, 189
Stonehouse, Ned, x, 51, 55, 58n16, 63
Strimple, Bob, 118, 123, 124, 136–38, 137n18, 139, 143, 148, 152, 155, 160, 167, 175–76
Student Christian Association, 30, 41
Student revolt, 152–53
students, 203
"Studying Theology as a Servant of Jesus," 205
Sukraj, Sunita, nanny job 189
Summit Church, 184
Sunday school, 3
suzerainty treaty, 97
Swagerty, Doug, 125, 127, 141, 195
Swagerty, Lois, 125, 127
Swain, Scott, 197, 202, 214
Sweeting, Don, 199, 203n39
Swinburne, Richard, 157
Systematic Theology, 211
Szathmary, Arthur, 44–45

Talbot, Ken, 207–208, 208n42, 208n43
Tanaka, Elizabeth, 148
Tanaka, Warren and Janice, 147–48, 148n5
Taylor, Bill, 77–79
teaching assistants, 75, 86, 102, 102n26, 124, 157, 171, 179, 196, 201
teaching load, 194–95, 202, 214
Temple, William, 38
Tennyson, Alfred, 19
tension, academic/pastoral, 72, 76, 77, 87, 89, 94, 208
term papers, 201, 210–11

Terrace Club, 26n2
The Academic Captivity of Theology, 208, 211
The Escondido Theology, 207
The Geneva School, 175, 178, 187–89, 191
The Master's Academy, 175, 181, 187, 188
The New Community, 105
theology, xvii–xviii
    definition, 94, 155
Theology of My Life, 213
theonomy, *see* Christian reconstruction
Thilly, Frank, 28
Third Millennium Ministries, 196, 205
Thomas, George, 38
Thompson, Lawrence, 39, 44
Tillich, Paul, 27n4, 75, 77, 83, 93
Tilley, Mike, 184
tolerance, 56, 167n8
Topical Memory System, 14, 32
Torres, Joseph, 153n17
Townsend, W. Cameron, 37n12
Tracey, Eleanor, 173, 178
Tracey, Michael, 178
Tracey, Tim, 173
tradition, traditionalism, 56, 61–62, 93, 117, 121–22, 122n50, 141, 151, 154, 160, 161, 161n31, 167, 203, 204, 216
transcendence and immanence, 95
traumatic events, 6
Trinity, 160n29, 204
Trinity Evangelical Divinity School, 164–166, 168, 199
Trinity Presbyterian Church, 154
triperspectivalism, *see* perspectivalism
truly Reformed, 67, 69, 71, 121, 129, 150, 156, 161–63, 164, 168–69, 178, 203
Tucker, Lem, 179n18
Tumin, Melvin, 38–39
Tuttle, Mike, 176
two kingdoms, 110, 192, 207, 216

Uganda, 104n29
Union Theological Seminary, 53, 73
United Presbyterian Church of North America, 3n4, 18n3, 69, 88
United Reformed Churches of North America, 149
University of Central Florida, 191
University Presbyterian Church, 185

Valencia Community College, 191
Van Brakel, Tony, 104, 106, 119–22
Van Gemeren, Willem, 100, 164
Van Til, Cornelius, x, 34, 35, 36, 41–42, 51n3, 52n7, 55, 58n16, 59–60, 62n21, 72, 73n2, 85, 86, 88–90, 92, 93, 95–96, 98, 101, 107, 114, 150–52, 160n29, 171, 204
"Van Til the Theologian," 150
Vanhoozer, Kevin, 103, 164, 194
Ventrella, Jeff, 199–200
victorious life, 36–37
Vietnam war, 78, 102n25
Vivaldi, Antonio, 175
Vlastos, Gregory, 39
Vos, Geerhardus, 57, 92

Walgren, Eric, 19–20, 20n6
Waltke, Bruce, 110n37
Warfield, B. B., 35, 51, 74, 98
Weeks, Gwendolyn Cummings, 67
Weeks, Noel, 67, 104n27
Weinrich, Carl, 38n13
Weisiger, Cary, 52
Weiss, Paul, 75–76
Wells, David, 162
Wells, Paul, 100
Welty, Greg, 157
Westerly Road Church, 37, 38, 47, 79, 109
Western medicine, 202n37
Westminster Orthodox Presbyterian Church, 77, 106
Westminster Shorter Catechism, 129

Westminster Theological Journal, 150–51, 207
Westminster Theological Seminary (Philadelphia), ix, xii, 35, 46, 50–72, 88–122, 123, 130, 133, 136, 137, 164–66, 174, 203, 209
Westminster Theological Seminary in California, 93, 123–63, 168, 173, 175–76, 199, 203, 208n43, 209
Westphal, Merold, 85
Whitcomb, John C., 37n12
Whitefield Theological Seminary, Lakeland, FL, 207–8, 208n42, 211n48
Whitehead, Alfred North, 75–76
Whitlock, Luder, 167–69, 171, 172, 179, 195, 198
Whitlock, Mary Lou, 172, 198
wholly other, 95
Wichmann, Russell, 14, 15, 38n13
Wild, John, 43, 86
Willow Creek PCA, 169, 169n12, 180
Wilson, Douglas, 166
Wilson, Robert Dick, 51n3
Wittgenstein, Ludwig, 40, 81, 81n14, 93, 138
Wolling, Rick, 79
women in church, 120, 149, 168, 172, 210
Wood, Ledger, 28
Woodbridge, John, 164
Wooden, John, 180
Woolley, Paul, x, 55, 57–58, 58n16, 58n17, 74n5, 98, 109–11, 117
World Harvest Mission, 92
Worship, 127–28, 177, 182, 200, 203
Worship in Spirit and Truth, 128
Wright, G. Ernest, 48
Wright, Mary Louise, 77, 78
writing, 118
Wycliffe Bible Translators, 69

Yale University, 25–26, 73–87, 94, 98, 104, 106, 166
Young, Edward J., 41, 51, 55–56, 58n16, 73n2, 98

Scripture Index

Exodus
3:12–15	97
6:2–8	97
20:2–17	97
33:19	97
34:5–6	97

2 Kings
6	xi

Psalms
	4
23	4
23:6	216
71:18	ix
103:1–22	97
104:4	28
119:97–100	xv
121	4
139	132

Matthew
18:15	xi

John
1:1–14	12
3:8	10
4:23	10

Romans
10:9–10	36

Galatians
3	173

First Corinthians
1:10	xii
10:31	12
11:28	120
13	4
13:13	11

Ephesians
4:32	xi
6:10–18	xii

First Thessalonians
1:5	11

Second Thessalonians
3:6, 14	120

First Timothy
1:1–7	xiii
3:1–7	209–210

Second Timothy

2:1	xii
3:5	34

Titus

3:10	120

Hebrews

1:7	28

James

2:14–26	114

Second John

10	120

www.ingramcontent.com/pod-product-compliance
Lightning Source LLC
Chambersburg PA
CBHW031808220426
43662CB00007B/571